ADVANCE PRAISE FOR
ALIVE DAY

"Gutsy, tightly written, emotionally powerful without an ounce of cheap sentiment."

—PHIL KLAY, author of *Redeployment*

"Astonishing . . . Both a love story and a gripping account of the cost of war from the unique perspective of a military widow, *Alive Day* serves as a crucial reminder of the aftermath of war and the kids left to clean up the mess."

—STEPHANIE LAND, bestselling author of *Maid* and *Class*

"Karie Fugett did not fight in a war. And yet her voice sings with deliberate, horrific, powerful, beautiful knowing about war and the human toll it demands. Her writing is an excoriating, bright-eyed indictment of a system built from the bones of mostly poor boys and girls who are promised that they and their families will be taken care of if only they sign on a dotted line and are then left to rot, struggling to claim benefits and treatment they've earned while their commanders in chief practice portraiture of their broken bodies and invoke their names for political gain. Fugett's words shine humanity on those of us who volunteered before we understood the actual cost, all while she stands before us an open wound, not begging for aid but demanding that we bear witness to the grotesque, the intimate, the absurd, the tender, without averting our eyes. A small penance for our forever sin."

—MATT YOUNG, author of *Eat the Apple*

"*Alive Day* is a riveting and clear-eyed memoir about love, class, war, and the consequences of all of those. This urgent and necessary book is a gift, a marvel, a reckoning. I wish every American would read it."

—JUSTIN ST. GERMAIN, bestselling author of *Son of a Gun*

"Shimmering with heart and humanity on every page, *Alive Day* feels like a book that Karie Fugett had to write. We owe it to her, to ourselves, and to every young person that the forever wars threw into the deep end of caregiving and loss to bear witness to her story and to never forget it. I know I couldn't if I tried. There are scenes from this powerful memoir that will forever be seared into my mind."

—SIMONE GORRINDO, author of *The Wives*

"In a society too often numb and indifferent and entirely too insistent on forgetting, *Alive Day* is an essential, urgent reminder of the cost of war and a savage, gritty, and romantic monument to those who pay it. Karie Fugett's memoir is deeply felt and disturbingly funny. I hope it pisses you off. We should be pissed off."

—LAUREN HOUGH, author of *Leaving Isn't the Hardest Thing*

"The only thing worse than war is waiting for someone you love to return from it. Karie Fugett's *Alive Day* is as true a war story as any I've read. Like war itself, it'll break your heart."

—ELLIOT ACKERMAN, author of *Dark at the Crossing* and *Green on Blue*

ALIVE
DAY

ALIVE DAY

A Memoir

KARIE FUGETT

THE DIAL PRESS
NEW YORK

Published in the United States by The Dial Press,
an imprint of Random House, a division of
Penguin Random House LLC, 1745 Broadway, New York, NY 10019.

THE DIAL PRESS is a registered trademark and the colophon
is a trademark of Penguin Random House LLC.

LIBRARY OF CONGRESS CATALOGING-IN-PUBLICATION DATA
Names: Fugett, Karie, author.
Title: Alive Day / Karie Fugett.
Description: First edition. | New York, NY: The Dial Press, [2025]
Identifiers: LCCN 2024048840 (print) | LCCN 2024048841 (ebook) |
ISBN 9780593231081 (hardcover) | ISBN 9780593231098 (ebook)
Subjects: LCSH: Fugett, Karie. | Iraq War, 2003-2011—
Veterans—Biography. | Military spouses—Alabama—Biography. |
Kinsey, Jimmy Cleveland, II, 1984-2010. | Iraq War, 2003-2011—
Veterans—Family relationships. | Iraq War, 2003-2011—
Veterans—Substance use. | Iraq War, 2003-2011—Veterans—
Mental health. | Disabled veterans—United States—Biography. |
United States. Marine Corps—Biography.
Classification: LCC DS79.767.V47 F84 2025 (print) | LCC DS79.767.V47 (ebook) |
DDC 956.7044/30922—dc23/eng/20250108
LC record available at https://lccn.loc.gov/2024048840
LC ebook record available at https://lccn.loc.gov/2024048841

Printed in the United States of America on acid-free paper

randomhousebooks.com
penguinrandomhouse.com

2 4 6 8 9 7 5 3 1

First Edition

Book design by Alexis Flynn

The authorized representative in the EU for product safety and compliance is Penguin Random House Ireland, Morrison Chambers, 32 Nassau Street, Dublin D02 YH68, Ireland, https://eu-contact.penguin.ie.

For anyone who has ever had to choose
when all they had were impossible options

When the rich wage war,
it's the poor who die.
—JEAN-PAUL SARTRE, *Le Diable et le Bon Dieu*

In America, both the dream and the nightmare
can be true all at once.
—YAA GYASI, "Why the Next Four Years
Will Be a Test for All of Us"

CONTENTS

III.

IV.

V.

ALIVE
DAY

PROLOGUE
November 2005

I wake up on a blow-up mattress next to a mountain of beer boxes with a pistol under my pillow. I'd noticed its hard edges on my cheek, felt around, and paused when my fingertips touched cool metal. I pull it out and hold it flat in my hands, stare at its angles and curves, consider the desolation of the barrel, trying to remember how the hell it got there. Cleve is already awake and pulling a yellow-and-blue-striped polo shirt over his head.

"Uh . . . what is this?" I ask.

He chuckles and sits down on the edge of the mattress. With pops and squeaks, it lifts my body and rolls me toward him.

"Don't worry about that," he says. He picks up a pair of camo-print cargo shorts that'd been crumpled on the floor next to the mattress, pulls them over his legs, and stands once they're at his thighs. My mind is somewhere else, struggling to piece together the night before. The sound of Cleve's zipper pulls me out of a trance. "I put it there."

He explains that the night before, he'd found Fowler, his nineteen-year-old Marine Corps buddy, frantic and sobbing with both arms extended, the pistol squeezed between his sweaty, trembling hands and pointed toward his wife. Earlier that night, Fowler'd found a love letter in the hidden compartment of a wooden box his wife kept in her night-stand. It was from another Marine in their unit. One of his best friends.

"Our baby's in the other room, you fucking psycho!" she had screamed, but Fowler remained. I imagine his face distorted by the puffy wetness of his crying, imagine his wife regretting saying those words the moment they fell from her mouth. Did she drop to her knees and beg for forgiveness, willing to do anything to save her own life? I wonder what I would do if I were looking down the barrel of a gun. They say that when someone is about to die, they see a montage of their life leading up to that point. Movies depict the moment before death as a reel of happy memories. Birthdays, graduations, first kisses—one after another after another. But when I imagine this young woman, her baby in the room on the other side of the wall behind her, I know she was thinking about her future, all the things she would miss out on, her parentless child. Cleve, a peacemaker among his friends, convinced his buddy not to shoot.

"Hey, man. This isn't you," I imagine him saying with both hands in the air as he slowly moves toward his friend. "Look me in the eyes. I love you, man. Put the gun down. I got you."

I wonder how much Fowler resisted Cleve's urging. Did he hand the gun over right then, or did he tighten his finger around the trigger? It has always made more sense to me that the person whose life flashes before their eyes is the one about to take the life of someone else: all those moments that chipped away at their humanity until, finally, they break, leaving an unrecognizable version of themselves looking over the edge of the abyss, unable to conceive of any other option but to kill. Fowler must have thought of something worth not going to jail for, because he lowered the gun and handed it to Cleve. I'm sure Cleve hugged him. Cleve was a huge guy, and when his arms wrapped around you, you were cocooned, safe, and, for a moment, protected from the rest of this terrible world.

I'd been so drunk, I had already fallen asleep when all of this went down. I missed the whole thing.

I'd flown into Jacksonville to visit Cleve the night before. I was still wearing my navy blue flight attendant uniform, with my long brown hair twisted into a bun, tiny gold-painted wings that said *US Airways* pinned to my chest.

When I turned the corner into Arrivals, Cleve stood next to the luggage carousel, his smile broad and his arms open. I dropped my suitcase and bounded toward him, flinging myself into his arms. Wanting to remember his scent, I pressed my cheek against his chest and inhaled: spearmint and spicy-sweet deodorant.

"I missed you, Fugett," he said with an Alabama drawl.

I nodded to say *Me too,* and squeezed him tighter.

"You're gorgeous in that fuckin' uniform," he said, and we kissed.

I thought: *This is our second first kiss.* Our first first kiss had happened years ago when we were kids—all lanky limbs and fickle hearts—blissfully unaware that it marked the first day of the rest of our life together. Or that I would end up being the love of his short life.

Cleve retrieved my suitcase, grabbed my hand, and led me outside. He loaded my bag into the trunk of his white Mustang, and I slid into the passenger seat.

"Ready to meet these crazy bastards?" he asked as he started the car.

The engine growled to life as I buckled my seatbelt and pulled down the sun visor to check my appearance in its mirror. My eyes—pale blue with prominent limbal rings—sparkled in the visor's buttery light. They were the one physical feature I'd always been confident in—the one thing I could count on being complimented on. Mascara had smudged below my right eye. I licked my index finger and wiped it away, then looked at Cleve. "Yep."

Jacksonville was a man's world, the whole damn town a bachelor pad. The main drag, which led to Camp Lejeune, wasn't much more than asphalt and spindly pines. The rest was car lots, strip clubs and tattoo parlors, chain restaurants, and a sad excuse for a mall. Young men with matching crew cuts roamed in packs on the sides of the road; colorful hot rods purchased with deployment money revved at red lights; and in the median of Western Boulevard, the Jacksonville Ninja, an anonymous man who felt as natural to the place as the pines, practiced his finest karate moves with a boom box on his shoulder. Background noise was artillery rounds and low-flying aircraft, both so loud they often set off car alarms. Few people were local; nearly all of Jacksonville's residents were transplants lured there by the Marine Corps with its fancy uniforms, cool guns, and promises of bonus money, healthcare, and retirement.

In a town full of bored young men, there was no shortage of house parties. Cleve took me to one straight from the airport, stopping only for a bag of McDonald's double cheeseburgers and a tank of gas. He warned me on the way, "These guys get pretty wild."

I rolled my eyes and laughed. Not even six months ago, I'd been living in Tampa, a place known for its nightlife; I'd survived plenty of parties like this. In Tampa I'd worked at a popular alehouse, which meant sleeping in, working late, then going to whatever rager was happening that night. House parties were often held at pastel-colored, palm-tree-lined mansions. Kids rolled blunts the size of cigars, pissed in the pool, streaked through the house, tripped, snorted, and fucked in the back rooms.

By nature, I was shy, but I'd grown to enjoy proximity to chaos and recklessness, the thrill of trying mysterious new things and surrounding myself with extroverted people. A sort of high came with the risk involved at parties: a fight could break out; someone was probably cheating somewhere; the neighbors could call the cops at any moment. I found it much more interesting than my life had been when I was a kid, with my ten o'clock curfew and Sunday morning church services. Besides, it was easy to fly under the radar, everyone too sloshed to judge me sitting in the corner, petting the dog, and observing the circus around me.

I shrugged. "Tampa was pretty wild. I'm sure I'll be fine."

"Well, Hamilton and his wife are swingers," Cleve said. "If they go in the back room with anyone, it's probably best you don't go back there. Sometimes they snort lines and shit, too, so . . ."

"Don't worry about me," I said. I reached for Cleve's hand and pulled it to my mouth for a kiss. "I'm not the innocent Foley girl you met in eighth grade."

"Well, that's for damn sure," he said. He winked, let go of my hand, and squeezed my boob.

When we arrived, a man wearing nothing but socks stood on a coffee table, swinging his dick in circles, screaming *Wooo!* over and over between glugs of his beer. Behind him, empty cases of Bud Light were stacked against the wall up to the ceiling. The air smelled like stale cigarettes and broccoli, and to the left of me, a man with Brillo-y pink hair sprawled across a tattered green couch, his head and one of his arms hanging off the edge.

"He took a Xanny bar," the naked guy said. "He's fine. Woo!"

Cleve made his rounds, saying hi to all his friends. I followed behind, holding on to the back pocket of his jeans. Five people in their underwear sat on the back porch, playing strip poker. It was mid-November and cold enough that you could see your breath. I thought they were crazy. A shirtless guy introduced himself by telling me he had a third nipple. "See?" he said, pointing to a spot in the center of his rib cage. It looked like the chicken pox scar I have on my chest, powder pink and slightly raised. I wondered for a second if my mom had lied to me and if I actually had three nipples, too.

"I am way too sober for this shit," I said, and Cleve led me to the beer. I drank as much as it took for my anxiety to slip away, for a messy confidence to take its place. I don't remember much else. The next morning, I woke up with the gun under my pillow.

"Just put it in your purse," Cleve says as we get dressed. "There aren't any bullets in it."

Gripping the gun cautiously, I push some tampons aside and cram the thing in my purse, noting how strange it looks next to my pink wallet. Being in possession of something that holds so much power scares me.

I'd never held a pistol before, only a shotgun once when I was nine. Dad had woken me in the wee hours of the morning and snuck me out of my room to drive me to the edge of my aunt's farm in Elberta, Alabama. We sat in a tree stand for hours before we spotted a doe. Dad placed the gun in my arms and positioned it toward her.

"Look through here," he said. "Do you see it?"

"Yeah."

The creature was apparition-like, peacefully grazing on soybeans in the dawn light.

"Put your finger on the trigger here," Dad said. He placed his index finger over mine. "Ready?"

I swallowed to loosen the knot in my throat. He pressed my finger, and the gun exploded, the recoil strong enough to leave a sore spot on my puny shoulder. The doe disappeared. We assumed I'd missed. But then I overheard my dad talking to my uncle about it. They'd found the deer dead in the woods not far from where I'd shot it. It was pregnant. I vowed I'd never shoot a gun again. Eleven years later, I am struck by the heaviness of the pistol in my purse. I don't trust that it doesn't have bullets, that it won't go off by accident. I don't want to look like a wuss, though, so I carry it anyway. I couldn't have known then that this was only the beginning. Soon, I would carry so much more than I ever asked to hold.

I

We gotta make a decision
Leave tonight or live and die this way
         —TRACY CHAPMAN, "Fast Car"

1

THE AMERICAN DREAM

Summer 1992

Grammie and Granddad's home was one story and brick and sat on a three-acre pecan orchard that pushed against a small forest. I was crouched under a pecan tree, thrusting a gnarled stick into the muddy grass. A storm was coming. I could tell by the way the wind had shifted, the air had cooled, the sky rumbled softly in the distance. Mom had called for me, but I wasn't ready to surrender to an evening trapped indoors. I ignored her and hid behind a tree, knowing she wouldn't come looking.

The stick hit something hard—a root or a rock—and snapped just as I looked up and saw a cat. It was around fifty yards away, fully exposed, and looking straight at me. With a spotted coat and mutton chops, it was more magnificent—and much larger—than any cat I'd ever seen. Slowly, I stood up, startling it. The cat darted away, disappearing into the forest. Though part of me knew the creature wasn't something I should fool with, I was disappointed that it had vanished so quickly. I'd always been drawn to mysterious and dangerous things. I just wanted to get a better look.

"Come back!" I yelled. But nothing.

I considered chasing it. Instead, I threw the stick and ran between perfect rows of aged pecan trees toward the screened-in back porch, swung the creaky screen door open, and kicked my muddy shoes off as quickly as I could.

"Mom!" I yelled. "Mom!" The door was already cracked open, and I pushed my body into it and ran inside. A warm, savory smell hung in the air as I ran across the living room toward the kitchen, where Mom and Grammie were chatting and pulling casserole dishes from the oven. Mom turned around and put a steaming dish on the bar that separated the living room and kitchen.

"Whoa! What is it, baby?" she said as she pulled off her oven mitts and laid them on the bar next to the food.

"Mom! Guess what I saw!"

"What did you see?"

"A cat! The biggest cat ever! It had a beard and was looking at me and it's gone now!"

Mom scrunched her face. "A big cat?" She turned to Grammie. "Are there mountain lions around here?"

Grammie stirred something on the stove with a wooden spoon before tapping it on the edge of the pot, laying it on the counter, and turning around to look at my mom. She was shorter and wider than Mom, with wispy blond hair and a thin mouth that sat in a crooked line. She put her hand on her hip. "Not that I know of. Could be. I bet it was that bobcat Johnny saw when he was mowing the other day."

"A bobcat!" I said. "Cooool. I bet it's still out there. I bet I could find it!" I started toward the door.

"Whoa, whoa, whoa! Hold your horses!" Mom said, shaking her head. She was tall with hair cut like Princess Diana's, only dyed black, and she was thin enough that it looked like she rarely ate. When she was worried, she couldn't hide it. The muscles in her body would tense, and she'd move rapidly, eyes squinting, head shaking, cheeks flushed. She'd become almost twitchy, her arms crossed and then at her hips and then crossed again within seconds. "Honey, bobcats aren't pets. They can hurt you."

I sighed dramatically. "Mom! It didn't seem mean . . ."

"They're very cute, but they have sharp teeth and big claws. Why don't you go change and get ready for dinner?"

"Can I just have ten more minutes?"

"No, baby. Go change," she said. She picked up my sister Kirsten, then licked her thumb and mopped it across Kirsten's juice-drenched chin. "Eat?" Mom said, and Kirsten repeated, "Eat! Eat!"

I groaned. "Fine."

I moped through the living room, down the hallway, and into the back bedroom that my two younger sisters and I shared. There were only three bedrooms at Grammie and Granddad's house: one for them, one for my parents, and one for us. We hadn't been in Alabama long, only a couple of months. After serving ten years, Dad had decided to leave the Army. I was just about to turn seven. He had been deployed every other year, fifteen months each time, and he wanted to be more present in our lives. Dad was as mysterious to me as that cat in the yard. Most of the memories I had of him were from videos he made while he was in Korea. He'd record himself reading me books from his barracks across the sea. The room he filmed in had unadorned walls, and my dad, an almost-stranger, would lie on a small bed in the center of it reading *Amelia Bedelia,* pausing every so often to adjust his thick-rimmed military-issued glasses.

After years of this, he decided he wanted to be home more. "If I stay in any longer, Karie won't know me," he said to my mom, and she agreed. She was tired of being a single parent. They used educational loans to buy a white Aerostar van and moved us from Washington State, where they had been stationed, to Alabama, where my dad's parents lived. They thought moving closer to family would be good for us. *Grandparents! Cousins! Aunts! Uncles! The American Dream!* I loved it. My sisters and I had cousins our ages who would visit us at Grammie and Granddad's house. We'd play on the swing set in the backyard, splash in puddles that collected in the ditch after storms, create clubhouses in the branches of fallen pecan trees. To me, it was perfect. But one morning, as I was looking through Granddad's drawers for a small box of foreign coins I secretly liked to play with, I overheard my parents complaining about how suffocated they felt. They were eager to find us our own home, but nothing about Alabama was as easy as they'd anticipated.

"We need you to find a job," my mom said to my dad at the dinner table later that night. Her body was rigid, her lips pursed. I took a bite of my corn casserole.

"I'm trying," he promised her. Looking deflated, his large frame shrinking in his chair, he closed his eyes and rubbed circles between his eyebrows. He'd gotten his master's in psychology online from Liberty University while he was in the military. It was his second attempt at getting a degree. The first was at Toccoa Falls College in Georgia. That's where my parents met. They'd both been involved with a school play, and on opening night, when it was time for my mom to take the stage, she was so overcome with anxiety, she couldn't do it. She hid backstage in tears. My dad, a lanky stagehand with a halo of brown ringlets, sat with her while she cried. He was taken by her blue eyes and thought her North Carolina drawl was cute. That week, he asked her if she wanted to go for a ride on his motorcycle, expecting her to say no. She was shy and soft-spoken, and he saw her as an innocent southern belle. When she said yes, he was elated. They quickly became inseparable, and eventually he proposed. She said yes again. By then, college had proven to be too difficult for Dad. He was losing interest and struggling to keep focused. If he wanted to have a family, though, he would need to provide for them. He didn't have family money to fall back on. The military, with all its promises and benefits, seemed like a good plan B.

Now, no longer in the Army and with no relevant work experience, he struggled to find a position that paid enough to provide for all five of us.

"Just take what you can get. I can get a job, too. We'll figure it out," Mom said. Kirsten squirmed in her lap, pawing at a spoonful of food that Mom brought to her mouth.

"I didn't serve for ten years to be poor," Dad replied. He put his fork down. "Maybe I should've just stayed in. Waited for retirement . . ."

"And spend half your kids' lives deployed while I play single mom back home? No. It'll get better. It has to."

I looked at my sister Kelsey, who was sitting next to me. I gently kicked her foot. When she looked up, I crossed my eyes and opened my mouth full of chewed-up food, attempting to ease the tension. She half-smirked and kicked me back.

———

My second-grade teacher, Ms. Christensen, wore dark red lipstick, her hair in a pixie cut, and she spoke with an accent thicker than I'd ever heard before. I struggled to understand what she was saying and failed my vocabulary tests because of it. I didn't recognize the words, so I'd spell them the way they sounded to me, rather than how I'd learned them. The second time it happened, Mom snatched the test from my hand.

"Another C minus! You know these! I know you know these!"

I stood there, nervously fiddling with the hem of my shirt. I remembered a snail I'd seen on the playground weeks before—soft and slow, but protected by its shell. I wished I'd been born with a shell to hide in. "I'm sorry, Mom," I said. I studied hard for school and didn't understand what I was doing wrong.

"No, I don't think it's you. It's this freaking redneck woman, this freaking redneck state!" Mom said, her face turning pink. She was starting to blame Alabama for all our problems. Moving to Washington State, for her, had symbolized success. Her family had lived in the same part of North Carolina since their ancestors came to America. She went to school in Georgia. Gave birth to me in Virginia. She always dreamed of leaving the South and living in a place with more opportunity and less stigma. The decision to move back to the South had been a complicated one, based on what she thought was best for her children rather than her own desires. It left her bitter.

Mom took a deep breath. "Sorry. Sorry, I shouldn't say that. She's nice . . . it's just . . ." she growled. "Look, spell *dress* for me."

I stood up straight. "D-R-E-S-S, dress."

"See! You know these! I'm talking to her," she said. She slapped the test on the kitchen counter.

"No, Mom!" I begged. I didn't want the teacher to hate me.

"Yep. I have to. This is ridiculous."

Mom didn't mention it again, but I assumed she called the school because, from then on, Ms. Christensen pronounced every word slowly, awkwardly drawing out and emphasizing each letter.

"Wwwwiiiissssse," she said during our next test, contorting her face.

Mom looked pleased when I came home a few days later with an A.

————

Dad eventually found a job in Florida, just across the bay, at a place called the Waterfront Rescue Mission. It was a transition program for folks who'd been homeless. My dad worked there as a counselor, making just over minimum wage. It was less than what he had hoped for, but it also came with a discount at the thrift store attached to the mission and access to the free food people donated. As soon as he got his first paycheck, we moved to a house owned by a family friend in Elberta, Alabama, the town where my dad's sister lived and where my elementary school was located. It had one stoplight, and its only restaurant was the Roadkill Cafe. The house, painted various shades of beige and brown, was built in the seventies, had wall-to-wall shag carpet, and was located at the end of a dirt road with scattered potholes and poisonous snakes that made a loud popping noise when we ran over them with our car. The house sat on an acre of land surrounded by large fields that grew seasonal crops—corn and soybeans and cotton. We adopted two dogs: a medium-sized brown mutt named Jamie and a husky named Ivan, who had one icy-blue eye and one hazel eye. The dogs would often disappear into the woods. They'd show up half a day later with deer parts they'd spent the night ripping apart in the yard. I'd watch them through my bedroom window, disgusted, wondering if they'd killed the animal themselves.

The house's yard had space for a garden. Early that spring, Mom tilled a small plot near the chicken coop, and when the soil was soft enough, she pressed her index finger a half inch into the dirt, then again two feet away, and again and again. She stopped at three rows of five and handed me a small fistful of black pear-shaped seeds.

"Put one seed in each hole," she said, pointing toward the first one in the top row.

I squatted in front of the plot, opened my tiny fist, and picked my first seed, placing it into the hollow in the earth that Mom had made.

"Now cover it with dirt," she said, her cheeks pink from the heat. "Like this." She placed a seed into a different hole and swept loose soil over it with the edge of her palm. She looked up at me and smiled, wiping sweat from her forehead with the back of her arm. She always seemed happiest when she was working on a project, discernibly more at ease when she was busy with something that made her feel productive. So much of me wished she'd slow down sometimes, hold me and enjoy quiet moments with me. But when Mom was still for too long, she got antsy. Her mind wandered and she'd start worrying about things that hadn't even happened yet. And when she was like that, it threw everyone in the house off. She was at her best when she had something to keep her busy.

I dug my fingers into the earth, raked soil over my seed, then repeated this until I'd sown the entire row. Mom had already finished the remaining two rows. I looked up at her and smiled.

"Good job, sweetie," she said. "Now we just need water and patience."

I stood up and admired my work. "When do the watermelons come?" I asked.

"Around three months, give or take," she said.

"Aww, forever!"

Mom laughed. "It'll be here faster than you think," she said, standing up. One finger at a time, she pulled the gloves off of her hands.

"Can I go look at the chicks?" I asked. We'd adopted twelve of them earlier that week. We kept them in a galvanized tub with mulch at the bottom and a heat lamp clamped to the side. I wanted to keep them in my room, but Dad had said no.

"You can look at the chicks, just don't pick them up, okay?" Mom slapped the gloves together and chunks of dirt fell to the ground. She stuffed the gloves in her back pocket.

I sighed. "Okay," I said, already running toward the detached garage where we kept them.

The chicks were tiny balls of peeping downy fluff. I petted their heads one at a time with my finger, said "It's okay, it's okay" as they scurried away. My favorite was a black one that didn't seem as scared as the others. It was curious. Instead of running, it came to my hand and nibbled the tip of my index finger. I named it Curtis after a boy I had a crush on at school.

By June, the chicks had grown into pullets and cockerels and were living in the shabby chicken coop at the edge of our yard. Plump watermelons lay in Mom's garden, just in time to enjoy with my sisters and cousins during the hot summer months.

"Put your hands on the wheel," Dad said. It was late July—a few weeks before I'd have to go back to school—and Dad thought it would be fun to let me sit on his lap while he drove down the dirt road we lived on.

Sitting in his lap felt strange. It didn't happen often. My parents were only affectionate in random spurts that were welcome but always caught me off guard. I turned to look at him. Having gained some weight since leaving the Army, he was bearlike. He even had a hairy face now that nobody forced him to shave. I hardly recognized him.

"For real?" I asked.

"For real." Dad smiled. He took my right hand and put it on the wheel, and then I put my left hand on it, too. Dad took his hands off, leaving me to steer on my own. I'd watched grown-ups do it from the back seat and noticed the wheel often jiggled left to right. I didn't know that it happened when driving over bumps. I just thought it was what you were supposed to do when driving. I shook the wheel back and forth as quickly as my small arms would let me, just like I'd seen it done before. Dad yelled.

"Straight! Go straight!" he said, pulling my hands off so he could take over.

I screamed as he wrapped his left arm around my waist and slammed on the brakes. It was too late. The car plowed through a bush and hit a barbed-wire fence, my body jerking forward into the steering wheel. It didn't hurt much. But it was scary.

"I'm sorry, Daddy! I'm sorry!" I said, starting to cry.

Still in the bush, Dad put the truck in park. "Are you okay?" he asked. He brushed my hair out of my face and looked me over.

"I'm okay," I said, fat tears rolling down my cheeks.

"Hey. That wasn't your fault, okay? I shouldn't have let you do that."

"Okay," I said. I rubbed my eyes.

Dad put me in the passenger seat and reached over to pull the seatbelt across my body. He smelled like musky cologne. After the belt clicked, he put the truck in reverse.

"Maybe don't tell your mom about this, okay?"

"Okay," I said. "Can we do it again sometime? I'll go straight . . ."

Dad laughed and put his hand on my head. "I don't think that's a good idea, Kare Bear."

"Okay."

I felt at peace in that home, our little haven tucked away in the woods. I was happy when we moved away from Washington State. There, I'd been keeping secrets I wasn't sure I could bear anymore. When Dad was deployed and Mom needed a babysitter, she'd leave us with the neighbor whose duplex was attached to ours. She intended for us to be watched by the woman, but sometimes the woman would leave us with her husband. He was tall with dark hair. In my mind's eye, he was featureless, his face just a blur of white skin. While my younger sisters and his toddler son were watching cartoons, he'd lead me down the hallway to a bedroom with one window, close the door behind us, and instruct me to take my pants off.

"Don't tell your mom what we do in here," he'd say. "She'll be mad at you if she finds out."

I'd nod, so scared I was unable to speak. He would instruct me to lie on a queen-sized bed with no headboard and white crumpled-up sheets. And then he would lift my body and put his head between my legs. When the warmth of his tongue made me feel as though I had to pee, he'd tell me to do it in his mouth. I was so ashamed, I wished I'd never been born. I never told a soul.

When my parents announced we were leaving Washington, I prayed to God I could leave my secret behind and never have to think about what I'd done ever again. Alabama helped me forget. I finally felt safe and hoped we'd live there forever. But at the end of the summer, my parents announced we were moving again. The thought of living in an unfamiliar place filled me with dread. Memories of the scary man appeared in flashes. I wondered if the next place we moved to would be safe, too. My sisters and I were given little warning. Then, just like that, we rehomed the dogs and the chickens and abandoned our garden to move to Florida, just over an hour away. My parents said we needed to move because the family was smothering them. If we weren't at church one Sunday, my dad's sister would call that evening to see if we were okay. A week couldn't go by without a surprise visit from someone. To Mom and Dad, it was invasive. They hated confrontation, though, so instead of setting boundaries with our family, they chose to flee.

At my new school in Florida, Ms. Hansen was enthusiastic and had a pet turtle we got to feed every day. She would dance in front of the classroom as she sang, "Six times six is . . . thirty-six!" We'd all giggle and sing along, dancing and squealing with delight. In the afternoon, I volunteered in the library, where I was taught the Dewey Decimal System and helped file catalog cards in tiny drawers. I loved walking up and down aisles of books, loved the quiet, the order. It was the opposite of home. Mom and Dad were overworked. Tired. They didn't have the energy to deal with the sound of kids screaming and running and playing. We'd be instructed to either watch cartoons or go to our rooms. One night, my sister Kelsey and I sat on the floor of our room, cutting up socks to make outfits for our knockoff Big Lots Barbies. Our dolls were dressed in crooked white skirts, white tube tops with thick knots tied in the back, white hats. We'd lost ourselves in the fun of it, forgetting for a moment that we'd gotten in trouble for cutting up socks before. We pretended our dolls were talking to each other in their new outfits.

"Hello, Miss Jenkens. Where did you get that beautiful skirt?" I said in a high-pitched voice.

"From Kmart," Kelsey said, spinning her doll as if she were showing off her outfit.

The floor was covered in scraps when Mom found us. She gasped and marched into the room, then snatched up the basket she kept the socks in.

"I told you not to cut these up! What is wrong with you? Do you think money grows on trees?"

"Maybe," I said, sarcastically. Kelsey looked at me with wide eyes.

"John!" Mom yelled toward the hallway, and then looked to us. "I'll let your dad deal with this," she said as she turned to walk away. I could hear my dad's footsteps coming down the hallway. I knew a spanking was coming, and Dad always made us pull our pants down first so that hand met bare ass. If two of us were in trouble at once, he'd make us stand and watch as the other was being hit. I stood up, ran to the door, and slammed it shut. I locked it and hid under the bed.

"Open the door," Dad said, firmly. He waited a moment before yelling, "Open the door!"

It was too late. What was done was done, and I wasn't opening that door. Kelsey crawled under the bed with me and we held hands, crying, as Dad kicked the door over and over until it fell off the hinges. He crouched to the floor and looked at us, hiding.

"Don't make me pull you out," he hissed. Kelsey scurried out from under the bed, and I followed. One by one, we dropped our pants and took our punishment.

In the summer of 1994, Mom and Dad couldn't afford daycare, so Mom made a list of every church holding a Vacation Bible School in our area. Each week, we were dropped off at a new church where we'd hear the same stories about Jesus and Jonah and Noah. We'd make crosses out of Perler beads and Popsicle sticks, and would eat the free snacks. Before the summer was over, we packed all our things and moved to a different neighborhood. We moved many times after that, almost always because of money. Between low pay and over a hundred thousand dollars of school debt, my parents struggled to build the life they'd dreamed of when Dad left the military. It didn't help that they were overly concerned with appearances. They couldn't bring themselves to live within their means. Evangelicals, they believed God made prosperous those who deserved a place in heaven. In other words, if you're poor, you're probably a sinner who deserves to go to hell. My parents spent the bulk of their money renting houses they couldn't afford and hiding behind those pretty walls, hoping no one would notice the shabby furniture inside. We moved so much because, eventually, their bills would catch up with them and they'd be forced to downsize. Then Dad would get a scant raise and rent another fancier-than-us home before having to downsize again. And again. And again. Meanwhile, we couldn't afford healthcare or daycare, and many of our groceries came from the bins of donated food at my dad's work. I learned from my parents that if you have to be poor, you'd better be good at hiding it.

At eight, I babysat Kelsey after school and in the summertime. By the time I was ten, I was babysitting both sisters, and my parents filed for bankruptcy. Not long after that, my parents got wrapped up in Amway after learning about it from a church friend who claimed it changed her life. Dad had recently gotten a new job that paid more, and Mom was hired at one of Amway's brick-and-mortar stores as a sales associate. We moved to the biggest house we'd ever lived in, a two-story home with a white picket fence, and filled it with Amway products— dish detergent, eye shadow, vitamins, you name it. They enrolled me in a private Christian school where my teachers were more invested in me than I was used to. They would stay with me after class to work on concepts I was struggling with. I joined cross-country and volleyball. I was making friends. I loved it there.

One night, Dad gathered us around the kitchen table. His eyes were wide and manic, his foot bouncing up and down under the table.

"Girls," he said with a huge smile, "we're gonna be okay." Kelsey and I looked at each other. I was eleven and she was nine and we had no idea what he was talking about. Kirsten, who was five years old, played with a pile of naked Barbies in the living room. "You'll notice things changing around here. Eventually, we'll be able to buy a house with a big yard. I'll even buy you horses if you want 'em!"

"A horse? Really?" I exclaimed. I had a collection of plastic horses with matted hair. I'd taught myself to draw horses. I dreamed of being a horse trainer one day. I was that girl.

"Yep. Really."

After that, Mom started taking us to mansions after school. There, we'd watch Disney movies on big-screen TVs or swim in large screened-in pools while she did dishes, swept, mopped, and made beds. These were the homes of the people who'd reached Amway's Diamond status. We were nowhere near that, and it felt like a privilege to be able to see how they lived. We got a new TV and a new stereo system. I got a huge keyboard for my birthday. For a moment, I thought maybe we would be normal, maybe even rich. Then, one day, my parents came to my sisters and me looking defeated. They'd taken out a large loan, thinking they'd strike it rich and be able to pay it back. But they were spending more money on Amway than they were making. It wasn't what they expected. We'd have to move again, this time to a house so small I'd have to share a room with my two sisters.

By the time I was thirteen, I had gone to six schools: four elementary schools and two middle schools. It was 1998, my dad had just been offered a position as a pastor at a small church in Foley, Alabama, and I would start over again. I thought I'd mastered letting go, but this move proved more complicated than the ones before it. This time, I was contending with puberty. Sometime after starting my period at twelve, I'd become aware of my body and how it was interacting with, influencing, and being judged by others. When I walked next to the highway to my favorite sno-cone stand, men yelled things at me, like "Hey, baby!" and "Whore!" At church, an older boy with body hair who always smelled like sour sweat said I was hot, said he wanted me to come swim at his pool sometime so he could see me in a bikini. I didn't know what to do with this new attention. I couldn't talk to my parents. They'd become distant, were more stressed than they'd ever been. Dad was gone a lot, even when he was supposed to be home from work. Mom was working odd jobs, like delivering newspapers before the sun came up and cleaning condos on the weekends. I didn't have friends to talk to, because I was never in one place long enough to keep any. I would have to navigate my new body on my own.

The night before I started eighth grade, I looked at myself naked in the mirror. All I saw were flaws. My hips were too square, my breasts too small, and my waist too wide. I hated my scars the most, relics of my nervous habit of picking. My legs were covered in them, cratered like the surface of the moon. My only female role model, my mom, wasn't much help. She always talked about how she would get plastic surgery if she could afford it. When makeover shows became popular, she devoured them. With each reveal, a brand-new version of the person would stand at the mirror smiling at their appearance, and my mom would sigh audibly.

"If I was on the show, I'd get rid of this turkey neck," she'd say, pinching the skin under her chin. "And my schnoz." She'd laugh at herself, then gaze into the distance. "I'd just tell 'em 'fix me' and let 'em have at it."

I would look at her as she spoke, trying to see what she saw. She was thin with pale blue eyes, and her skin was bronze from lying out on the back porch on sunny weekends. She was great at thrifting stylish clothes on a strict budget. I always thought she was beautiful. But she insisted the flaws were there until I saw them, too. *Okay, fine, maybe her nose is a little big,* I started to believe. *I can kind of see the neck thing, I guess. Sure, her clothes could be more fashionable.* And then, as a girl who looked a lot like her mother, I'd look in the mirror and see the same flaws in myself.

2

THE ONES WHO WOULD FIGHT

August 1998

I noticed Cleve on the very first day of eighth grade. He was taller than most other boys, a football player with a collection of *South Park* T-shirts—a cartoon I wasn't allowed to watch—and more friends than I'd ever dreamed of having. He seemed to always have an audience and a funny story on hand to keep them entertained. When he walked, there was a buoyancy to his step, a confidence in the way he held his shoulders, even though he also seemed a little nerdy. At times Vin Diesel and at others Dustin Diamond, he was a paradox, and I found it captivating.

It took me months to finally introduce myself. Instead, I passed the time playing MASH, a game drawn on a piece of paper meant to "foretell" the future. I'd cheat, playing over and over until it predicted Cleve and I would be married, live in a mansion, and drive my dream car: a yellow Volkswagen Beetle. I'd kept all the papers that promised our perfect future in a shoebox under my bed, along with a Coke wrapper Cleve had left on his desk once, a few of my favorite Pogs, paper folded into a fortune-teller, a *Backstreet's Back* CD, and my diary.

I made contact at the urging of my friend Fiona, whom I met in band class. The first time she spoke to me, in the third week of school, she tapped my shoulder and said, "Those are my shoes."

I turned around to see a petite, black-haired girl's manicured finger pointing toward my feet. I looked down at my shoes and then back at her, confused.

"Huh?"

"The tear near the toe on the right foot," she said. She pointed to a minor imperfection on my brown leather sandal. "Those were mine. I wanted new ones because they're torn. My mom donated them last month."

I felt sick, the urge to flee rushing through my body like flames on dry grass. Almost all of my clothes were secondhand, but nothing like this had ever happened before. I'd hoped nobody could tell my clothes were old, but now I was certain they could. I imagined throwing my flute at Fiona and running out the door, never to return.

"No, they aren't," I said in an almost-whisper.

I turned away from her and held my flute with clenched fists. I willed myself to disappear, imagining I was invisible through the rest of class.

When the bell rang, Fiona pulled me into the hallway and apologized.

"That was my bad," she said. She pinched her eyelashes, then looked at her fingers before wiping them quickly on the front of her plaid skirt. "I noticed you before and thought you had a cool style. It's different from what other kids here wear. When I saw the shoes, I got excited. I'm dumb. Sorry."

Fiona swayed as she spoke, nervously zipping and unzipping her Tommy Hilfiger bag. I could tell it wasn't easy for her to admit she'd been an asshole. I appreciated her courage, even if I still hated her for doing that to me in front of our classmates. I wondered what she meant by "different." I hated that word. Like lava, it filled my core with heavy, burning anxiety. I didn't like standing out. All I wanted—more than anything else in the world—was to fit in. But when I arrived at Foley Middle, I was shocked by how the girls dressed. While I wore baggy jeans, flannel button-downs, and skate shoes, the girls at Foley wore bootcut jeans, Birkenstocks that looked to me like duck feet, and form-fitting, tummy-revealing tees with names like Calvin Klein or Ralph Lauren written across the chest.

I forced a smile. "It's okay," I said.

She asked if I was new and when I said yes, she invited me to sit with her at lunch. She became my only friend that year.

Fiona—like many of the kids at Foley—had known Cleve since elementary school. When I told her I had a crush on him, she squealed.

"Oh my gosh! Don't do that!" I crossed my arms and scowled at her.

"Oh, please!" she said, rolling her eyes. "I'm allowed to be excited if I want."

She told me Cleve hadn't always been that tall. Just a couple years before, he was short and thin with dorky, oversized glasses. Then, last year, he shot up in height, becoming one of the tallest boys in school. Suddenly, he was getting more attention from girls.

"You should write him a note," Fiona said with a wide smirk and a wild look in her eye. I hadn't expected her to get this excited about a dumb crush.

"Nooo." I shook my head. "No way, José. Not happening. What if he doesn't answer? I'd die."

"He's really nice! And you're so pretty! You *have* to talk to him!"

It took months. I waited until the next semester, using the solitude of winter break to mull over the pros and cons of making my feelings known. And then, in late January, as the words "I did not have sexual relations with that woman" echoed through every television screen and radio speaker in the country, I decided to write Cleve a note. Anything to get Fiona to shut up about it. I kept it simple. *Hi, I'm Karie. What's up?* I wrote on a piece of yellow notebook paper. I arrived at English class early to avoid being seen and placed the carefully folded note on his desk before leaving again to go to the bathroom, even though I didn't actually need to go. I tried to pee. I paced a little. I washed my hands. I fixed my hair. By the time I got back, half the class had arrived, including Cleve, who sat in front of me, just to the right. The note was gone. That day all I heard from my teacher was wordless nonsense: "Wah-wah wah-wah-wah." I was too busy daydreaming about my future with Cleve, too distracted by the perfection that was the back of his egg-shaped head, his ears protruding just like Will Smith's. So dreamy.

At the end of class, he left without looking at me, and I wondered if I'd made a mistake.

The next day, I sat nervously at my desk, damp palms tucked under my thighs, waiting for class to begin and regretting the whole thing. *Had he even gotten the note?* I thought. *What if someone else picked it up? If he did get it, what if he doesn't want to talk to me? What if he tells his friends?* I was spiraling.

I pretended I was reading my textbook as Cleve passed through the doorway. I ran my finger down the page and pointed at a random word, tapped on it: *Verb. Oh, yes. Verbs are so verby.* I looked up to the right and made my best deep consideration face. Cleve placed his gray backpack on his desk, unzipped the front pocket, and pulled out a folded note before turning toward me and putting it on my desk. We made eye contact and held it for the first time. He smiled. I smiled. My heart thundered in my chest. I tucked the note in my pocket so the teacher wouldn't take it. After class, I pretended I was looking for something in my purse until Cleve left. I couldn't handle more eye contact. It was too much. Once he was gone, I headed to my locker, where I hid behind the door and pulled out the note. *hi. i'm cleve. nuthin much. are u new?*

Over the course of a week, we swapped notes until he asked for my phone number. The night he called, I stretched our corded phone as far as I could, making it just past my bedroom door. I lay on my stomach, kicking my feet back and forth, my face numb from grinning so wide. I listened to every word he said as if I were studying for a test. He told me his full name was Jimmy Cleveland Kinsey II, but people already called his dad Jimmy. That's why everyone called him Cleve. He was raised behind a field that grew soybeans, corn, and cotton, in a trailer with broken-down cars parked in the front yard. The trailer hid in the shadows of pine and oak woods at the end of a dirt road named after his grandfather. He'd lived there his entire life, something I tried to imagine but couldn't. Cleve was technically his parents' second child after a baby boy who was born with a hole in his heart. The baby didn't live longer than a month, so Cleve grew up the oldest of four. From what I could tell, he was an excellent big brother: loving, supportive, protective. But he was hard on his siblings, too. "There's no room for fuckin' up when you're a Kinsey," he told me. He knew they would have to fight for what they wanted because they weren't born with money.

It must have been springtime when we shared our first kiss because he had been leaving fresh-picked flowers on my desk. Cicadas sang as he walked me home after school each afternoon, the air thick with humidity. Those awkward walks were lessons in early love: How to Hold Hands; How to Speak Without Running Out of Breath; How to Stop Giggling Like a Fool. One day he stopped me under the bleachers of the football stadium.

"Can I kiss you?" he asked.

He stood in front of me, a baby mustache budding on his upper lip, brown eyes longing for a yes, a dumpster steaming in the heat behind him. It was finally time for the lesson I had been waiting for: How to Kiss.

"Yes," I said meekly, and he pulled me into him.

He smelled like cheap cologne and sweat, and the dumpster smelled like hot Coke and something rotting. His mustache tickled my lips. *Maybe I love him,* I thought.

He walked me home almost every day after school. It was the only time we could find to be alone. The walks were usually quiet and awkward, us holding hands, me smiling nervously and struggling to come up with interesting things to say. He'd look over at me and nudge his shoulder into mine, smirking. I'd look at him sheepishly from the corner of my eye, giggle, and nudge back. He always kissed me before we parted. It was all so sweet.

A few weeks after our first kiss, I found him after football practice and broke up with him. I'd heard he had a crush on a cheerleader. While there was no way to know for sure if it was true or just a rumor, cutting off the relationship felt safer than risking being heartbroken.

"I'm not really ready for a relationship, I don't think," I lied. I stared at my feet as I kicked a rock loose from the soil. When he didn't respond, I looked up. His eyes were closed, his fingers laced and resting at his mouth as if he were praying.

He nodded, his mouth in a tight line. "I get it. I understand." His eyes opened, large and longing like a puppy dog's. "Can we stay friends?" he asked.

I smirked. "Duh. I mean, I hope so."

"Good," he said. We stood in uncomfortable silence. He scratched his head and then pulled at the chest of his white T-shirt to fan himself. It was hot out, and he was sweaty from practice. I folded my arms and looked at the ground again. I swayed side to side, something I'd always done when I was nervous or forced to stand still for too long. "Well, shit." Cleve sighed. "Can I at least get a hug?"

Relieved that he had broken the tension, I chuckled. "Duh," I said. I wrapped my arms around his waist and squeezed. I paused to inhale him—all sweat and grass and soil—unsure if I'd ever get a chance to again. As I began to pull away, he grabbed my arm and gently pulled me back toward him. My chest tightened as he kissed my forehead. My cheeks burned. Despite my decision to break up with him, there was no doubt I still had feelings. I didn't know if I was making the right decision, but I knew I was making the safe one and that was good enough for me. We remained friends after that. An intensity that was hard to ignore buzzed between us, but we never acted on it. He started calling me "little sis," and I found comfort in the idea that I had someone looking out for me.

By the time I was in high school, Mom often slept on the couch and cried more than she smiled. She didn't have friends or family she trusted, so she came to me, her eldest daughter, with her problems. I was in ninth grade when I came home from school and found her sitting on our faded sectional with her head in her hands. The wall behind her was covered in chicken-themed decor: chicken figurines, chicken wallpaper, chicken art. She called her knickknacks her "finds." It wasn't that she particularly loved chickens. It was just that, in Alabama, chicken decor was plentiful and cheap in thrift stores. She always said that even with little money, it was important to her to make her house feel like a home. She was good at it, too. No matter where we lived, the air smelled like cinnamon, and the floors were so clean you could eat off of them.

"Mom?" I said, inching toward her cautiously. Sometimes when she was like this, she got mean. If she were a chicken, I imagined she'd be a rooster with extra-long spurs. When there was no sign of danger, she was pleasant, even if always on a mission and not paying much attention to us kids. She'd flit through the house with Febreze in one hand and a duster in the other, always doing ten things at once. But when she felt threatened, she had a short temper and sharp tongue. She didn't scare me, necessarily, but I also didn't like being verbally lunged at. I spent a lot of time in my room with the door closed.

Mom looked up at me and shook her head. "Apparently your dad doesn't care about clothing his own kids," she said. "I have to freaking hide money from him. I should have enough to buy you new jeans soon." If her spurs were out this time, they were directed at Dad, not me.

I had rarely seen Dad anywhere besides Sunday morning church in months. There, he was cheerful, funny, and warm. People loved him. But he spent the rest of the week at his job or locked in his room. When he emerged, he had a scowl on his face. He'd avoid eye contact and tramp to the kitchen, dig around in the fridge, then carry an armload of food back to the room and close the door behind him. "Fat ass," my mom would say under her breath. She resented that Dad used food as a coping mechanism when we had so little of it to begin with.

"Thank you, Mom," I said. I chewed my lip to distract myself from my increasing heart rate. I wished I didn't need so much. I saw the way Mom would skip a meal so we could eat until we were full, the way her face scrunched when our feet grew too big for our shoes again. "I'll see if I can pick up some hours at work."

I'd taken a job at a restaurant that catered to tourists. I was called a "passer." The uniform was jeans, a collared shirt with the restaurant's logo, and red suspenders. I walked around the room with large pots of southern food.

"Black-eyed peas!" I'd yell, dragging my feet as I weaved between oversized wooden booths. "Getcher black-eyed peas!"

Hands would wave in the air until I scooped gray blobs of beans onto all of their plates. The place's motto was "Home of the Throwed Rolls," because we also pushed around carts of big, warm rolls and hurled them across the room to whoever wanted them. On the days roll-throwing was my job, I often landed at least one directly in someone's sweet tea. Dark amber liquid would fly through the air, and the whole room would laugh and holler. When people asked what I did, I told them I worked at the redneck show, because it seemed like tourists only came to the restaurant to get up close to the wild and weird Alabamians. And we performed for them, too. We'd pretend to spill pitchers of tea in people's laps, only the pitchers were filled with molasses too thick to pour. We pretended to be holding pots of food, but when people asked for a scoop, we'd pull out a stuffed racoon with tongs instead, jiggling it above the table as everyone screamed or laughed, all while country music played in the background.

Despite my promise to my mom, I knew I couldn't really pick up more hours. I didn't have time for it with school. But I'd learned from Fiona that what you couldn't buy, you could steal. You just had to be smart about it. All my makeup and half my wardrobe was stolen.

"I'm sorry," my mom said. She began to cry. "I'm doing the best I can."

"You don't have anything to apologize for, Mom," I said, putting my hand on her shoulder. I considered hugging her, but couldn't. We weren't a hugging family. The thought of embracing her made my skin crawl, and I hated myself a little for feeling that way. I'd read somewhere that certain tree species' branches never touch, no matter how big they get. When the trees are fully grown, rather than their branches reaching toward each other, rivers of space form between them. It made me sad. It was called crown shyness, and it was what my family had.

As time went on, my parents continued to fight, and though they tried to hide it, we could hear them yelling in their bedroom. Mom would call Dad *lazy, deadbeat, waste of space*. She was working just as much as he was, but he wasn't helping her with chores or the kids. It wasn't fair. She was sick of it. She wanted a different life. He'd take her yelling for a while before finally shouting back, "Would you just shut up!" He'd storm out of the room and redirect his anger toward my sisters and me.

"Go to your room!" he'd demand, his voice a demonic baritone that seemed to force its way out of him. We knew not to challenge him when he was like that. We would scamper away.

Kelsey eventually went to live with my dad's sister in the next town over, leaving Kirsten and me behind. It was no secret that my parents were struggling to take care of all three of us, so my aunt offered to take Kelsey off their hands. My aunt and uncle had money. Kelsey would have her own room now. She would go to a private Christian middle school. She would take tumbling classes and try out for the cheerleading squad. My aunt and uncle would take full financial responsibility for her. I wasn't sure why they chose Kelsey, but I assumed it had something to do with her being the same age that Anna Lynn, their daughter who had died as a toddler, would have been. Kelsey and Anna Lynn even had similar features—curly blond hair and blue eyes.

I was fifteen, and it all seemed to happen overnight. Once Kelsey was gone, she quickly became a stranger whose world I could only imagine. My aunt and uncle thought it was important to keep us separated. I'd been caught a couple of times sneaking out at night to be with friends, so the adults in my family thought it was too late to fix me. But Kelsey was still young enough—only thirteen years old—to keep from following the same path. The few times I did visit her, I couldn't believe the way she was living. She had Clinique makeup, Bath & Body Works lotions and sprays, clothes from the Limited Too. I was furious with jealousy and lonelier than ever.

A few weeks after Kelsey left, I came home from work to my mom alone on the couch again, looking melancholy. I sighed, bracing myself for what she was about to say.

"We need to have a chat," she said. Still in her mismatched pajamas, she picked up the TV remote and turned off the *Law & Order* rerun she'd been watching.

I rolled my eyes. Something about seeing her sitting there on the couch made me angry. She looked pitiful. I knew this was about Dad. It was always about Dad, and I was tired of hearing about it. *Get up and fucking leave,* I thought, but said, "Do we have to right now?"

"Don't roll your eyes at me. This is serious."

"Is it, though?" I said sarcastically. I'd become increasingly smart with her, especially when Dad wasn't around. Mom took a deep breath. I sat on the opposite end of our sectional, pursed my lips, and looked at her wide-eyed. "I'm listening."

She looked at me with an intensity that gave me chills, black mascara smudged under both eyes. She spoke warily. "Something happened to your dad last night." She paused, searching for the right words. "He . . . he saw things that . . . weren't there."

"What does that mean?"

"I'm not sure," she said, shaking her head. "It's something we have to figure out."

I crossed my arms and leaned back. "But what did he see?" I asked. Now she really had my attention.

She took her glasses off, rubbed the bridge of her nose, then put them back on. She looked up at me. "Spiders?" she said. She seemed almost twitchy as the word came out of her mouth. "And a cannonball?"

I chuckled, though none of this was actually funny to me. "A . . . cannonball?"

Mom shrugged and nodded. "We were watching a movie, and there was a cannonball, and he thought it was real. He jumped behind the couch to hide. After he calmed down, he told me some things that were a little disturbing." She shook her head. "I probably shouldn't even be telling you this."

"Too late now. What exactly happened?"

She looked at the floor and clasped her hands in her lap, rubbing one thumb with the other. "He's been listening to radio stations with nothing but static, searching for messages from God. I don't know how long that's been going on. But then, yesterday, he saw colorful spiders crawling all over the floor."

"So Dad's schizo . . ."

Mom scoffed. "Don't say that. That's rude. We don't know what's going on, but he's sick. So if we seem off right now, that's why."

"Sorry," I said. "I just don't know what to say. This is really fucking weird."

She glared at me. "Don't use that kind of language around me," she said, before her body softened. "I don't know what to say, either."

Cleve called that afternoon asking if I wanted to go skinny-dipping. I agreed, but under one condition. "I'm keeping my underwear on."

He laughed. "Yes, ma'am."

"Pick me up on the corner by the church at eleven," I said, then hung up. Mom would never give me permission to go, but I needed out of the house. I'd have to sneak out.

That night, I stripped to my underwear and ran toward the water as the other kids cheered my name. In my family, nudity was sinful. But it was dark enough that I figured nobody could see me. I ran as quickly as I could to hide my body in the inky water. The moon glowed bright and reflected on the waves, all flickering light as far as the eye could see until the water turned into constellations. I sank neck-deep and went limp, giving way to the waves. Floating on my back, I stared at the sky, trying to figure out if I was looking at the Milky Way or a cloud, wondering if my mom would discover I'd left.

Cleve waded over to me and took my hand. "Watch this," he said. He pulled my hand gently through the water, and behind it was a spar-kling green trail.

"Whoa," I gasped. "What is that?"

"Bioluminescence. It happens out here sometimes. Pretty, huh?"

I'd never seen anything so magical in my life. We splashed and spun and watched as the algae wrapped around our bodies like fairy dust. Afterward we sat on the sand, wrapped in towels and drinking beers. When I told him about what was happening at home, he told me his home life wasn't great, either.

"Daddy's always spendin' his money on booze. He leaves Mama at home to go to bars. I love him, but Mama doesn't deserve that." He looked down and shook his head. "Pisses me off."

I nodded and dug a fistful of sand. "As soon as I'm old enough, I'm leaving. I don't care where I go."

Cleve shrugged. "Kinsey blood runs deep here. Messed up as my family is, I think I'd miss 'em too much."

I grumbled, then rested my head on my knees. "Not me."

Cleve looked at me and smirked. "You say that now."

"I'm serious. I know I'd be better off."

The truth was, it was hard for me to imagine anything different from what was in front of me. My parents never had conversations with me about my future. It wasn't on their priority list. Everything was about surviving one day to get to the next. If I was going to find a better life for myself, I would have to do it on my own. But I had no plan. Everything seemed far-fetched when I tried to envision what I wanted to do when I grew up. I didn't have money, I wasn't making good grades. I figured my best bet would be to get married and be a good wife and mother. I cringed at the thought.

I looked up at the sky and remembered a weird Burger King commercial where Whoppers were being thrown out of an airplane followed by skydivers who caught them in midair. I thought the commercial was silly, but the idea of skydiving stuck with me. I imagined an open door, a leap, wind against my body, falling, falling, falling. I imagined the thrill of the unknown, the terror of possible death, the adrenaline rushing through me, making me forget, for a moment, everything else in the world.

"God, I just want to go skydiving right now. Maybe one day you could take me when you get your pilot license," I said, nudging him with my elbow.

Cleve smiled. "When I get my pilot license, we can go wherever you want."

"A safari in Africa?"

"Maybe so."

A year later, I was sixteen and repeating the tenth grade. I began isolating myself at school. I quit extracurricular activities, stopped turning in assignments, and ate my lunches in a bathroom stall so no one would notice me eating alone. After school, I hung out with kids who'd already graduated, friends I'd met years before when they were seniors and I was a freshman. I'd begun dating one of them over the summer, a persistent twenty-year-old named Jonathon who'd had his eye on me for a while. One night, he snuck in through my bedroom window. He begged and begged for me to have sex with him until I gave in. He took my virginity on my bedroom floor. When he was done, he stood up and zipped his baggy jeans.

"That was nice. Betcha didn't know what you were missing, huh?" he said. I half-smiled as I pulled my pajama pants back on. "I have to get outta here," he told me. "My boys are expecting me to come out. Wanna hang tomorrow?"

"Sure," I said as I pulled my hair into a ponytail. I already knew I was going to ghost him. I didn't care about Jonathon, I just didn't want to be alone. It was as if the light in my life had been switched off, and I was crawling in darkness, feeling around for anything at all to hold on to. He just happened to be there.

Around that time, my aunt said that she wanted to adopt Kelsey. She reminded my parents that I was a bad influence and that she had the means to give Kelsey the life she deserved. Mom wasn't convinced. She'd known my aunt since college and had never liked her much. The distance between them had only gotten worse since Kelsey moved. So, when she called to talk about adoption, Mom was pissed. I sat on the couch, watching her pace and scream into the phone.

"That's my kid! My kid!" she yelled. She stopped in front of the kitchen. "Oh, you think so?" She pulled the phone away from her ear and put the receiver to her mouth. "Try me! I'll call the police!" she said before hanging up.

Mom brought Kelsey home that night, and, in a rage, my aunt threw all of Kelsey's belongings in a dumpster. In less than twenty-four hours, Kelsey went from being the star cheerleader at her private school to the unknown new girl at a mediocre public school. Heartbroken, she cried on and off for days. I wanted to comfort her, but I didn't know how to cross the ocean between us. She was distant after having been told that I was bad news, and I was bitter that she'd gotten special treatment while I was stuck at home feeling neglected.

One afternoon, Kelsey and I argued over whose turn it was to use our shared computer. The bickering grew louder and louder, until Dad barged into the room. Everything after that happened so quickly: his hand around my neck, my body pinned to my parents' bed by his body, his face strained and only inches above mine.

"Shut the fuck up!" he spat. "Shut the fuck up, or I'll snap your neck! I'll fucking snap your neck."

I'd never heard him say *fuck* before. I'd never felt his hands around my throat before. Mom stood in the doorway screaming. Kelsey screamed, too. I cried as all my options presented themselves in a flash. *Would he really snap my neck?* I thought for a second, then: *Survive! Survive!* I decided I would have to kick him between the legs and run, but I hesitated, afraid to touch him there, afraid to hurt him. He pushed his weight into my throat again, repeating those words: *Snap. Neck. Fuck.* I held my breath and kicked. He rolled off of me, and I ran. I thought my legs might collapse under me. I wanted to stop, to scream, *It's not fair it's not fair I hate you!* But adrenaline carried me past my sister Kirsten, who was ten now and wailing, and out the door. I tore a decorative fall wreath from the door on the way out. I felt insane; if anyone got in my way, I would tear them apart.

I didn't know where I was going. I had no plan. All I had was instinct urging me to flee and my mom's wreath clenched in my angry fist. A fierce game of tug-of-war between love and hate was playing out in my mind, and it left me feeling dizzy, seeing red, raging. I threw the wreath—adorned in plastic flowers and foliage—into the ditch that lined the edge of our front yard. It bounced off the ground, and for a moment I was filled with a sense of satisfaction as cheap shrapnel flew off of it in all directions.

That year, I'd torn one of my sister's chain necklaces in two after a fight, ripped my parents' car's visor from its hinge, thrown a bag of trash across our living room. Sometimes at night, I'd sneak out of my house and vandalize things with friends. We'd smash lights shining on signs at the entrances of neighborhoods fancier than ours, we'd egg teachers' houses, and at construction sites we'd knock over porta-potties. It felt good to destroy things, like pressure being released. I yearned for that feeling you get when your parent sees you—like, really hears you and wants to help you succeed or find happiness or, I don't know, have an okay day. But my parents didn't seem to notice that I was struggling. The yearning turned to rage turned to a physical thing—a knot at my core that, when provoked, demanded I expend as much energy as possible as quickly as possible. Sometimes that meant destroying something. That always got people's attention.

"Fuck you!" I screamed, watching the wreath settle in a puddle in the ditch. "I hate you! I hate all of you!"

Part of me was afraid of my neighbors seeing me losing my shit in the yard—our messiness on display. But another part of me wanted people to witness it. I was exhausted by trying to keep our family's dysfunction hidden, by the fear that people would find out we were frauds rather than the perfect family we pretended to be at church. I wondered if freedom could be found in letting the world see us, cheap decor, rainbow spiders, torn shoes, and all. More importantly, I knew the easiest way to hurt my parents was to expose their most profound shame: our broken family.

I only came back home because I had nowhere else to go. The sight of the wreath lying in the same place I'd left it caused a pang in my throat. Like my father, I was capable of violence. *Is this how it starts?* I wondered. What happens once anger leaves the body and becomes a thing in the world, like a battered wreath? If the tiniest flap of a butterfly's wings can cause a tornado, what could this rageful destruction do? *You didn't deserve that,* I whispered to the wreath before stepping into the damp ditch to retrieve it. I hung it back on the front door, a mess of twigs tangled into a misshapen circle.

My mom, sisters, and I stayed at Motel 6 that night. In the car on the way there, Mom said she was done.

"He finally crossed the line," she said, her hands gripping the steering wheel firmly at ten and two. "I'm sorry I let that happen to you."

I rolled my eyes and rested my head against the window. I took a deep breath. I hated how she caved under the stress of Dad's mental illness, the minimum wage that hardly paid the bills, and the three children no one was helping her raise. She was no longer capable of giving what I needed from a mother—she'd been checked out for years—and I was bitter about it. But I also felt bad for her. She wasn't even able to meet her own needs anymore. Who did she go to when she needed comfort? Love? Reassurance? Looking at her clutching the steering wheel, all I saw was defeat. I was angry, but I also wished I could protect her. At sixteen, all I could do was relieve her of the burden of my pain.

"I'm fine," I said. "Dad was just in a bad mood. It's fine."

After two nights at the hotel, we stayed at Grammie and Granddad's for a week before going back to Dad. "He's my best friend," Mom said. "I can't just leave him." I knew it was also because God didn't like divorce. It would take a lot more than my dad attacking me for my parents to break their wedding vows.

We went back to the house we called home. The wreath, accentuated by the muted coral door on which it hung, greeted us. *Welcome back to hell,* it said. The house smelled like ripe trash and apple-cinnamon candles. A forgotten pot of murky water full of soggy spaghetti noodles sat on the stove. Our cat, named Kitty because we could never settle on a real name, ran to us and wrapped her chubby body around Kirsten's ankles, mewing for ear scratches and food. I didn't want to be there. Home is meant to be a refuge; this was no home, but I couldn't think of a single place where I felt safe.

That next Tuesday, a woman from the front office interrupted Miss Daniels's lesson to whisper something in her ear. She turned on the mounted TV, which showed a large building I didn't recognize, a plume of smoke rising from it. I thought it was a movie before I realized it was the news broadcasting from New York City. And then a plane appeared and hit the identical building next to it. My teacher screamed, and my skin tightened with goosebumps, my eyes filling with tears, though it didn't feel like crying. I still wasn't sure what was going on.

A student asked what we were all thinking: "What's happening?"

The teacher hesitated before saying she wasn't sure.

The news anchors repeated the word *terrorist, terrorist, terrorist.*

I was confused and afraid. We all were.

When class was over, I walked out to an uncommon stillness in the hallway. Rather than a river of adolescent humans moving from one class to the next, it was more like coagulating blood, clumps of kids hugging and crying and expressing their disbelief. One girl's voice echoed, "My mom is there!" I didn't know if she meant New York City or the buildings themselves.

After some time had passed, I was much more concerned with failing high school and the news that Fiona was pregnant than I was with terrorists. Hallway chatter went back to new boyfriends and Friday's party. It seemed everyone had moved on. It hadn't occurred to us that our country might go to war, and that if it did, we'd be the ones fighting it.

3

SOULMATES

October 2002

Kelsey and I sat on the floor of our shared room, rummaging through our belongings, trying to decide what we would throw away this time.

"Emily's mom has an attic full of things from when she was a kid," Kelsey said. Her hair—thick, dirty-blond curls—fell in her face as she shoved a pile of colorful school folders into a black trash bag. She pushed a piece of hair behind her ear and rolled her eyes. "She has report cards from when she was, like, five. It's like our parents don't even care."

"You wish we had that?" I asked. I'd considered whether it was something I wanted. Our parents always threw away our things when we moved. It was like we were just another disposable, unimportant thing in their lives that took up too much space. Although it had made me sad in the past, I couldn't tell if I still felt that way. Anger had choked out all the other emotions a long time ago.

"Yes."

I looked up at her and tilted my head. "I'm sorry."

Earlier that day, our parents had dropped a bomb: Mom had gotten a better-paying job in Tampa and we had two months to pack our things and say goodbye to our lives in Foley. The way they told us rather than talked to us about it was cruel. At seventeen years old, I was finally in the eleventh grade. I'd been feeling a bit more optimistic that year, too. I'd made a few friends, had pulled my grades out of the gutter, and was starting to grow a bit more confident in my body. Kelsey and I weren't children anymore, we were damn near adults, and the news we'd have to move was crushing. Kirsten, who was much more easygoing and eager to please our parents, didn't seem as bothered as we did. She'd been so young for most of our moves, only seven when we finally landed in Foley. She hadn't known what it was like to say goodbye to friends over and over again.

"It's not your fault," Kelsey said.

"I know. But still." Kelsey and I had grown closer. As the eldest sister, I felt responsible for fixing things but was rarely able to, so I often felt like a failure. I wanted to tell my sister that our parents cared, that they had no choice but to get rid of our things because we had moved so much. But I wasn't sure if I believed that. I wasn't sure if they considered us at all when we moved.

While Foley had been far from perfect, we'd lived there longer than anywhere else in my lifetime. Imagining leaving the place I'd only just started to figure out, imagining starting over *again* made me want to scream. I'd been in this position before and knew exactly how it would go. Eventually, I'd lose touch with everyone I cared about. My life here would fade into the past. I'd struggle to fit in and would find myself alone all over again.

I couldn't bear the thought of moving to Tampa, so I decided to run away. I waited until the night before the move. I knew if I waited until then, it was unlikely my parents would come looking for me. I carefully opened the window of Kelsey's and my shared room and tossed my suitcase into the front yard. It hit the grass with a thud, and then, my body halfway out the window, I heard a whisper.

"I knew it!"

I froze. Kelsey was awake. "Go back to sleep," I said. I closed my eyes and willed her to lie back down.

Kelsey sat up. "Take me with you! I don't want to move, eith—"

"Absolutely not," I said, shaking my head. "You need to go with Dad." Mom was already in Tampa by then. She'd gone ahead of us to start her new job. "Please don't say anything, okay?" I pulled myself back inside and sat on the windowsill, rubbing my eyes in frustration.

Kelsey flung the comforter aside and stood up. "If you don't take me, I'll wake him up."

"Are you fucking serious right now?"

"Please," she pleaded. Her eyes, tears welling in them, glowed in the window light.

"Fuck." I paused to think. I imagined how hard life could get for us. I was planning to live with an eighteen-year-old boy I'd been dating for only a couple of months. I knew it was risky, and I didn't want Kelsey to get caught up in my drama. But I also didn't want her ruining this for me. And the thought of leaving her behind with my parents made me feel bad. I shook my head. "Would you please just stay? Please?"

"I wanna come with you!"

With clenched fists, I shook my head. "Fine! Damn it. You have to get a job!"

"Okay!" She nodded enthusiastically. "I can get a job!" She crouched next to her bed and felt around under it, searching for her duffle bag.

"Just fucking grab some clothes and a toothbrush and come on," I said as I started out the window again. "I'll be on the corner in front of Emily's, waiting. You've got ten minutes."

Fifteen minutes later, as she crawled out of the bedroom window, I noted that she'd left it open. She was also empty-handed.

"Where's your stuff?" I asked as she walked toward the car. Her eyes were puffy and pink.

"I'm too scared. I can't do it," she said. The bottoms of her floral pajama pants were wet from walking through the damp yard. She stopped in front of me and pulled at a scrunchy she wore on her wrist. "You sure you want to do this?" She sniffled.

I shrugged and looked at my boyfriend in the front seat. He was checking himself out in the mirror and tapping his fingers on the center console. I could tell he was getting impatient. "Yeah," I said, turning back toward her. "I can't live with them anymore."

Kelsey started crying and leaned in to hug me. "Please be safe."

"I'll be fine," I said, patting her back before pulling away. "You're the one who needs to take care of yourself. Don't take any shit from them, okay?"

Kelsey nodded and wiped her eyes with the back of her hand.

"I have to go," I said, opening the car door. "I'll wait until you're back inside, though." I wanted to say *I love you*, but I couldn't get the words out. I regretted not saying it as soon as she closed the window behind her. Kelsey told me later that when Dad realized I'd run away, he seemed irritated, and he never mentioned staying to look for me. I would be eighteen in less than a year, and he didn't think it was worth the fight.

I was gone for nine months. During that time, I didn't talk to my parents much, save for a few check-in phone calls letting them know I was still alive. I quit school and got a job doing hair wraps for tourists at a Gulf Shores souvenir shop that had a giant purple octopus for an entrance. By spring 2003, George W. Bush announced that America would be invading Iraq, but I was too preoccupied to notice. The guy I'd run away with had become abusive. He was arrested after picking up our mattress off of the floor and hitting me with it, over and over, as my head bounced off our bedroom wall. Despite the abuse, leaving wasn't easy. I'd fallen in love with him and wondered if he might change after he was arrested. I also wasn't sure living with my parents was any safer. But I had to make a choice and decided to bet on my parents. One month before my eighteenth birthday, I called them in tears and begged them to let me live with them. They agreed, but not without making it very clear they didn't trust me. I didn't trust them, either.

So much had changed. My parents could afford a rental with a screened-in pool and enough rooms for each of us now. They also seemed calmer and they fought less often. Dad could afford a counselor, and he was taking medications that helped with his mental illness. He'd drift through the house toward the kitchen, whistling to himself as he poured a glass of root beer before sitting on the living room couch and opening a giant book that looked like it was meant for a college classroom. He'd take turns bringing the glass to his mouth and turning pages, audibly sipping the soda, ice click-clacking against the glass, his face cracked with a subtle grin. I hadn't seen him this content in ages. He was even telling his cheesy dad jokes again.

"Did you get a haircut?" I asked one evening as I passed him in the hallway. I'd noticed his hair looked shorter. "Looks nice."

"What? Why would anyone do that?" he chuckled.

I looked at him, confused. "Because it got too long?"

"But I didn't just get *a* hair cut," he said, enthusiastically. "I got *'em all* cut!" He looked pleased with himself.

I rolled my eyes and laughed. "Wow, Dad."

I could tell he was trying with me. But he still made me nervous. Something at my core was uneasy with him, always ready to fight or flee. He never mentioned the day he attacked me. It was almost as if I had made it up. While I would have appreciated an apology, I settled for pretending it never happened.

Meanwhile, Mom spent much of her spare time renovating and decorating the home. She painted red accent walls and moved lamps from one table to another until she had the exact aesthetic she was going for. Her fashion sense had become more bohemian. She wore jewelry handmade by locals and patterned tops made of flowy natural materials. She still kept the house spotless, only now there were no chickens to be found. They had been given back to the thrift stores where she'd bought them, more modern decor in their place. She bought the expensive candles, too, and, as always, kept them burning anytime she was home. In the afternoons after work, she'd put on her oversized shades and sit in a lounge chair next to the pool, sunbathing with her arms slack at her sides. She didn't cry on the couch anymore.

While my parents were far from rich—the house was located in a neighborhood of aging homes on small lots, our cars had high mileage and faded paint, and my parents still had massive school debt—they had, for all intents and purposes, done the thing Americans love to tell poor people to do: they'd pulled themselves up by the bootstraps. They could pay their bills. The kitchen cabinets were always full of food. They were starting to pay off some debt. On the surface, they even seemed happy. Unfortunately, however, the damage had already been done to us kids, and there was no amount of strap-pulling that could fix it.

Kelsey was angry and expressing it with a recklessness I recognized. She was sneaking out at night, dating older boys, drinking, and doing drugs. She reminded me of me, only in Tampa, there was much more trouble to get into than there had been in Foley. Tampa was a dangerous place for an aggrieved teenager, something I was about to discover for myself.

I spent the next year and a half searching for more ways to numb myself. On most days, I slept in, waking up around noon to work at an alehouse where I was a hostess. When my shift was over, I'd get drunk at a local bar that never carded me or at house parties where I discovered cocaine and ecstasy and Xanax. By the time I was nineteen, I was getting high almost every night, often in strange places I'd never been with people I'd never met before.

On Myspace, I posted pictures of myself posing suggestively. I learned how to use makeup to accentuate my best features—my eyes, my lips. I'd position my webcam toward the bed, put on a low-cut, lacy top, and look at the camera like I wanted to eat it. I was getting more attention from men than I ever had before, and I liked it. Messages asking to meet came in daily from strangers claiming they wanted to take me on dates. When they'd pick me up, though, they'd suggest we go back to their place. What I hoped for was a boyfriend. But most of them just wanted to fuck. So, I drank, and I got high, and I let them have sex with me. Anything to feel a semblance of affection or love, even if it ultimately left me feeling disgusted and empty.

Around that time, I befriended a stripper named Marianne. I was shocked by her lifestyle. She lived in a luxury apartment complex, drove a pearlescent white Lexus, and had a walk-in closet with more name-brand clothing than I'd ever seen. Her nails were always done, and her long, blond hair was always perfectly curled. When I'd stay the night at her house, we'd make out and cuddle on the floor, watching movies. She was the first girl I ever slept with. Sometimes, I'd try on her work outfits: five-inch stilettos, neon fishnet dresses, pasties. I'd strut around her house, sipping on whatever alcohol she had lying around. I wasn't nearly as graceful as her, more like a baby giraffe learning to walk. That didn't stop me from considering becoming a stripper, too, though. I wanted her life. I started frequenting the club she worked at. I'd sit next to the stage with a stack of dollars in my hand, let her wrap her legs around my neck. I'd try to imagine being her.

After a party one night, my friend OD'd in the passenger seat on the way home. I was riding in the back seat when the driver pulled over and panicked, unsure if he should call 911. We'd all snorted coke earlier that night, and he was afraid of going to jail for driving while intoxicated.

"Are you serious? Who fucking cares!" I yelled, pulling my cellphone from my purse. I thought my heart might explode. I dialed 911 as quickly as I could, certain my friend would die and I would be arrested. With the sleeve of my shirt, I wiped sweat from my face. My head was throbbing.

When the ambulance arrived, I was leaning through the passenger door, tracking my friend's pulse. Though he was pale, clammy, and unresponsive, he never stopped breathing. The siren stopped as the ambulance parked, red light pulsing all around us. Paramedics pushed me aside and took over, strapping my friend to a gurney and hauling him to the nearest hospital. A policeman questioned me and the driver as he shined a flashlight into our eyes.

"Are you under the influence of drugs or alcohol?" he asked, only inches away from my face.

"No, sir," I lied. I wondered if he could see I was shaking.

Somehow, we didn't get arrested, and our friend survived. But that night turned out to be the wake-up call I needed. I'd been punishing myself for too long. It was time for a change.

I sat in a crowded room in downtown Tampa, scribbling small circles onto a bubble sheet with a freshly sharpened number two pencil. By the end of the day, I was the proud recipient of a GED. I lay in bed that night, thinking about the overdose that had happened months before. *Never again,* I thought. It was time to grow up, time to figure out my purpose in life.

I found a job ad online for flight attendants and applied on the bulky, used desktop computer Dad had stolen from his job for me. He had given one to each of my sisters and me the prior Christmas, and though the computers were ancient and ugly, it was the most incredible gift I'd ever received. He eventually admitted he'd stolen them from one of his jobs as the company he was working for was upgrading their equipment. They'd put all the old computers in the hallway, intending to donate them, and he wanted us to have a good Christmas, so he took them. Imagining my father sneaking those massive computers out of the building and into his car was both comical and sad to me. They were huge. It couldn't have been easy. Were there security cameras? Was he afraid of getting caught? I'd never felt more loved by him. I'd never respected him more. I'd never pitied him more.

Soon after I turned in my flight attendant application, US Airways flew me to Charlotte for an interview. It was only the second flight I'd ever been on, the first since a church mission trip to Peru when I was thirteen. After a grueling interview process, I was offered a job. I thought I'd made it in life. For the first time ever, I hoped to take care of myself without anyone else's help. My plan was to live with my parents in Tampa and commute to Charlotte, where I'd share a hotel room with five other flight attendants in case I needed to crash some nights. Once I'd saved enough money, I'd decide whether to get an apartment in Tampa or move to Charlotte. But after a two-week-long training in Dayton, Ohio, I came home to Tampa to disheartening news. Mom and Dad were moving again. To Alaska. Weary from a lifetime of being dragged around, I hardly reacted. I pursed my lips, went to my room, and resigned myself to living in the hotel room in Charlotte full-time until I figured something else out. My parents threw me a bone and said I could use their white Dodge Intrepid until I got on my feet. They weren't sure how to get it to Alaska, anyway.

A few months later, I stared at the screen of the computer in the lobby of the hotel I'd been living in, a photo of Cleve glowing back at me. It had been taken in Fallujah, during Cleve's first deployment. In it, he wore desert camis and a pair of Costa sunglasses. He sat in a chair made of green sandbags, his posture nonchalant, leaning back with one leg folded over the other. To the right of him lay a large rifle on a makeshift table made of two-by-fours and plywood. Behind him was a wall made of cinder blocks, with barbed wire in loops across the top. He'd sent me a message on Myspace. It was the first time I'd heard from him since high school. Now, only days before my twentieth birthday, I thought, *He's not a kid anymore. He's a man who's been to war.* And, it turned out, he was stationed at Camp Lejeune in North Carolina, only a thirty-minute flight from Charlotte.

I'd always told myself I would never date someone in the military after seeing what happened to my parents. But I hadn't anticipated this: already having feelings for someone. Before Cleve messaged me, before social media existed, I had assumed we'd never see each other again. I had daydreamed about him over the years, wondering what might have been. The prospect of a second chance thrilled me. I believed in soulmates, and I couldn't help but wonder if Cleve was mine.

4

UNUSUAL OBJECTS

August 2005–March 2006

"Why the military?" I asked. Cleve and I talked on the phone almost every night and had for months.

"I don't know," he responded. "What else was I goin' to do? Thought about college, but I don't have that kind of money and didn't wanna go into debt. Also, my grades." He laughed to himself. "I didn't like school much, anyway."

"Same," I said. "But college sounds kinda cool. Sometimes I look at the courses at the community college for fun. I doubt I'd get accepted, though. High school dropout and all that. Womp womp."

"You're one of the smartest people I know," he said. I could feel myself blushing.

"Oh, please."

"Girl, don't even. I coulda listened to you talk forever when we were kids. You were always thinkin' about things from a different perspective than me. Made me see things in a unique way. I miss those days," he said.

"Me too." I paused. My face hurt from smiling. "We're here now, though. And somehow you're a Marine, which, I'm still just . . ." Cleve had never mentioned joining the military when we were kids, so when the image of him in Iraq had shown up in my inbox, it caught me off guard.

"I know. I know. I guess . . . lookin' at age twenty in the eye and still not havin' any direction in life wasn't sittin' well with me. My whole life, I watched Mama and Daddy grind themselves to the bone workin' and livin' in that trailer that's all but fallin' in on 'em now. I had to do somethin'. This way they don't have to take care of me anymore. Maybe I can even get 'em a new trailer one day." He spoke softly now, nostalgia permeating his voice. "Maybe help 'em retire before they die. I'm the oldest, ya know? It just always felt like it was up to me to get 'em outta that hellhole."

"'Murican Dream," I said sarcastically. It made me angry to think that Cleve had to sign up to go to war to get the things he needed to live, while others benefited from his sacrifice from the comfort of their homes, living in abundance with every option in the world available to them. It wasn't fair. And sure, it was possible that, *if* he survived the war and *if* he played his cards right, he could one day use the money, insurance, and education the military provided to pull himself up into the middle class. But help his parents, too? It was hard to imagine after seeing what I'd seen with my own parents.

"It ain't that bad. Some of the best men I ever met are Marines. Someone's gotta do this job. Might as well be me. I didn't have any direction or plans to make anything of myself. At least it gives me some purpose, havin' something to fight for."

I considered, for a moment, what exactly our country was fighting for. It had never really been clear to me. Some people said it was to defend ourselves from terrorists, some said it was to free the Iraqi people, and others said it was all just for oil. Before I could ask his opinion, Cleve said he had to run.

Three months later, I flew to Camp Lejeune, met Cleve in the airport, and went with him to that party. The next morning, I woke up with the pistol under my pillow. The military was never told about the gun incident. Everyone who knew what happened kept their mouths shut to protect Fowler from possibly being dishonorably discharged. When I asked Cleve whether Fowler's wife was safe, he assured me it was a onetime thing; he promised that he and the other Marines in his unit would keep an eye on their buddy. *Just in case.* I couldn't believe how nonchalant he and everyone else seemed to be about it. *A man threatened to kill his wife,* I thought. I decided the Marine Corps was another planet, and I was only visiting. I stayed out of it.

I flew to see Cleve as often as possible after that. It didn't add up to much because I was on call six days a week, and I could only ever stay for one night at a time. But when I did see him, I made up for every *no* I'd ever given him when we were kids. We were inseparable: sneaking away to kiss, to make love, to lie around memorizing each other's faces.

On one of my visits, Cleve surprised me with a day trip to New Bern, North Carolina, the town *The Notebook* was set in. The film adaptation was one of my favorite movies, and I'd told him I wanted to visit. We lost track of time, and I missed my flight back to Charlotte. "I'll just take the next one," I said assuredly. "It's totally fine." But when I arrived at the airport, the next and final flight of the day had been canceled.

"Maintenance issues," the gate agent told me, her voice a punch to the gut. I missed my shift the next morning and was promptly fired. I had two thousand dollars in savings, the Dodge Intrepid my parents had let me borrow, and whatever I could fit in the back seat. I didn't know what to do, but I knew I wanted to be close to Cleve. I drove to Jacksonville and parked in the Kmart parking lot just down the street from Camp Lejeune. It was close to base, and I figured no one would notice me while I figured out what I would do next.

New Year's Eve had come and gone, and the weather was so cold that the trench coat I used as a blanket was hardly warm enough when the car heater wasn't running. For two weeks, I'd been confined to the two front seats, and I was starting to feel claustrophobic. I'd memorized every cigarette hole, every scratch, every stain in the upholstery of the cramped car.

"It's a Great Day to Be Alive" played on the radio one night as a man hunched in the window opposite me, his body backlit by the glow of a streetlamp. He pressed his nose to the glass, cupping his hands at his temples, dark eyes squinting—searching—before meeting my own. A streak of breath fogged the glass. He waved. *Cleve.*

I unlocked the door to let him in. He swung it open and plopped his body into the passenger seat, the smell of sweat and grass and oil flooding the car. Still in his uniform, he had just gotten off work. He was a mortarman, and his job, according to him, was to "blow shit up." The radio sang: *Now I look in the mirror and what do I see?*

"You scared me," I said, leaning in for a kiss. He tasted salty, like a peanut shell. "How was work?"

Cleve sighed, then leaned against his door, tucking his left boot under his right camouflage-clad thigh. I imagined mud streaking across the seat as his boot slid across it. Because the car had become my home, I tried to keep it tidy, at least in the front, where I lived. I considered asking him to keep his feet on the floor, then decided against it. I was sure he'd had a long day. I wanted him to feel comfortable. "I still can't find a place for you to stay," he said. "But I think I figured out what we could do."

I shrugged, settling into the seat and leaning my head back. He'd asked his friends who lived off base if I could live with them. They'd let me stay overnight on my visits, but none of them knew me well enough to take me in for an unknown amount of time. I understood. I didn't want to be a burden. This was nobody's problem but my own. "Well, if you mean I could move to Alaska, I'm starting to think that might be the only option. It just sucks. I don't wanna leave you and I really don't wanna live with my parents in the tundra."

Cleve shook his head. "Hell no, you're not leavin'! No," he said again, pausing. "I was thinkin' . . . what would you think about . . . I was just thinkin' the past few days that maybe we could get married or somethin'."

I was shocked. I hadn't expected this. My body tingled with adrenaline; my heart pounded in my chest. I tried to imagine a future together. *What should I say?* I wondered. Part of me wanted to scream *Yes! Yes! Yes!* But it was as if there were two of me, and the other me was shaking her head, saying, *You know it's too soon to be considering marriage!* It *was* too soon to be considering marriage. I had just turned twenty. Cleve and I had barely gotten to know each other as adults. But I was also living in my car and was quickly running out of money and options. Marrying him would at least offer some security. I'd have insurance and we'd be able to get a place on base after he deployed. I imagined what it would be like to marry a military man. I thought of the videos my dad had sent from Korea—how that was all I knew of him for so long—and of my mom raising us alone. I had sworn I would never do that to myself.

"Whaddya think?" Cleve asked with the same longing in his eyes I'd seen when I was thirteen and he had asked to kiss me for the first time. My chest ached with love for him. *What's the worst that could happen?* I thought. *Divorce? Heartbreak?* That seemed like nothing compared to moving to Alaska and losing him again. Marrying Cleve was not only the best option I had, it was also the one I wanted.

"Yes," I said. "Fuck it. Let's get married."

Cleve leaped out of his seat, grabbed my face, and kissed me. He pulled away and, with his hands still on either side of my face, said, "Karie Fugett's 'bout to be my wife." He smiled. I smiled. He wiped a tear from my cheek.

"These are happy tears, I promise," I said.

A few days later, on January 11, 2006, Cleve and I eloped at the Jacksonville County courthouse. It was just the two of us and his two best Marine friends, Carson and Baker, as witnesses. My hair was in a ponytail, and I wore bootcut blue jeans and a slouchy tan sweater. I'd gotten ready in the bathroom of a local park. Cleve wore his desert camis, soiled from a day's work. There was no ring, and there were no pictures. After the ceremony, Carson's wife, Brittany, said she would consider letting me live with her while our husbands were in Iraq. Although I'd met her before, she saw me as an outsider—only a random girlfriend she wasn't interested in getting to know. She and the other wives had been standoffish with me. But now I, too, was a Marine wife, and she was willing to give me a chance. Brittany and Carson also had a five-month-old son named Dillon. Cleve convinced her I could help babysit. A day after the wedding, Brittany and I shared a bottle of cabernet on her front porch. We hit it off immediately, and I moved in before the end of the week.

————

Cleve was starting to prepare for his second deployment to Iraq. I wanted to see his room at the barracks before he left, so he snuck me in two nights before his unit was scheduled to depart. Typically, civilians weren't allowed after hours, but Cleve was friends with the guy on duty. To be "on duty," I learned, meant you were in charge of making sure no shenanigans were going on in the barracks. The guys who lived there rotated shifts, and most of them were friends, so they often turned a blind eye to things—and people—that were technically not permitted.

As far as I could tell, Camp Lejeune was mostly parking lots. It had few trees, and what wasn't paved was dirt and weeds. The barracks were redbrick and shaped like shoeboxes, with two rows of white railings lining the walkways that encircled the buildings. At dusk, the moon sitting just above the horizon, we made our way up the stairs. I smelled cigarette smoke and noticed a crushed beer can crammed into the railing. We reached Cleve's floor, and a man in a military-green T-shirt and gym shorts passed us, carrying a box of belongings too big for his arms to wrap around. Another man ran up behind us, passed us, and almost knocked the guy with the box over.

"Reiser, you motherfucker!" the man with the box yelled.

"Sorry, man! Girl's waitin' in the car!"

Around the corner, two men with medium-reg haircuts and Bud Lights in their hands peed off the side of the balcony. Cleve grinned and grabbed my hand. "What the fuck do y'all think you're doing?" he asked the guys.

"What's up, Kinsey?" the shorter of the two said, zipping up his pants before reaching his hand out for a low handshake.

"You think I'm goin' to touch that hand, Burns? You're outta your mind."

"Aw. Fuck you too. Who you got there?"

Burns looked at me with a flirty smile, his teeth too big for his face. I smiled back and caught myself chewing on the inside of my mouth, a nervous habit I'd had since childhood.

"This is my wife, Karie," Cleve said before pulling my hand up for a kiss.

"Hi," I said. I shifted from one leg to the other and put my free hand in my pants pocket.

"Shit, I didn't know you got married, man!" He scanned my body. "Not bad, not bad."

Cleve squeezed my hand. "Yeah. It's been two months."

"Well, congrats, man." Burns turned to me and patted Cleve's shoulder, which was nearly eye level to him. "You got a good man here."

I nodded and looked at Cleve. "Yeah, he's pretty great."

I wondered what Burns made of the fact that his friend was married to someone he hadn't known existed until just then. He acted as if it was normal. It didn't feel normal. Later, I'd find out it was commonplace for guys to elope just before going to war. I assume a lot of young military couples get married for the same reasons we did: it makes sense financially; war is uncertain, and love is safe; knowing you might die makes people do crazy shit.

Everyone in the barracks was cleaning, packing, or drinking. Some were doing all three. When we got to Cleve's room, Baker, Cleve's friend who'd been at the courthouse when we were married, was cross-legged on the floor, digging through a giant green duffle bag. He looked up and smiled. "Kinseeeey!" he said, then looked at me and nodded. "Hey, Karie."

I smiled and waved.

"Sup, Baker," Cleve said. "You still gettin' ready for that sandbox?"

"Fuck yeah. I don't want my mom finding some of this stuff if things go wrong, you know?"

"I hear that," Cleve said.

I wondered what he felt he had to hide before deploying: secret love letters, porn, incriminating emails?

"Which bed's yours?" I asked, and Cleve pointed to a single next to the entrance. I sat on it and examined the room while the guys chatted. It was small and gray with a set of bunk beds on one wall and Cleve's bed on the other. At the back were two sets of metal closets and drawers with a mirror separating them. The place was as drab as a hospital. I wondered if they weren't allowed to have stuff on the walls or if they just hadn't taken the time.

"Where's the bathroom?" I asked.

Though I did need to pee, I was mainly curious to see what the bathroom looked like in a place shared by so many men.

Cleve pointed to the back right of the room. "Through that door. Watch out, it's messy. We share it with the boys next door. Six Marines in a bathroom is no joke."

"Noted," I said, making my way to the back.

The bathroom was small, containing only the essentials: toilet, shower, and sink. No color, no candles, a couple pairs of shower shoes parked at the door, and anime porn on the back of the toilet, which, I guess, could be considered art. It wasn't as dirty as other bachelor pads I'd seen—I was happy to note a lack of pubes on the toilet seat—but I still hovered, just in case.

When I was done, there was another guy in the doorway of the room with a black trash bag thrown over his shoulder. "They didn't tell me a lady was here."

"She's cool," Cleve said.

"Well, could I interest *you* in some porn? Only five dollars."

"Say what?" I asked.

"Get outta here, Cortez," Cleve said, starting to push him out the door. "She doesn't want any of your used porn."

"Hey now!" I said. "What do you have?"

"Oooooh!" Cleve and Baker yelled simultaneously.

Cortez pushed past Cleve. He opened the bag and pulled out a fistful of DVDs.

"Well, let's see here. *The Anal Girls of Tobacco Road, Good Assternoon, Sperms of Endearment, Ultra Kinky #79, Hooters and the Blowjob, Unusual Objects . . .*"

I laughed. "That's quite the assortment. What's *Unusual Objects* about?"

Cortez handed it to me, Cleve and Baker dying of laughter in the background. I wanted to get a rise out of the guys, so I said, "I'll take it."

The night before deployment, Cleve and Baker came over to Brittany's place for a sleepover because they didn't want to spend their last night in the barracks. On a whim, we decided to watch *Unusual Objects*. We gathered around the TV in our pajamas, drinking Bud Lights Cleve bought because he was the only one old enough to purchase alcohol.

Brittany put her six-month-old to bed and gave us the go-ahead to push play. Though we'd thought it would be funny to watch porn stars put "unusual objects" like golf balls and shampoo bottles in their bodies, it was actually pretty horrifying—anything to get our minds off war, I guess. We were all relieved when the DVD was so scratched it stopped playing just before a woman sat on a sprinkler head. Carson stood up. "Welp. Who wants to watch *America's Funniest Home Videos*?"

We woke up with the sun the next morning. Brittany stood in the living room in sweats, her hair in a knot on the top of her head, her baby on her hip. She'd done the deployment thing once before, so she chose to stay home and feed Dillon while I dropped off Cleve and Carson. Baker drove himself. Brittany kissed her husband goodbye, and we piled in the truck.

"Any last requests?" I asked, buckling my seatbelt.

"Meat'normous!" Carson shouted from the back. Burger King was one of the only fast-food restaurants on base, and many of the guys in Cleve's unit, especially those who lived in the barracks, ate there daily.

The truck lurched as Cleve jumped in his seat. "Meat'normous!"

Cleve was very serious about his love for Burger King. Once he told me he wanted Burger King's Whopper-scented cologne. When I went to buy it for him, it was sold out. I imagined Marines across America spraying the smoky-smelling liquid on their necks every morning before reporting for duty.

After we ate, we drove to the barracks, where multiple buses were parked in a line, duffle bags stacked around four feet high and ten feet across in the grass in front of them. We got out of the truck, and Carson took off almost immediately.

"Later, Fugett," he said as he ran away from us. I'd kept my last name because I wanted to save my name change for a real wedding. I yelled after Carson to take care of himself.

Cleve and I hugged. We hadn't slept much the night before, and the morning had gone by quickly. Until that moment, what was happening hadn't settled in. I began to cry.

"Please be safe."

"Don't worry about me, baby. This ain't my first rodeo."

"I know, but . . ."

"I'll be fine, sweet girl." He put his hands on my cheeks. "I love you."

"I love you, too."

He gave me one last kiss on the forehead and took off, vanishing into a sea of uniforms. He would be gone for seven months. I sat in the truck, smoking a cigarette and watching the buses pull away. When they were out of sight, I closed my eyes. I took a deep breath. When I opened my eyes again, I could hardly see my hands, my arms, my thighs, through the tears and smoke. I wondered if I was disappearing. I thought of my mom, the weight of my tiny body on her hip as my dad left her for Korea. I wondered, *How did I get here?*

5

ALIVE DAY

March 13, 2006

Dillon crawled in circles on the carpet, the TV behind him glowing with reports of destruction and death. Though it had been only days since the boys left, it felt much longer.

"Three people died in Iraq yesterday," Brittany said as she watched the news and flipped through a *People* magazine, her gaze switching from page to screen and back. "I wonder how long it takes them to call the families."

"How can you watch that shit?" I asked as I passed through the room.

"If I don't know what's actually happening, my brain just makes stuff up and that's always worse. Oh no!" Brittany jumped out of her chair and ran to her son. "That's not for you, baby boy." She took a picture frame from his hand, then picked him up over her head to sniff his diaper. She kissed him on the cheek and placed him in his playpen.

"You just haven't found good enough distractions," I said. Cleve's unit had been sent to fight the Battle of Ramadi. It was dangerous: fighting in the streets, virtually no law and order. Cleve called it the most hostile place in Iraq. His unit's job was to secure the city center, and it was very likely that someone would die or be wounded. "Cannon fodder," I once heard someone call units like Cleve's. The units that were young. Uneducated. Replaceable. Expendable. The idea that these men were simply pawns, meant only to put a barrier between the enemy and the higher-ranking Marines who were considered more valuable, made me sick. I was starting to wonder if this had been part of our country's plan all along: let poor people struggle to survive so that when the time comes, they can be lured into the military by the promise of food and healthcare and shelter in exchange for using their bodies to protect the rich and powerful.

Watching the news was like watching the sun set: the result was inevitable. Someone in Cleve's unit was going to get hurt. Someone would die. The news reported seven service members had died in Iraq since the day our husbands deployed. I knew because Brittany was keeping me updated. Watching all the world's pain and suffering on a tiny screen from the safety of my home has always been difficult for me, a reminder of how small I am, of how little power I have. There was nothing I could do about any of it. If something was going to happen to Cleve, something was going to happen to Cleve. For my own sanity, I needed to focus on things I could control.

I sat down at the computer Brittany kept in her bedroom and wiggled the mouse. The screen came to life. Firefox still had all the tabs I'd pulled up the day before: Monster.com, Coastal Carolina Community College, a list of things to do in the area. I had even looked up guitar lessons. I'd wanted to learn to play since childhood. Lessons were too expensive, but a girl could dream.

"How are those distractions working out for you?" Brittany asked that night with a smirk on her face. She was sitting across the dining room table from me, eating a bowl of macaroni and cheese. Brittany had tried to avoid thinking about the war during her husband's first deployment, but it didn't work. She wasn't convinced I'd be any more successful at it than she'd been.

"Shut up," I said. "How long before they can contact us, though, for real?"

"Last time, it was sometime in the second week. They'll probably have computers. I'm not sure if they'll have Myspace, but they had AIM last time."

While I waited, I wrote Cleve letters. I mailed him a letter every day so that once they started arriving, he'd have something each night to cheer him up. I printed off pictures of him and placed them around my room, including one under my pillow. At night, I would pull it out and stare at it, wondering where he was, what he was doing, and if he was okay. Boredom and loneliness have a way of making time stretch. Combine the two, and you might be stuck in a single moment forever. This deployment had only just begun, and it already felt unbearable. On the fifth day, he finally called.

"It's not pretty out here," he said. "I sure miss those pretty eyes of yours."

"I miss you, too. Are you okay?" I could hear voices in the background.

There was a long pause before he answered. "Yeah, I'm fine. Y'all doin' all right?"

"Yeah. I think there's a lag. Something's wonky. Our power got turned off a couple days ago, but we—"

"Yeah. It's always like that," he interrupted.

"Ah. That sucks."

"What, your power was turned off?" he said.

"The lag is so annoying." I laughed uncomfortably. "But yeah, the power's fine now. We figured it out."

There was another long pause, then Cleve said, "Okay, good. We'll get paid soon. It'll be more 'cause I'm deployed. Help Brittany with bills or whatever you need." He'd given me access to his bank account before he left, and because we chose not to live in on-base housing, he had some extra money from getting married that he insisted I use while he was gone. We'd talk about money again when he got back.

I waited a second until I was sure he was done.

"Thanks, babe. I applied to a bunch of jobs, too. I also applied to the dental hygiene program. Then I'll be the moneymaker taking care of you."

Pause. "You goin' to be my sugar mama?"

Pause. "I can be your sugar mama."

Pause. "Hey. Gotta run," he said. "I love you. I'll try to call ev . . ."

"Oh, okay. I . . . damn it, this lag. I love you, too."

Pause. Cleve laughed. "Bye, baby."

Cleve called every day at first, sometimes multiple times a day, and he always seemed relieved when I answered. I learned to keep my phone on me so I didn't miss him. When I slept, my cellphone sat next to my pillow with the volume turned all the way up. By the end of the second week, Cleve called less, and when he did, he didn't say much.

"I'm just busy s'all," he said when he called for the first time in four days. I'd asked him if anything was wrong. His answer made sense—of course he was busy—but it didn't explain the shift in tone. There was a heaviness I couldn't pinpoint. Something was being left unsaid. *He's at war,* I told myself. *This isn't about you.* But I couldn't help feeling like something else was going on. The way we'd gotten married left me feeling insecure. I'd wondered from the moment he proposed whether he'd felt obligated to do it because I was living in my car. I wondered if he regretted making such a huge decision so hastily. I heard an explosion in the background, but he didn't react.

"Well, I love you," I said, and he said it back. "When will you call again?"

"I dunno," he said, and that was that.

When I told Brittany I was feeling insecure, she was careful but honest.

"You need to take care of you," she said. We were drinking beers on her bed. We'd just put Dillon to sleep. "I know him, and he's going to take care of himself."

When I asked her what she meant, she shrugged and shook her head. "I didn't expect to be close to both of you. I just want you both to be happy."

Brittany and I had become inseparable in the few months since we'd met. We did everything together. We did each other's laundry. We cooked each other food. We cried and laughed together almost every night over bottles of wine. She was the closest friend I'd had in years. But despite our budding relationship, she'd known Cleve longer than me. She was conflicted about who she should be most loyal to.

"I need you to promise me you won't say anything to him," Brittany said quietly.

"I won't," I promised.

"Well, you aren't the first girl he's brought here."

"What do you mean?" My heart was starting to race.

She sighed and took a swig of her beer. "He proposed to his ex like six months before you two got together. She said no and they broke up, or maybe they weren't even actually together, the story changed a few times, but I'm pretty sure they keep in touch. That's all I know for sure," Brittany said. She exhaled. "You okay?"

When I tried to respond, I just cried. Cleve hadn't mentioned this ex before, even though he'd asked her to marry him not long before he messaged me on Myspace. I was already afraid he'd only wanted to marry me because he felt bad that I was living in my car, and now I wondered if he was looking for any wife at all to get the extra benefits from the military. I wondered if he even loved me. Was I just a rebound?

"I know he loves you. It's not that," Brittany said. "I don't know what it is, really. He's just . . . Kinsey. You know how guys are."

I knew how guys were. I thought about the twenty-year-old who took my virginity when I was sixteen; the shadowy figure who molested me when I was six; the Tampa men; the married pilots who were always trying to hook up with the young flight attendants. Now Cleve was keeping secrets from me, possibly even using me as a rebound. *What is this game I'm playing?* I wondered. *Where is the rule book?*

"What do I do?" I asked, but I already knew what I would do if I had to.

I could feel the instinct I'd learned from my parents kicking in: I wanted to run. I was already going over escape plans in my mind before Brittany could answer. But I didn't have a lot of options. Cleve was financially supporting me until I could find a job.

"I don't know," she said. "But I'll help no matter what you decide."

Two days later, the phone rang. When I picked up, silence. "Hel-looo?" I said a second time.

"I just don't know what I'm doin' in this life anymore," Cleve said finally.

A knot grew in my chest. It was happening, I thought. He could have been talking about anything, but I knew in my gut he was gearing up to say getting married had been a mistake. He'd been so quiet with me, and now the news about his ex. Something just wasn't right. Unsure of how to respond, I waited to see if he'd say anything else. When he didn't, I asked if he was okay.

"Some days I feel like this is it, ya know? Like, maybe I'm not comin' back this time. This is my destiny or some shit," he said.

That was not what I'd expected. I'd been so distracted by what Brittany had told me and by how quiet he'd been that I almost forgot where he was. I grappled with asking about the other girl. *Who is she? Do you call her, too?* I wanted answers, but I decided to wait. He needed me to comfort him.

"Please don't say that," I said. "Just get through the next few months. Then you'll be home with me, and this will be behind you. I'll take care of you," I said. "I love you."

"Thanks," he said. "I'm just all in my head. It's fucked-up out here."

"What can I do?" I asked.

"Just somethin' I have to deal with on my own," he said. There was a prolonged pause and a deep sigh, and then, "I don't think I can keep doin' this relationship."

There it was. So quiet. A whisper, almost. Infuriatingly quick and straightforward.

"What do you mean?" I asked. "Please don't say that."

"We shouldn't have gotten married, Karie," he said. "I messed up."

I begged him to take it back. It was the war, I tried to convince him, something in that hot, foreign place, something temporary that was clouding his judgment.

I pleaded. I begged. All he could say was sorry. I cried into the phone for too long, then heard a sigh and a click. I spent the rest of the day in bed, crying and cursing at pictures of him. *What was it about me that made me so easy to leave?*

When I woke up the next morning, I decided I wouldn't let the sadness keep me from being productive. If there was one thing I'd learned from moving so frequently as a child, it was how to adapt quickly. I pulled myself together and began planning my next move. Brittany said I could live with her no matter what happened with Cleve, and I was grateful. I had some interviews lined up, and to my surprise, I'd been accepted to the dental hygiene program at the local community college. The plan seemed solid. I could breathe now.

"What a mess," Brittany said one night as we sat on our back porch, drinking wine and smoking cigarettes. "The boys changed in Iraq last time. Who knows what will happen with Nick and me." Nick was Carson's first name. Everyone except for spouses called the guys by their last names. Brittany shook her head, rolled her eyes, and took a sip of wine. "He hardly even pays attention to his son. It's probably because I had him when he was deployed. There's no connection there. Nick left when I didn't look pregnant at all, then *boom,* he comes back to a baby screaming in the back room."

"I'm sorry," I said. I'd gotten the sense that she felt stuck. I knew what that was like. I had felt that way for most of my life. "I'm glad we found each other."

She raised her wineglass. "It's hard not to be bitter sometimes. I was dragged out here for love, then left in the dust of war." She took a drag of her cigarette. "You know Nick and I met in high school? He chased me. I kept saying no, but finally I gave in. I fell hard after that. Life is crazy. Now it's two years later, I have a baby, and I'm the one waiting."

I thought about Brittany—the way her shoulders slumped, the way her hair hung stick-straight at her shoulders, her calming voice, her half smile. She was only twenty years old and already so tired, so resigned.

"You think this is a phase?" I asked. "Maybe they'll go back to normal after they get out?"

She shook her head, her hair glowing the color of wheat under the porch light, june bugs winding in the air and slamming their bodies into the sliding glass door as if they'd been drinking, too—*clink, clink . . . clink.*

"Who knows? The best thing we can do is look out for ourselves and each other and hope they get their shit together."

I nodded. "Cheers to that."

Cleve called back, apologizing. He still wouldn't promise anything about the future of our marriage, but he did say he loved me. There was a lot of silence, then he said, "Burns shot himself in a porta-john yesterday."

Suddenly the space between us seemed infinite. "My God. Cleve. I'm sorry." I felt like such an asshole for acting like my own issues were life-or-death when he was across the world fighting a war. "I wish I could hug you."

"I . . ." he gasped. "I had to clean out his fuckin' body. I had to put him in a . . . I had to put him in a fuckin' body bag," he sobbed.

Helplessly, I listened as Cleve's sobs turned to wet, heavy breaths, then to silence. And then he had to go.

Cleve was a big dude: six foot three and 225 pounds. I'm not sure I had ever seen a man cry, so it was difficult for me to imagine his eyes producing tears, his large male body heaving as he fought to catch his breath.

Over the next three days, Cleve called at least twice daily, always ending with *I love you*. This time, I tried not to overanalyze the conversations despite my insecurities. Meanwhile, Brittany and I made care packages for Cleve and Carson. We filled two boxes with snacks, socks, drinks, and anything else we could think of that might cheer them up, including Listerine bottles filled with whiskey.

"Military wives' trick," Brittany said.

"You don't think someone'll notice?"

"They didn't last time . . ."

It was April Fools' Day when I got a message on Myspace from Cleve's brother, Nathan. He was the only person in his family who knew Cleve and I had gotten married, but we rarely spoke, so I knew something was up. The message was quick and to the point: *Cleve's hurt. if you don't know, call me.*

The nausea was immediate. I yelled for Brittany to come as I dialed the same number I'd memorized in high school. She pushed the door open with Dillon on her hip.

"What's going on?"

The phone was still ringing. I put my hand over it and whispered, "Cleve's hurt."

"Oh my God! *Hurt* hurt or is he . . ."

I waved my hand at Brittany and mouthed, *Hold on! Hold on!* Someone was picking up the phone. It was Nathan, thank God, but he didn't have much information. The military was looking for me because I hadn't had an address or phone number to give them when we submitted paperwork for my military ID. Cleve was alive, but his foot was hurt bad enough that he might lose it. A bomb, Nathan thought. While his parents were mostly scared for their son, they were also upset about the marriage. They had only found out about it when the Marine liaison called them trying to find me. They didn't want to talk to me. I was okay with that.

I stayed up through the night smoking cigarettes and telling stories about Cleve with Brittany as if he'd died. The military liaison officer called me the next day. He didn't give me much information. He confirmed Cleve was alive and well. An improvised explosive device had hit his Humvee, and his foot was severely injured. He was in Germany, getting ready to be flown to the States. He'd be at Bethesda Naval Hospital in less than twenty-four hours. He gave me an address and a phone number.

"Is there anything else I should know?" I asked.

"Sorry, ma'am, that's all the information I have."

"Will I have a place to stay in Bethesda?"

"Yes, ma'am. Someone will meet you at the hospital with all that information."

"And I just call that number when I know I'm coming?"

"Yes, ma'am, so they can meet you. We have someone there all hours."

"Well." I paused to be certain I had no more questions, biting at my thumb's cuticle as I thought. I couldn't think of any. "Okay, then. Thanks so much."

"Very welcome."

I closed my phone, tucked it into my back pocket, turned to Brittany, and shrugged. She'd been standing next to me, listening to the phone call.

"That's it?" she said.

"Thaaaat's it."

"It's really just his foot?"

"I guess so? I'm not sure that guy really knew what happened. Sounded like he was passing on info from a piece of paper."

"Damn. This is crazy town."

"Right? Cleve was hit by a bomb. At war. After only three weeks. I mean . . ." I shook my head, mouth agape.

"Well, I can drive you so you don't have to fly," she said. "I want to see him, anyway."

"Can I hug you?" I asked.

She looked at me like, *Well, obviously,* and opened her arms.

Cleve called during our drive to Maryland. It was quick. He'd been flown from Ramadi to Baghdad, then Baghdad to Germany. In Germany, doctors performed surgery on his leg to stabilize him for the flight back to the States. He said he'd be in Maryland a few hours before me.

"I'm okay," he said. "They got me, but I'm okay. I love you."

That should have confirmed that he expected and wanted me to come be with him, but I couldn't shake the words *I can't do this anymore.* I wondered whether he felt obligated to call: wounded men are supposed to call their wives. It didn't matter now. Whether he liked it or not, I was coming. *I'm gonna love the shit out of you until you love me back,* I thought.

Brittany and I arrived at Bethesda Naval Hospital sometime after midnight. The hospital was asleep except for the liaison officer who waited for us, his office a fluorescent sore in an otherwise low-lit and shadowy space. I was delirious from lack of sleep, too many energy drinks, and the anticipation of seeing Cleve again. The liaison officer—who introduced himself as Addair—was just a little older than me, in his early to mid-twenties. He was tall and thin with piercing hazel eyes, a sarcastic attitude, and a subtle limp. I wondered if he always worked in the middle of the night or if he was only there for me. He handed me a stack of paperwork to fill out. I'd had a headache for hours now, and the brightness of the paper, the tiny words covering each page, made me feel like my head might pop. Brittany sat patiently in the corner, holding Dillon, who'd fallen asleep on the ride over.

"What's all this for?" I asked, gesturing to the forms.

"Just some red tape," he said. "Non-medical attendant pay, info we'll give to the Navy Lodge where you'll be staying, stuff like that."

The military would pay one non-medical attendant, or a primary caregiver, just under two thousand dollars a month as long as the patient had to be away from their duty station (in our case, Camp Lejeune) while receiving treatment. I got stuck on the word *month.* The dental hygiene program started in four months. I wondered for a moment if

I'd still be able to go, then shooed the thought away. *Cleve. I've got to get to Cleve.*

When I finished, Addair told us the baby wasn't allowed in Cleve's room. Because he'd just gotten back from Iraq, he could be contaminated with who knows what, and it wasn't safe.

"I don't mind waiting," Brittany said. She kissed Dillon on the head. "As long as he's asleep, I'm fine."

Though I hadn't known Brittany long, she'd shown me a kind of friendship—one of kindness, patience, and selflessness—that I hadn't found in many people before. I put my hand on her shoulder, careful not to wake Dillon. "Thank you. Seriously."

Addair's and my footsteps echoed in the hospital lobby as we made our way to the elevator. When we reached Cleve's room, Addair instructed me to put on a yellow paper gown, a mask, and gloves. I opened the door. A lamp in the far corner draped the room in soft light. Cleve was in the bed closest to the door. At first, I thought he was asleep. I was afraid to walk toward him, afraid of what he would say when he realized I was there. But then, he moved. His eyes opened, and he turned to look at me. For a split second, his face was blank, and I swore he was mad and would tell me to leave. But then, he smiled.

"There she is." He reached out his good arm—the other had been hit by shrapnel and was being held by a giant piece of foam that looked like Swiss cheese—for a hug, and my uncertainty melted away. "Come here. I missed those freckles of yours."

I walked over to him and kissed him on the forehead. "What the hell did you let them do to you? I told you to be safe," I said.

He looked down at his leg. "War takes what it wants, I guess. I was just along for the ride."

It was apparent he was high on pain meds. His movements were a little too fluid, his words slurred.

"Can I see it?"

"Sure. They got me good," he said, lifting the sheet from his left leg. It looked like something you might find at a butcher shop, a large chunk of bloody meat wrapped in what looked like cellophane. I gasped.

"They said your foot. That's your whole damn leg."

"Oh, yeah. The whole damn thing. They put rods in my thigh before I left Germany. The bottom half's goin' to take a little more time to figure out, but they said I should keep it."

Addair walked into the room.

"I hate to break this reunion up, but it's well past curfew, and I need to get you and your friend checked in to your hotel room. Visiting hours start at eight in the morning. You can continue catching up then."

"Aw, come on, Addair. You can't give a broken man some time with his wife?" Cleve said.

I smiled.

"Trust me, you'll have plenty of time together in the next few months," Addair said. There was that word again. *Months.*

"Will we be going back at all before then? Are people usually here that long?" I asked.

"It depends on the injury," he said. He looked at Cleve and made a clicking noise with his tongue. "I'm no doctor, but I'd get comfortable if I were you."

I sighed. I would have to forget about college, at least for now. "Okay," I said, nodding. "I'll get comfortable, then."

As Addair left the room, he tapped his hand on the wall and said, "Happy Alive Day, man," over his shoulder. Later, Cleve would tell me that every wounded service member celebrated what they called an alive day. It was the day they almost died at war but survived—the day they were given a second chance. I wondered what Cleve's alive day meant for me.

II

Society can give its young men almost any job and they'll figure out how to do it. They'll suffer for it and die for it and watch their friends die for it, but in the end, it *will* get done. That only means that society should be careful about what it asks for.

—SEBASTIAN JUNGER, *War*

6

HOSPITAL LIFE
April 2006

I slept well that night, considering. I'd been given a room at the Navy Lodge, a hotel where family members of the wounded stayed, located on the same base as the hospital, about a mile down the road. The rooms were dated, with gold filigree wallpaper, prints of foreign landscapes, and maroon bedspreads made of thick, itchy material. The beds were comfortable enough, and the rooms came with a kitchenette, complete with a double burner, sink, and fridge. Our room had two queen-sized beds. Brittany's son slept in a Pack 'n Play. In the lobby, you could rent VHS tapes and books. This would be my home for . . . I had no clue how long this would be my home. *Months,* apparently.

Day one, we were greeted by a clear sky and cherry blossoms, their petals riding the wind in waves. April in Maryland was stunning. We ate breakfast at Burger King, which was on the same street as the Navy Lodge—a couple of sausage-and-egg biscuits and orange juices. We made the mile-long hike up a hill and across a bridge to the hospital, Dillon on Brittany's hip, then on mine, then back on hers. He still wasn't allowed in Cleve's room, so I watched him in the waiting room while Brittany caught up with Cleve. The waiting room on Cleve's floor was decorated in shades of gray and had large windows looking out onto the hallway, where patients rolled by in wheelchairs or beds pushed by nurses. I never liked hospital waiting rooms. So much nervous energy: families sitting in silence, flipping through magazines, tapping feet, munching on Cheetos from the vending machine.

When Brittany was finished visiting with Cleve, she took Dillon from my arms.

"He's happy you're here," she said, bouncing Dillon on her hip. "I want you guys to work out."

"Really?" I asked, and she nodded. "Well, looks like we'll have plenty of bonding time."

Brittany headed home a few days later. "If shit hits the fan, you know where to find me." She laughed as she started her truck. Though Brittany initially came across as meek, when you got to know her, she was refreshingly forthright. I appreciated the balance. We hugged, I thanked her, and she headed back to Camp Lejeune.

Sometime in the first two weeks at Bethesda, Cleve's surgeon, Dr. Gupta, said confidently, "He's the perfect candidate for leg salvage." Dr. Gupta told us that, years ago, with an injury as severe as Cleve's, they would have amputated his leg before putting him on the plane. Since the beginning of the war, however, they'd learned a lot about the injuries coming out of Iraq. "You're going to be a bit of a guinea pig, Lance Corporal, but we have some of the best doctors in the world. We'll take good care of you."

The words "guinea pig" made me uncomfortable. I wondered if the doctors really thought Cleve had a chance of keeping his leg or if they just saw his injury as an opportunity to do a science experiment. I learned that most of the soft tissue had been blown off his calf—leaving the shredded skin and muscle that remained hanging from exposed bone. His tibia and fibula were shattered. His femur was also fractured in multiple places, but doctors in Germany had placed a rod in it before he was sent back to the States. I stroked Cleve's head and stared at his constricted pupils and flushed cheeks.

"Thanks, Doc. I don't care what you have to do. I just wanna keep it. I can't lose my leg."

Cleve looked down at his broken body. His toes and foot drooped forward, cold and crusted with blood and dead skin. If he wanted to be a guinea pig, I would support it.

"I understand, Lance Corporal. We're going to do the best we can to keep it. You should be in surgery in a few weeks, and if everything goes as planned, you'll be out of bed and in physical therapy a month or so after surgery."

Dr. Gupta told us there were no guarantees, but he would do everything he could. When he left the room, Cleve flopped his head to the side to face me. His eyes were alien-like, their pupils so small they were nearly lost in the brown of his irises.

"Take a nap," I said. "Everything's gonna be okay."

Hospital life was boring. Day one looked like day two and three and every other day up until his leg reconstruction surgery, which wouldn't be for weeks. Cleve had to have countless wound-cleaning surgeries before he could have the big one. They wanted to be sure his body was free of shrapnel debris or anything else that could cause infection. He had cleaning surgeries every few days. He was also on several medications I could hardly pronounce, all of which made him sleep a lot. While he spent the majority of most days in surgery or sleeping, I spent my days watching him sleep, eating too much vending machine food while watching him sleep, and exploring the hospital's maze of hallways after I couldn't watch him sleep any longer. I felt out of place in this world of doctors and patients, illnesses, injuries, and prescriptions. Cleve and I had yet to address the breakup phone call. It felt silly to bring up something that suddenly seemed so trivial. And he never brought it up. Though it hovered over me like a ghost, I decided to assume the best. I was twenty years old, a military spouse, and, now, a caregiver.

Whenever Cleve was awake, I asked him questions. The most important: *What the hell happened?* He said he'd been driving a Humvee along a dirt road in Ramadi the day he was injured. He said the streets were blanketed with improvised explosive devices—IEDs—or homemade bombs, often hidden in piles of trash or broken-down vehicles. The one that hit him had been hidden in garbage on the side of the road. When men nearby saw Cleve's Humvee approach, they triggered it.

"That one just snuck up on us," Cleve said as he lay in his hospital bed, naked except for a white sheet woven between his legs and around his lower torso. He stared at the ceiling as he spoke. Curtains were pulled around his half of the shared hospital room, separating us from the world.

"You didn't see it? Were you the only one out there?" I asked. I was sitting cross-legged in a stiff, plastic-lined chair next to his bed. I'd positioned it so it faced him. I leaned forward, my chin resting on my arms on his bed.

"Nah. They told me over the radio, but I didn't hear it in time. There was a row of us that day. I wasn't the first. I had my leg propped up on the dashboard as I was drivin'. You're not supposed to do that, but I probably would've lost my leg if I hadn't of done it.

"All of a sudden, I heard a voice over the radio. *Kinsey! Kinsey! Watch out!* Then, before I knew it, *BAM!* A double-stacked IED. That son of a bitch blew the door right off my side." He laughed to himself. I didn't laugh. I was stunned, paralyzed by the image of a world lined in bombs.

"I barely remember the explosion," he said. "All of a sudden, I come to on the ground. My boys were draggin' me to safety, stabbin' me with shots of morphine, others were shootin' back and forth. I looked down, and my leg was bent toward me, the opposite way a leg should bend. It was like a limp noodle draped across the top of me."

I reached for my water on his bedside table and took a sip. "Could you feel the pain? You must have been terrified."

"No. Really, I didn't know what the hell was going on. The morphine had me feeling pretty good. Disoriented mostly. My boys got in there and took care of things."

"It sounds like hell," I said.

Cleve and I sat in silence as I played with his hair. I couldn't stop staring at his face, searching for the boy I had met so long ago, wondering what our future would be. He looked wan, his brown hair disheveled, eyes gaunt and painted in dark circles. He had been so muscular when he deployed, with strong arms and a healthy layer of pudge that I loved. But he was losing weight rapidly from lack of appetite and being in bed for so long. Soon he would hardly look like himself.

I asked him what a double-stacked IED was. He grinned and sat up in his bed.

"Well, it has twice the power." He held his hands out wide to show how large it was. "It was a big son of a bitch. The explosion is bigger, so it's more powerful. More dangerous. I'm lucky I'm alive."

I had never heard of an IED until Cleve's injury. He told me that day that they could be made with marbles. When the bomb goes off, the marbles explode, glass shards shooting in every direction toward their victims. As he spoke, I imagined the innocent balls of glass I played with as a child, white with blue cat-eyes in the center, the same shade as my mother's and my eyes. The toys wait in darkness, forced to play in a war they weren't designed for.

The picture of Cleve's Humvee, taken by one of the guys in his unit after he was shipped back to the States, was uncanny. It didn't make sense for such a powerful thing to be destroyed that way. On the driver's side, where Cleve had been sitting, there was no door. In its place was shredded metal. The frame at the bottom of the vehicle was bent, and the engine's guts were exposed. Cleve's seat was missing entirely. I wondered how much of his body had been left behind.

At first, I hated the men who hurt him. I hoped that the other Marines were able to find and kill the bastards who did this. I wanted revenge. But as time passed, I found myself wondering what the men's names were. What they had had for breakfast that morning. Whether they had families. I wondered what it was exactly that made them want to do it. To kill. I wondered how many of *their* loved ones had been wounded or killed in the war. I thought about how much they must hate us, too.

Addair knocked on Cleve's door sometime after lunch. I was just about to leave so Cleve could take a nap, had just kissed him goodbye, when I heard a voice.

"Rudy Giuliani's here today. You want to see him?"

I didn't know who that was, but Cleve did.

"Sure," Cleve said. He felt around for the buttons on the railing of his bed and adjusted it so he was sitting upright. Moments later, a balding man with big white teeth and a fancy suit rounded the corner. He stood over Cleve, holding his hand out. Cleve shook it.

"How are you holding up?" Rudy said.

"Good, sir. I'm doing good."

"I'm glad to hear it," he said. He looked around the room. "They keeping you two busy?"

"Eh," Cleve said.

"It's kinda boring," I said, gesturing toward the room.

"I bet. I bet."

"It's fine, though," I assured him. I didn't want to sound like I was complaining. "We're just happy he's alive."

"Of course," Mr. Giuliani said, patting Cleve on the arm. "Hey, uh, have you two seen *The Sopranos*?" Cleve and I looked at each other and shook our heads. "I have a box set of every season if you're interested. I can grab it after I make my rounds and bring it back up. Might give you guys something to do while you're here."

"Yeah," Cleve said. "That's really nice of you, sir."

He stayed to chat another few minutes, then left. That evening, he returned to our room with two red gift bags. I was curled up in a chair next to Cleve's bed. Cleve had fallen asleep. Mr. Giuliani tiptoed into the room and put the bags on a table next to Cleve's bed. He pointed to them.

"As promised," he whispered.

"We really appreciate it," I replied.

"You two take care," he said with a pensive look.

I smiled, and he quietly slipped out the door.

We watched every one of those DVDs over the next few months. *The Sopranos* became one of our favorite series.

At the hospital, it was routine for celebrities to visit. Someone came almost every day, accompanied by Addair, holding a white clipboard. Several people had already shown up at Cleve's door, but he was often asleep, too high, or just not in the mood. When George W. Bush showed up, Addair asked us if we wanted to meet him, and Cleve shook his head no, hardly awake after a surgery. I was disappointed, but I pulled the curtain around Cleve's section of the room anyway. I decided if he couldn't meet him, I couldn't either. When the President walked past the curtain to meet Cleve's roommate, I watched his shadow. I listened to that famous Texas drawl of his as he thanked the man for his service. We were so close to him. Now, thinking about that day, there are so many things I wish I had said: *Why are you here? Do you feel bad at all? We're just kids and you sent us to fight a pointless war! Do we even matter to you?* But I didn't yet understand the mess we were in. Instead, I sat in silence.

Cleve's mom and dad arrived from Foley two weeks after we did. It was the first flight they'd ever taken in their lives. Because the military paid for everything, they could spare a week of work to visit. I was nervous. Neither of us had told our parents we had eloped. But after Cleve was injured, the whole damn world knew. My dad and I only spoke to each other when necessary, so I didn't know how he felt about it. My mom wasn't thrilled, but she had decided it wasn't a battle worth fighting. "If it's what you want, I guess I have to support it," she'd said. That was good enough for me. Cleve's dad seemed indifferent. He wasn't the kind of man to overthink things. But when Cleve tried to explain the situation to his mom over the phone, she was very blunt: "Well, I think that's right near stupid, don't you?" Cleve told me to brace myself for her arrival. "Mama's pissed. Nobody messes with Mama when she's mad."

The day his parents arrived, they hovered over his bed with their hands on their hips.

"Them ragheads got my boy, didn't they?" his dad said, shaking his head. Jimmy was tall and thin with an unkempt goatee and a University of Alabama T-shirt tucked into belted jeans. I cringed at the word "ragheads." Cleve's mom stood there in silence as Cleve and his dad went back and forth for a while. I stood in the corner, afraid to do anything that might remind them I existed. They hadn't acknowledged me, other than a few nods and a side-eye from his mom. She walked over to Cleve and brushed her hand through his hair.

"My baby," she said. Shorter and heavyset, with silky, medium-brown hair past her waist, Penny was her husband's physical opposite. She put her hand on Cleve's cheek. "You're a hero, ya know that?"

Cleve patted her arm. "I love you, Mama."

The *Today* show wanted to feature a family at Bethesda Naval Hospital for their Easter Sunday special. Cleve thought it would be cool, so we volunteered. The show's reporters came with pretty faces and bright lights. Cleve was bedridden but eager. We answered their questions the best we could and, days later, watched excitedly. Onscreen, Cleve came off as pitiful lying there in that bed. It was clear he was high on pain medication, his answers unnaturally enthusiastic, his eyes wide and piercing. He was shirtless, wires reaching from his chest to an array of machines. And his accent seemed thicker onscreen—so did his parents'. The producers had cut everything I'd said out, only mentioning me once as "his wife, Karie," and showing a second-long clip of me giggling like a fool. When the episode was over, we turned off the TV.

"Never thought I'd be on TV," Cleve said.

"Pretty cool," I replied. I didn't let Cleve know it, but I was embarrassed by how they'd portrayed us. I decided to be more careful about who filmed us in the future.

Cleve's parents and I ate lunch together at the bowling alley on base. His mom remained quiet, stiff as stone, but his dad and I bonded—sort of. After eating our French fries and chicken fingers, we lingered on the porch, where a swarm of bumblebees buzzed.

"He's missed y'all," I said, and his dad grinned.

"That boy's my pride and joy."

I smiled. "He knows that."

"How'd y'all meet?" his mama asked, raising an eyebrow.

"Middle school," I said, and she sneered. "We dated, or whatever you want to call it, for a little bit in middle school."

"Oh, really? I don't remember you."

"I'm not born and raised, and I kinda kept to myself. My grandpa is the pastor of the church down the street from your house, though.

Maybe you've seen his name on their sign?" I was hoping my grandfather's reputation as a good Christian man in the community would make her like me more. It didn't seem to work. Later, I would find out Cleve's mom thought of me as a "Yankee." I didn't have the right accent, wasn't from the right place, didn't wear the right clothes. Someone I didn't know who claimed to know me told her I was "strange." Typical small-town rumor-mill stuff. Her suggesting I wasn't a Southerner upset me. So many people in my parents' generation moved away from their hometowns in search of good jobs and better lives, leaving my generation with shallow roots. I realized for the first time that I didn't even know where my ancestors were from. I was my parents' daughter, my grandparents' granddaughter, and it ended there. I couldn't help it that my parents had left their hometowns in the South or that the military stationed them west for a few years. I was born in the South, everyone I knew lived in the South, every*thing* I knew was in the South. I thought of myself as a Southerner—thought of Foley as my hometown—but Cleve's mom made me wonder if it was true. Who was I, really?

Standing across from me on the bowling alley porch, she pursed her lips. "Well, I guess we gotta get to know each other now, don't we?" She rolled her eyes.

"I guess so," I said. The interaction made my stomach hurt. I wished Cleve was there to be a barrier between us.

His dad pointed to my face and jumped back. "Hey, girl, a bee's in your ear!" he yelled.

I screamed and ran down the stairs of the porch, swatting at my face. He belly-laughed. "I'm just messin' with ya," he said, and we laughed together. He must have felt the tension, too, and I was relieved he'd found a way to break it. I liked Jimmy. I saw Cleve in him.

His parents could only stay a week. They didn't work the kinds of jobs that offered paid vacation, and they had bills to pay and mouths to feed. After they left, I was, on the one hand, relieved to have Cleve and our hospital back to myself. On the other, it had been kind of nice to have visitors, even if one of them didn't like me.

Cleve's feelings were clear. "I just want my mama," he cried. He was much more emotional on the medication: higher highs and lower lows.

Witnessing a wounded Marine bedbound and weeping for his mother was heartbreaking. I crawled into the bed with him and held his head in my lap. Besides strangers, they were the last visitors we would have for the rest of our stay.

Just after sunrise, I sat in the corner of Cleve's hospital room, watching as two nurses rolled his bed away from me. It had been a month since his family's visit and it was time for Cleve's leg reconstruction surgery. Once I was alone, I scanned his room. The lamp's soft light fading in the harshness of the rising sun in the window. A blinking computer screen. *Beep, beep, beeps* coming from the hallway. The smell of iodoform and antiseptic. Empty space where my husband used to be. And a hollow, nauseated feeling I'd endured so many times before. It was an insecure hope. I knew from experience that where there's hope, disappointment is lurking, waiting for its turn. I'd been hopeful every time we moved to a new home. When my parents announced we'd be rich. As I crawled out of my bedroom window before my family left for Tampa. Experience had taught my body to brace itself for the worst-case scenario.

7

UPHILL FROM HERE
May 2006

Time warped, every minute its own eternity. I sat in the waiting room for hours, even though the Navy Lodge was only a thirty-minute walk away. I sensed that my role as Cleve's non-medical attendant meant that I was supposed to wait at the hospital. I had an entire deflated couch that looked like it had been plucked from a nineties sitcom to myself. Other family members whose loved ones' bodies had also been broken by bombs or guns or whatever other man-made killing machines sat or stood or paced around the room. Though there were parents and siblings, most of us were young women—wives, girlfriends, and fiancées. There we were, suspended in time, waiting for someone to tell us our future. So much space pulsed between each of us, negative repelling negative. This was my couch and that was her corner and that was her recliner and that was her patch of carpet. I was afraid to start a conversation with anyone, afraid of their pain making my own heavier. I assumed they were afraid of me and my pain, too. So there we sat, islands within an island.

I wondered what the other non-medical attendants had sacrificed to be there. Did they put off college, too? Did they quit jobs or miss birthdays or cancel fun trips? Did they miss their families? Somewhere out there were women in their twenties who went to class every morning, went on dates with boys, went to parties with their friends on weekends. The simplicity of their lives was something I both envied and looked down on. The military often reminded me that I was a "wounded warrior's caregiver." They told me I was "strong, brave, and essential." I understand now that the military relies on young spouses like me as cheap—sometimes free—labor. Military brass knows what to say to make young women think their labor is their duty. But at the time, I believed those pretty words: Courageous. Self-sacrificing. Brave. Hero. Believing those things about myself felt good. I was part of something important. I was useful. Other women's lives, carefree and selfish, seemed shallow in comparison. Sure, I wanted to go to college, and I missed parties and friends, but I was also proud of the sacrifices I was making. For the first time in my life, I had a purpose that felt worthy.

I'd just finished my lunch when Cleve's doctor called to say his surgery was going well, even if it was taking longer than they'd initially expected. He didn't detail why; he just explained that this was normal, and it would be a few more hours. He'd call me when Cleve was on his way to the ICU. I could visit him there briefly, but then they'd have to keep him overnight. When the call ended, I decided to go back to the Lodge. It didn't sound like the surgery would be over anytime soon. I stopped at a vending machine and stocked up on snacks, my pockets and purse bulging with junk food.

When I arrived at my room, I locked the dead bolt and dumped the food on the bed. I took my pants off, put a CD into my CD player, put my headphones on, and sat cross-legged in front of the pile of food. I ate the Cheez-Its and then the Honey Bun, washed it all down with a Barq's root beer. I wasn't even hungry. I just needed to be doing something, to feel something solid fill the void growing inside me.

I'd just opened a bag of Skittles when I caught a glimpse of myself in the mirror shoveling the candy into my mouth like a zoo animal. *Gross*, I thought. I always did that: Act before I think. Do whatever feels good in the moment and regret it later. The things that felt good were rarely actually good. Drinking, smoking, overeating, even shopping and sex. For so long, it seemed as though the key to my survival was to bury things: my feelings, my disappointment, my fear, my loneliness, my anger. Distract, distract, distract. It was all about finding something riskier, more exciting, more delicious, than the panic I was feeling. Abusing my body while dissociated was easy, but not so much with a mirror in front of my face. I took the headphones off, gathered the leftover snacks in my arms, and threw them in the trash. They weren't in there for a minute before I dug them back out and put them in the drawer next to the bed. Just in case.

I lay on my bed with my arms at my sides and stared at the popcorn ceiling. I saw a spiral. A face with crooked eyes and a large nose. Constellations. *I have to let the dental hygiene program know I'm not coming. There's no way I can go to college now. I'm never gonna be anything. Why am I such a fuckup? I wonder how Cleve is doing? What if Cleve dies? Could he die? It's just leg surgery, he can't die. Can he?* The song "Grey Street" by the Dave Matthews Band played from somewhere on the opposite side of the room. My phone's ringtone. I sat up and realized I had the bed's comforter tightly clenched in both hands. I crawled off of my bed and onto the other. Lying on my stomach, the upper half of my body hanging off the bed, I rifled through the pile of dirty laundry I kept hidden in the space between the bed and the wall, frantically slinging clothes behind me like a dog digging for a lost bone.

"What the fuck?" I said to myself. I was always misplacing things. I tried to remember which pair of pants I had been wearing. *The dark jeans,* I thought, and then the phone stopped ringing. I hoped it wasn't the doctor. "Idiot." I found the jeans, the phone tucked in the back pocket. I flipped it open. A missed call from Mom. *Thank God.*

I crawled back into my bed and called her back.

"Hey, honey," she said.

"Hi, Mom. You rang?"

"Just checking in. Cleve's having the big surgery today, right?"

A keyboard click-clacked in the background. She must've been at work.

"Yeah," I said. "He's still there."

"You doing okay?"

"I guess so. Waiting sucks," I said, tucking the phone between my shoulder and ear, and picking at the pink polish on my thumbnail. "I hope this is it. I hope this works, and then we can go home."

"Well. That would be nice, wouldn't it?"

"Hey, Mom. I have to tell you something."

"Uh-oh. What is it now?"

"No, nothing that bad. It's just that it sounds like we're gonna be here awhile. I know I told you I got into that school, and you were excited. I think I have to push it off. I think it's the right thing to do."

The click-clacking stopped and she exhaled into the phone.

"Honey . . ." I knew she was going to ask if I was sure. Though Mom supported my marriage to Cleve, she wanted me to have my own thing, too. A way to take care of myself if things didn't work out.

"I've already made my decision, Mom. I'm sorry. It's just another year."

"You don't have to apologize. You're an adult," she said.

I didn't feel like an adult. I felt like a kid with no clue what I was doing.

The day dragged on. I'd fall into a shallow sleep for a few minutes then jolt awake, worrying about having missed a call from Cleve's surgeon. After a while, I pulled my new laptop out of the bedside table's drawer. I'd bought it, along with some clothes, food, and a small digital camera, with money we were given from a nonprofit called the Semper Fi Fund that assists vets with everything from paying bills to making their homes handicap accessible. When we arrived at the hospital, the Semper Fi Fund wrote me a check for $2,500 so I could buy necessities for my stay. I was grateful, because I hadn't packed enough clothes, I didn't have a computer to keep in touch with people, and I didn't have much money for food. Eventually, the monthly non-medical pay from the military would start, but it would take time for all that paperwork to go through. The Semper Fi Fund filled the gap. The fund was meant to meet the needs of service members where the military failed to. As the war raged on, more and more needs were unmet and more nonprofits seemed to be stepping in to save the day. It just seemed like another cog in the military machine: young men went to war, returning home injured, relying on spouses and girlfriends and parents for their care, and letting these nonprofits pay the bills.

The ability to browse the internet in bed felt luxurious. I'd never had a laptop before. That cinder block of a Dell was a window to the rest of the world when my corner of it had shrunk down to an 880,000-square-foot hospital, a hotel room, and a road connecting the two. I looked through pictures friends had posted, read blog posts I'd missed, and caught up with Brittany on AIM. Dillon was pulling himself up to stand. One of the guys in Cleve's unit, Hamilton, was almost shot in the head by a sniper, but he happened to be wearing his Kevlar helmet incorrectly, and it saved his life. Jacksonville was getting a new Olive Garden. Eventually, I emailed the person I'd been in contact with at the community college, letting them know I wouldn't be attending that fall. My heart sank. I wanted more than anything to prove that I was more than just a high school dropout. I pressed send, shut the laptop, and closed my eyes. The computer was warm under my hands. I tried not to cry, but I couldn't help it. While we felt stuck in time in the hospital, it was clear the rest of the world was moving along as usual, unconcerned with whether or not Cleve and I could keep up.

It was beginning to get dark. *Sex and the City* reruns played on the TV. Just as Charlotte found out her dog, Elizabeth Taylor, had gotten knocked up after an orgy at the dog park, my phone rang. Cleve was out of surgery. Things had gone well, and I could see him now. With no one to impress, I put on my pajama pants and a jacket and slid a pack of cigarettes into my purse, save for the one I planned to smoke. On the way there, I tried to imagine what Cleve's leg would look like. The doctor said they'd be taking the latissimus muscle from his back and sewing it onto the area where his calf used to be. They would take skin grafts from his thigh. I imagined Frankenstein's monster—scraps of body parts pieced together, thick skin buckling in between crooked stitches. It was so late. Walking through the hospital's main entrance reminded me of the night I arrived: nobody around, the lights dimmed. My footsteps echoed in the empty lobby. I stared at my feet as they slapped against the shiny tile, "Yankee Doodle" playing over and over in my mind to the rhythm of my steps.

I'd never been in an ICU. I remember it as wires and screens and plastic machinery that looked intelligent, even sentient. Masked men and women in scrubs scurried around the room. I stood there waiting for someone to make eye contact and ask me what I needed. At first, nobody did. I could feel the anxiety rising in my chest. *I look like a Muppet without a human,* I thought. I pictured too-long, scrawny arms hanging at my sides, a dumb grin splitting my face in half, and all the space my body took up as I waited for someone to tell me what to do.

"Ma'am?" Someone had noticed me. "Are you here to see someone?"

"Yes!" I said, relieved. "My husband. Cle— Um . . . Jimmy Kinsey? I'm his wife . . ."

"Right over here," she said, and led me through a tight maze of medical equipment.

The space Cleve's bed occupied seemed to float in the center of the room. If I moved a foot in any direction, I would have bumped into something that looked expensive, so I was careful to make myself compact. Cleve was asleep despite the fluorescent lights, the beeping, and the chatter among staff. I didn't want to wake him, but I needed to touch him to know that this was real, that he was still okay. I reached out to his hand, ran my fingers along his index finger, noted the roughness of his knuckles. I took a deep breath. *All uphill from here,* I thought.

I met Cleve in his new room the next morning. He was high on Dilaudid but didn't seem to be in pain.

"Check this out," he said, pointing to his leg. It bulged in places no leg should bulge and looked more like raw chicken, skin side up, blue and purple and white. It didn't bleed from any one wound: the entire thing was a wound and bled out all over. He had metal rods about half an inch thick boring into his flesh and attaching what we later learned was called a *halo.* It circled the outside of his leg, like steel beams holding a bridge, supporting the pieces of his shattered bones. Before Cleve's injury, I would have said that a wound like his would make me queasy. But faced with the reality of it, my instinct was to do whatever I could to fix him, and that was the end of it. The nurses eventually taught me how to clean his leg. Sometimes the holes around the rods oozed pus and needed to be cleaned with a mixture of hydrogen peroxide and water, and the entire wound, which spanned from his ankle to his knee, needed to be rewrapped with gauze at least once a day. I'd sit on the edge of his bed with a pile of Q-tips, dip them in the solution, and carefully clean green and yellow pus from around the pins. I'd open a fresh pack of gauze and carefully wind it around the wound, tucking it into itself to keep it taut. I'd kiss him on the forehead, lie down next to him, and we'd both stare at it, wondering what would be next for us.

Two weeks after Cleve's surgery, twenty-five thousand dollars showed up in Cleve's bank account. It was TSGLI money, also known as Servicemembers' Group Life Insurance Traumatic Injury Protection. You could get up to a hundred thousand dollars depending on the type of injury you had and how long you were inpatient and needed the assistance of a caregiver to do basic tasks like using the bathroom and bathing. There was a body part price list. On it, each injury someone might sustain during war was listed, accompanied by the dollar amount the military deemed that body part worth. The 25K was what Cleve's leg was worth.

"Baby, look at this," Cleve said. I looked up from my laptop.

"What's up?" I was updating my Myspace blog about Cleve's surgery. I tried to keep up with it for friends and family. I was in the middle of a sentence.

"Just come here."

"Okay," I said. I put the laptop down and walked over to his bed. When I looked at the screen, I was speechless. I'd never seen that much money before. "Shit."

"I know, right?"

"That's a lot of money." We were both quiet for a minute, thinking. "Weird to think half a leg is worth 25K to the military, though. Like, who came up with that?"

"It's worth more to me," Cleve said with a sigh.

"I know, babe."

"We need to get a car. Something big enough for the wheelchair and bags when we travel," he said.

I nodded. "Heal first, and then we can figure that out."

Cleve looked at me with a mischievous grin. "You should get in this bed so we can celebrate."

I looked at his leg, at the sheets stained with blood. "You've got to be kidding."

"Do I look like I'm kidding?" He looked down at his crotch. He already had a hard-on.

"Cleve!" I whisper-yelled.

"What?" He grinned and wiggled his eyebrows up and down.

"What if we get caught?"

"They just took my vitals. They won't be back for a while." He patted the bed next to him.

I sighed and got up to close the curtain around the bed. "I wish we had locks on the doors," I said. I unbuttoned my pants and took them off, followed by the tattered cotton panties I definitely wouldn't have worn had I known we were going to have sex. I draped my clothes on the armrest of the chair and slid it closer to the bed so I'd be able to reach my clothes quickly if someone came in. "You have to stop grinning like that." I smirked and rolled my eyes.

"But I'm so excited."

"I know you are," I said as I crawled into the bed. Cleve was already naked under the sheet, as usual. He pulled the sheet aside, exposing his naked body—both familiar and not—and I climbed on top of him, careful not to accidentally hit his wounded leg. He ran his hands from my thighs up to my waist then pulled our bodies together. "Are you sure you're okay?"

"I'm fucking great," he said as his eyes rolled into the back of his head.

I nodded and took a deep breath, closing my eyes and imagining our first time together, away from hospitals and nurses and bloody sheets, not a care in the world, and so fucking excited to finally feel our naked bodies against each other. I moaned as I lost myself in the memory.

It had been a month since his surgery, and though Cleve's leg seemed to be healing, his doctors were worried about blood flow. Dr. Gupta had to stitch together many tiny veins from the remaining pieces of his leg to the muscle flap, and if they didn't work correctly, the tissue would die, and they would be forced to amputate. Dr. Gupta stopped by one day to test the circulation of the newly constructed leg. He had Cleve sit up in his hospital bed and lower his leg to the ground. Each time they lowered it, his leg turned purple, and blood dripped out, collecting in a crimson puddle on the floor. It was called venous congestion, and it wasn't a good sign. But according to Dr. Gupta, there was still time for improvement.

"I'm gonna start calling you stink foot," I said the following day as I cleaned out the pus around Cleve's wound. I'd already gone through a stack of Q-tips. I piled the dirty ones on a brown paper towel on the windowsill.

"Aw, that's fucked-up," he said, laughing. He propped himself up to watch what I was doing. "I hope it gets better soon. I'm ready to get out of this damn bed. I'm sick of looking at this room."

"Don't blame you. Let's talk to the doctor about getting you into a wheelchair. Seems mental health has to count for something, too, ya know?"

"Yeah, 'cause I'm 'bout lose my mind. It would be real nice to breathe in some fresh air."

I finished cleaning his leg, balled up the Q-tips in the paper towel, and threw them in the trash next to the bathroom.

"I need to wrap your leg. Where's the dressing?"

"Over here," he said, patting around his bed, then pulled a roll of tightly wound gauze from under his sheet and handed it to me. I sat on the bottom edge of his bed and wrapped his leg cautiously, weaving between the pins, careful not to touch the wound. I was afraid of hurting him, though he claimed most of it felt numb. That evening we spoke with Dr. Gupta about getting Cleve out of bed.

A couple of nurses brought us a wheelchair the next morning. I sat in the corner of the hospital room, recording Cleve's first ride with our new camera. With a cherry sucker in his mouth, he hopped on one leg to his new mode of transportation, and the nurses strapped his wounded leg flat in front of him on a wooden board so it wouldn't bleed out. He turned around and pulled the sucker out of his mouth, then pointed the red ball on a stick at me.

"You recording this?"

"Yeah, I've got it."

He smiled and waved, then put the sucker back in his mouth and settled into his seat. Once he was strapped in, the nurses moved his chair around to ensure it worked properly.

"All right, you're ready to go," one of the nurses said before turning to look at me. "Ms. Kinsey, don't push him too fast. His leg is tied to the chair and we don't want him flipping." Most people affiliated with the military forgot I had a different last name. To them, I wasn't Karie Fugett. I was Mrs. Kinsey. I didn't mind it. I liked being reminded I was his wife.

"Got it," I replied.

I turned the video recorder off and positioned myself behind Cleve, pushing my weight into the handlebars and wheeling him out the door of his room. When we reached the hospital's lobby, just before the main entrance that led outside, a young man missing every limb but his left arm rolled toward us in a wheelchair being pushed by someone who looked to be his father. The chairs' wheels nearly touched when Cleve raised his hand for a high five.

"Looking good, man," Cleve said.

Their hands met with a strong clap. On contact, the young man's body fell to the opposite side of his chair; he had to catch himself with his one arm before falling out. His dad stopped pushing and leaned forward to steady his son. The young man's smile was wide and sweet.

8

FUCKING *LISA*

"I miss my friends and family," Cleve said as he pushed the button that released more Dilaudid into his body. "I just wanna go home."

"I know, babe," I said as I stood up. I pulled his sheet, which was crumpled at the end of his bed, up over him and tucked it under his arms. The bottom half was streaked with blood and pus. "This is where you need to be right now. Just focus on getting better, okay? Pretend it's a vacation or something." I half-smiled and rubbed his earlobe between my thumb and index finger before kissing him on the forehead. "I have to go. It's getting dark."

"Worst vacation ever," he huffed. "When'll you be back tomorrow?"

"Probably after breakfast. Does that work?"

Cleve nodded. "Love you."

I blew him a kiss as I walked out the door.

Most nights, I slept in Cleve's room to keep him company, which usually meant sleeping in an uncomfortable chair beside his bed. It wasn't restful, so occasionally I forced myself to sleep in my room at the Navy Lodge. The counselor who checked in on the patients and their families every few weeks always reminded me that I needed to take care of myself if I wanted to properly take care of someone else. So, I tried. I knew Cleve was where he needed to be, safe in the care of doctors and nurses. But I tossed and turned in my bed, worrying about him, afraid he was lonely. He'd always been gregarious. People loved him—his sense of humor and jolly disposition—and he thrived on that love. But after being hit by the IED, his only visitors after his parents left were doctors and nurses, celebrities and politicians, and me.

I remembered hearing about a company, typically meant for kids, where you could build a custom stuffed animal. I sat up and grabbed my laptop to look it up. I was excited to find that I could make a toy on their website and have it shipped. I chose a moose for no other reason than it was cute. I chose blue boxers for the moose's outfit because I assumed he'd live in the hospital bed with Cleve, who was usually naked or in boxers. I didn't want the moose to be overdressed. I added a music box that sang "You Are My Sunshine." I knew it was cheesy, and I second-guessed myself for a moment, but Cleve was cheesy, and I knew he'd love it, so it stayed.

A week later, I got a call from the post office in the hospital basement saying I'd received a package. The basement was like a mall food court. It had a Pizza Hut, a Subway, and a small store where you could buy military souvenirs like shot glasses and decals for your car. I grabbed an Italian BMT from Subway and then picked up my package. I sat at one of the food court tables, set the unopened box on it, and took a bite of my sandwich. After eating half of it, I pulled my keys from my purse, slid one of them along the tape, split the box in two, and opened it. The moose was cuter in person—soft, sweet. I pushed the button on its foot, and it began to sing: *You are my sunshine, my only sunshine, you make me happyyyy when skies are gray.* I propped it up against the napkin holder so we faced each other.

"I guess you're my dinner date today," I said. "Want a bite?" I lifted my sandwich toward the stuffed animal. "Well. More for me, then." I shrugged. This was the most company I'd had outside of Cleve's hospital room in weeks. I took a few more bites, then wrapped the rest in case Cleve wanted it.

As I walked into Cleve's room, I could hear Jerry Springer's enthusiastic, nasally voice.

I knocked on the doorframe. "Heyo."

Cleve sat up in his bed. He was beginning to look frail. His meds made him lose his appetite, so he'd been losing weight since he arrived. He pointed to the TV.

"This dude married a horse." He laughed.

"You know what, I don't even want to know. Have you eaten today?" I raised the Subway bag with the half-eaten sandwich.

"I had a can of Ensure this morning. Had some Jell-O and a ham sandwich for lunch."

"Well, eat this." I pulled the sandwich out of the bag, unwrapped it, and spread it onto his bedside table. I wheeled the table toward him so he could reach it more easily. "It's not warm anymore, but it's still good."

"Aww, thanks."

I smiled. "I have something else for you," I said. I sat in the chair next to his bed and pulled the stuffed moose out of my backpack. "I hate thinking of you here alone when I'm gone, so I got this little guy to keep you company." I pressed its foot. "It even sings!" I said, handing it to him.

Cleve didn't respond right away. He just held the stuffed animal in his lap and stared at it. He closed his eyes, and I wondered if he thought it was too childish. When he opened them again, he crossed his arms and looked directly at me. "I don't deserve this," he said.

"What? Yeah, you do."

"No. I don't deserve you. I'm a piece of shit, Karie." He started shaking his head. "I'm a fuckin' piece of shit."

"What are you talking about? Whatever it is, just . . ."

"I cheated on you." He began to sob. "It was over Christmas break. When I went home. I don't know what I was thinkin'." My heart began racing. I didn't know what to say. I'd flown to see him that November. We were saying "I love you" by Christmas, and we eloped two weeks later. I wanted to cry, but I refused to do it in front of him. "I'm so sorry, Karie."

"Who?" I asked. He kept shaking his head. He started crying harder. "Fucking who, goddamn it!"

"Lisa," he said.

"Lisa? High school Lisa? Are you serious?" Lisa was a friend of Cleve's from childhood. She was the girl he took to prom. I always suspected they had a romantic thing going on, but he swore to me and everyone else he knew that the relationship was platonic. In fact, he went out of his way to insist he wasn't into her. *She's fat,* he'd say. *She's annoying. Obsessed with me. Doesn't know how to take a hint.* It was so obvious in retrospect.

"I'm sorry. I don't know why I did it. I was drunk. I wasn't even thinkin'."

"Is that who you proposed to before me?" I asked.

He looked shocked. "I didn't—"

"Don't fucking lie. I know you proposed to someone."

He hung his head. "Yes," he said. "I can explain."

I scoffed. "What a sack of shit. I don't want an explanation. I'm gonna go now." I started toward the door.

"Please," Cleve pleaded. "I love you. I didn't realize how much until now. I'm so sorry, Karie. Please . . ."

I shook my head. "Stop fucking saying that! You sound pitiful," I said. "I don't know what I'm gonna do, but I can't be in this room right now." As I walked out the door, I could hear Cleve break into uncontrollable sobs. I almost stopped from turning the corner into the hallway. Part of me wanted to console him, but most of me was angry and wanted him to feel terrible.

When I stepped out of the hospital, the night's crisp air hit my face, and there I was again, alone. I walked into the parking lot and stood in a dark spot away from the streetlamps to hide the tears streaming down my face.

"Fuck him," I spat. "Fuck marriage. I'm such an idiot. So fucking stupid." I was mad at myself for falling for someone I hadn't actually known that well, at least as an adult, for trusting that person would protect my heart. I was beginning to realize that love was a weakness. I hated how attached I became to men and how much I needed the validation of being wanted by them. Still, so much of me wanted to turn around and go back to Cleve. An ambulance siren wailed in the distance, and I knew it was on its way to where I was standing. I began my walk down the now too-familiar road to my hotel room, unsure if I'd ever go back to that hospital.

The phone was already ringing when I got to my room. I was sure it was Cleve. I'd turned my cellphone to silent and, though we didn't talk on the landline often, he had the number in case he needed it. I ignored it at first, throwing my suitcase on the bed and haphazardly filling it. I emptied each drawer by the armful. It gave me the same satisfaction destroying things once did. All I could think about was *Lisa*. Fucking *Lisa*!

"Bitch. She's not even pretty, Cleve!" I yelled to no one as I shoved my underwear into one of the zipper pockets. "Why is it so fucking hot in here?"

I turned the air conditioner on high and rooted around in my purse for a hair tie but couldn't find one. I pulled a small scarf from the suitcase, pushed my hair back, and wrapped the scarf around my head, tying it in a knot at the top. My phone had stopped ringing and I figured Cleve had given up and would be asleep soon. I resented him for it. I'd struggled to sleep since arriving at Bethesda. Whenever I did fall asleep, I had nightmares about war, about bombs, about Cleve dying. I was so tired. Meanwhile, the medicine Cleve was taking made him sleep more than sixteen hours a day.

I threw the final wad of clothes into the suitcase and tried to close it, but it was too full. I'd been shopping using the money from the Semper Fi Fund. Though I tried to stick to necessities, I couldn't resist the urge to buy a few things that made my life a little brighter, like the laptop and camera. I also bought some clothing from Target that I didn't necessarily need, but it made me feel good. It was exciting to be able to buy brand-new clothes. Cleve even encouraged it. He knew I'd spent most of my life shopping at thrift stores or stealing. "Spend as much of it as you want," he'd said when I asked how much of the money I could have. "As long as I can spoil you, I'm goin' to." I blushed, kissed him on the forehead, and promised I wouldn't spend it all. Something about spending money and buying things I wanted made me feel fulfilled, at least temporarily.

I sat on the bed next to the overstuffed bag, my head in my hands. How was I going to get home? I still hadn't received non-medical attendant pay, and there wasn't enough of the Semper Fi Fund money left to buy a plane ticket. Brittany was my only option.

"I'm so sorry I have to ask," I said after gathering the nerve to call her. I hated asking for help.

"Stop apologizing. I'm happy to come get you." She paused. "God, Kinsey, why? I wish I could say I'm surprised, but I guess I'm not. I love him, but he just . . ."

"You know what? Don't even finish that sentence. I don't have the energy to be more upset."

"Okay," she said. It sounded like she was doing dishes, the sound of plates clinking and water rushing in the background. "He does love you. I call him sometimes to check in, and he just talks about you the whole time. I'm not saying you should forgive him, but I thought you should know. He would have been alone there without you. He knows that."

"Things do feel different since we got here."

"Well, I can leave first thing in the morning."

"Thank you. I'll repay you somehow, I promise."

She laughed. "Karie, that's dumb. It's not a big deal."

I laughed too. "You're a good friend."

"I know."

"Brittany?"

"Yeah?"

"I really do love him."

"I know."

"What if I decide to stay anyway?"

"Then I'll support it. I'll support whatever you do."

"Okay."

"I'm still gonna yell at him for being stupid," she said.

"I love you, dude."

"I love you, too. Call me in the morning and let me know what you decide to do."

I hung up and went outside to smoke a cigarette and think. I saw two options. I *could* tell myself everything that happened before the hospital didn't matter and forgive him. After all, living together in the aftermath of war had become the most pivotal point in our relationship. The fear, the loneliness, the uncertainty—it bonded us in a way no one would understand. But was it enough to forgive cheating?

I could also get a job, go to school, and start over on my own. I thought about our quick relationship, how we eloped without any planning. Everything happened so fast, and then everything changed just as quickly when he was wounded. Pacing, I took a drag of my cigarette.

"Damn it," I said as my body started back toward the hospital as if on autopilot. Who was I kidding? I knew it would be harder to forget our time there than to forgive him for cheating. Being in such proximity to death, I'd found a much clearer understanding of how fragile humans are, how fleeting life is. I had a newfound appreciation for the present moment, for small gifts like window light dancing across the floor on sunny afternoons, or every single precious breath. I knew Cleve felt it, too, and it bonded us in a way that was difficult to articulate. It was as though we existed in our own world, one only we could access. He had become my family. I couldn't just leave him. I could hardly imagine living without him. I needed to at least hear him out.

I walked so fast my calves burned. I had to catch him before he passed out. I lit another cigarette as soon as I finished the one before. I wiped sweat from my forehead with the sleeve of my zip-up hoodie, and I argued internally about whether I was making the right decision. I couldn't help but think about the guys I'd dated in Tampa. *They were so much worse,* I reasoned. I thought about my dad. He *hurt* me, and I still went back to live with him.

I reached the bridge and noticed a shadowy figure in the middle of the street. It wasn't entirely shaped like a human but was too small to be a car. I slowed down and crossed the road to get farther away from whatever it was. And then the figure rolled into the light of a streetlamp.

"The fuck?" I said to myself, and then yelled, "Cleve! What are you *doing?*" Just like that, I was more concerned about his health than I was about Lisa. I started running toward him. He stopped and dabbed his face with a white towel he had hung around his neck like a scarf. He'd made it about a quarter of the way up the bridge, which was challenging in a wheelchair, even if it wasn't far. When I reached him, I noticed he was barefoot and was only wearing a robe and boxers.

"You're not supposed to be out of your room this late. Your leg isn't even propped up."

"Karie."

"It's gonna bleed out. Aren't you cold?"

"Karie! I don't fuckin' care! Please don't leave. I love you. I love you so fuckin' much. I can't be here without you."

"I don't know what—"

"No, listen," he said. "I know I fucked up. It's been tearin' me up since Ramadi. It's why I was bein' so weird. But even since then . . . things changed after I was injured. You've been here by my side. Just me and you. You've been my rock in here. It's made me realize how much I love you. I am beggin' you, baby girl, please believe me. I am so sorry." He began to cry. "Fuck. I'm so so sorry."

The tough exterior I'd armored myself with when I left the hotel—the speech I thought I'd make when I saw him—fell away. "Please don't cry, Cleve," I said. I bent down and wrapped my arms around him. "It's okay. I'll be okay."

He pulled me in so tight. "No, it isn't. It's not okay. But I just need you to believe me that I would never do that now, and I'm so sorry. I'm so fuckin' sorry."

I pulled away just enough to look him in the eyes and hold his face in my hands. "Hey. *Hey*. Listen to me."

"Okay," he said.

"You hurt me. That *fucking* hurt. It still fucking hurts."

"I know. I'll never be able to forgive myself."

"But, look. I'll stay. Okay? I can stay, and we'll figure something out. I won't leave you here alone."

"You're too good for me," he said, and I wished he'd just stop talking. I didn't think I was too good for anyone.

"No. I'm not. I just love you so much my judgment's all clouded up." I shook my head.

I wondered if I would regret forgiving him. All I knew for sure was that I couldn't leave him alone in that hospital. We walked back to his room together. I planned to drop him off and return to the hotel, but he was so upset.

"I'll stay with you tonight," I said.

"Wanna sleep in the bed with me?"

"I could hurt you."

"I'll be fine. Just sleep on my right side," he said, reaching for my hand. I took it and climbed into the bed. I curled up next to him and laid my head on his shoulder.

"We haven't slept a whole night holding each other since before you left for Iraq," I said.

"I know. We should do it more often."

"Yeah."

"Thank you for stayin'," he said. "I can't do this without you."

"Don't do that again."

"Swear to God."

"I love you."

"I love you more."

9

LANDSLIDE

June 2006

"Kinsey. Valentine," Addair called from the doorway. "Y'all wanna meet Stevie Nicks?"

Cleve straightened himself in the bed, adjusted his thick-framed, military-issued glasses, commonly referred to in the military as "birth control glasses," or "BCGs," and looked at me for an answer. I wasn't sure who Stevie Nicks was, but it had been an exceptionally dull couple of days; the celebrities usually brought decent conversation and, sometimes, gifts. I nodded.

"Wife says yes," Cleve said, then looked to his roommate for a response.

Valentine was the latest of Cleve's roommates. There had been many, between being moved to different rooms after nearly every surgery, and with new men constantly arriving from the war. Valentine had been shot in the face by a sniper. The bullet entered his jaw and exited at the back of his neck, just below his skull. His jaw was so damaged that doctors had to remove what was left of it, leaving his face soft and deformed. His fiancée, Iris, sat next to him just like I sat next to Cleve: all day, every day. Because Valentine couldn't eat, doctors placed a tube in his neck, and every few hours they'd pour liquid into it, drool oozing from what used to be his mouth, Iris tenderly sopping it up with a rag. A framed picture of the two of them sat on the windowsill next to the cans of Ensure I'd lined up for Cleve. In the photo, Valentine was un-recognizable: handsome, with a strong jaw and bright hazel eyes. Iris sat in his lap smiling, wearing a sundress with pink flowers, her curly black hair arranged neatly over her shoulders.

Valentine picked up the dry-erase board he used to communicate and scribbled something in black marker. He showed it to Iris. "We're okay," she said to Addair with her angel voice, pulling the curtains around their portion of the room for privacy. She looked at me and winked before disappearing behind the pale-blue fabric.

Cleve was naked from the waist down, as usual. Even visitors weren't motivation enough for him to get dressed.

"Are you ever going to put pants on?" I joked. A week before, the commandant of the Marine Corps had come to visit to present Cleve with a Purple Heart. A photographer took pictures of the commandant pinning the medal to Cleve's navy blue hospital gown and then stand-ing at attention. Cleve lay in the bed, his arms rigid at his sides, as if he were at attention too. The commandant said something that I've since forgotten, and then their bodies relaxed, and the two shook hands. Cleve and I received the photos a few days later, and in one of them, if you looked closely, you could see Cleve's balls hanging out of the sheet. We laughed when we saw it, but I was also a little mortified.

"I may never get a chance to live my life without pants again, Karie," he replied, only half-joking. "I have a bum leg. Let me milk it."

I couldn't argue with that. Two and a half months had passed since Cleve had been wounded in Iraq, and he was still inpatient. He hated being stuck in that bed. Who was I to take away something that brought him joy, even if I thought it was ridiculous?

I stood up. "If you must be pantsless, at least let me tuck the boys in." I straightened his sheet out and tucked it securely between his legs. I bent down to check all angles. "All right, weirdo. I think you're good." I looked at Addair and gave him a thumbs-up.

Stevie walked straight to Cleve's bed and sat on it right next to his wounded leg, which stuck out of the sheet like a prop in a horror movie, a hunk of scarred pink flesh. Her perfume filled the room with citrus and flowers. She put her hand on Cleve's arm, her nails perfectly manicured, a ring on every finger.

"How ya doin', honey?" she asked Cleve. There was a velvety raspiness to her voice, an effortlessness in the way she moved that put me at ease.

"Pretty good, pretty good. On the mend," Cleve said. He told her about his surgeries and about being sick of the hospital, and about how he was ready to see the monuments if they'd just let him out of that bed.

"Well, you're a real hero. It's not right you have to stay in here all day," she said. "I've got faith you'll be out of here soon." She turned to me. "How about you, sweetie? How are you doing?"

I wanted to say the hospital sucked, that I was sick of eating Subway sandwiches and cafeteria food, that Cleve sometimes cried for his mom, that I missed my mom, too, that we were just a couple of scared kids. Instead, I said, "I'm fine. Just doing my best to keep this guy from falling apart."

She asked where we were from, and we told her about Foley's cornfields and live oaks and big skies and about the white sand beaches of Gulf Shores that we'd taken for granted most of our lives but would give anything to go back to.

"We met when we were thirteen," I told her.

She put her hand on my cheek, and I thought she might cry. "You kids don't deserve all this," she said. Her hand was soft, like a fresh-picked peach warmed in the sun, and I didn't know what to say. "I brought you something," she said, handing Cleve a small black box. Inside was an iPod Mini. "I put my own playlist on it," she said as she signed the box with a silver paint marker. "I hope you like it."

"Hell yeah," Cleve said. "I never had one of these! Thanks, Ms. Nicks."

"Oh, no, honey. Call me Stevie."

Addair came into the room with a Polaroid camera. "You guys want a picture?"

Cleve and I said yes, and we all posed. She signed that, too, thanked us for our service with a hug, and left.

"Do you know who she is?" I asked Cleve once she was gone. "She was really nice."

"Please tell me you're joking."

I shrugged, sheepishly. My Christian upbringing had kept me sheltered. I often didn't know things I thought I should, and I hated when people discovered my ignorance. "Come on! Stevie Nicks! Fleetwood Mac?" He nudged my shoulder with the back of his hand and started singing, "I took my love, and I took it down / Climbed a mountain, and I turned around . . ."

"Oh my God," I said, realizing who she was. "Stevie Nicks was in your bed."

"Yeah! And now we have a Stevie Nicks playlist on a Stevie Nicks iPod!"

Cleve opened the box and pulled out the tiny white device. I crawled into his bed and curled into him as we scrolled through the list of songs she had chosen for us, his heart monitor beeping in the background. He pulled out a pair of earbuds and gave me one. He pushed play, and the music began: "I took my love, and I took it down . . ."

Valentine went into surgery a month later and was assigned a different room. The guy who replaced him, Arpin, was a talkative, pudgy soldier who'd been shot between the legs.

"I lost all of it," he told us with a chuckle. "Dick, balls." He pointed to himself with both thumbs. "This guy's never gonna fuck again."

His tone was jokey, which somehow made his situation sadder. I'd seen missing eyes, missing limbs, and missing jaws. Heads caved in, massive pink scars, and melted skin. Over time, seeing people with major wounds became as normal to me as putting keys into the ignition of a car or pouring a glass of water. But this guy was different. Something about him got to me. Clothed, he looked like there was nothing wrong. Someone might even say he'd been lucky. He could walk, he could talk, he could see. He was energetic and he entertained Cleve and me by playing burned CDs on a boom box he'd brought with him.

"You like Dashboard?" he asked me.

"Fuck yes, I do," I said.

We discovered that Arpin and I had both listened to Dashboard Confessional to get through bad breakups. He turned up the volume, and we mouthed the words to "Vindicated." We dramatically lowered ourselves to our knees when the chorus played, while Cleve tolerated our emo shenanigans. Cleve was a Johnny Cash and Alison Krauss kind of guy. Arpin and I were on the floor singing when the nurse entered the room.

"Time for vitals," he said.

"Aw, man," Arpin complained as he turned the music off and crawled back into his hospital bed.

Despite Arpin's cheery mood, something felt off. He smiled just a little too much. He talked a little too fast. When I asked Cleve about it, he said that at night, when the hospital went dark and still, he could hear Arpin sobbing to himself.

"If I lost my dick, I'd be crying at night for my mama, too," Cleve said. "I'd rather have anything taken but that." He grabbed his crotch and shook his head. "Poor bastard."

Though Cleve considered himself lucky compared to many of the other guys ("I got all my limbs intact," he'd say, "I can't complain"), he was still struggling with his new identity as a wounded warrior, as disabled. He admitted to me that he was beginning to feel invisible, especially in his wheelchair. He said people didn't take him seriously in that thing, said people wouldn't look him in the eyes. This new version of him made it easier for me to forgive him for cheating. He hardly seemed like the same person he had been before he was wounded. Being upset about it almost felt unfair, like blaming him for something someone else had done. The day after he told me about Lisa, we talked about it one more time, and then I said I didn't want to hear about it anymore. We would start over, and that was the end of it.

Cleve began using his crutches more, even though his leg wasn't fully healed, even though gravity's pressure pushed blood to his wound, filling it like a bloated water balloon, all swollen and purple, small rivers of red dripping into his shoe. Cleve's desire to use his crutches made sense to me, even though I didn't like it. Witty, confident, and tall, Cleve had always been the center of any group. He had always been hard to ignore. Though being upright had to hurt, he preferred that to the pain of suddenly feeling unseen.

Being upright had other perks. After a week or so of proving he was mobile, Cleve was approved to leave the base, the last step before being approved to leave the hospital for good. His first request: to see the monuments.

"What if we figure the car thing out first, then we can drive ourselves?" I said.

Cleve agreed. We spent the next couple of days looking at SUVs. We needed something big enough for his wheelchair. We also knew we'd be traveling and moving at some point. "Didn't you say you like Nissan Armadas?" he asked.

"Yeah. But this is your car. Get whatever you want."

"I've been looking at a Mustang for me. This should be your car."

I shook my head. No one had ever gotten me something that expensive before, and it made me feel uncomfortable. "You don't have to do that. Just get what you want. I'll obviously drive it when I need to."

"Baby. I'm goin' to spoil you. I don't care what you say. This is your car."

Tears welled up in my eyes. It was so important to him that I felt taken care of, too. It made me feel loved, despite also feeling uncomfortable with the cost. I wiped my eyes. "And now I'm crying. What is wrong with me?" I laughed.

"Let's look at Armadas," he said.

We took a taxi to a dealership a few days later to test-drive a mint-green Armada with cream-colored leather seats. Cleve and I both test-drove it and agreed it was perfect, but I thought it was too expensive.

"We should look at some cheaper cars, too," I said. We were still sitting in the Armada. The salesman was standing a few yards away, staring at us.

"I like this one. We'll put 10K down and can get a loan for the rest."

"That's still a $45,000 loan, Cleve. Maybe we should wait and think about it." Though the money he received for his injury felt like a lot now, we were spending it quickly and I worried about how we would make money in the future. No one had talked to us about what retirement would look like other than to say that he'd eventually be receiving disability payments—but we didn't yet know how much those would be. I also wasn't sure if I'd be able to work if he continued needing a full-time caregiver.

Cleve shook his head, got out of the car, his crutches in tow, and tottered toward the salesman. We sat at the man's desk for an hour, filling out paperwork and making phone calls until Cleve was only approved for 30K.

"We could put more down," he said.

"Okay, no. Absolutely not." I looked at the salesman. "Do you have anything similar within this price range?"

"Let me see," he said, tapping away at his keyboard. "Let me see, let me see. Oh! Any interest in an Escalade?"

"Yes," I said. "Let's look at it."

The Escalade was a shimmery beige, and the interior had gray leather seats with faux wood trim. On the back of every headrest was a screen.

"You're joking," I said. "What in the world would we do with those?"

Cleve looked at me, smiled, and shrugged. "I bet a baby would love those."

"What?" He caught me off guard. We'd never talked about having kids.

"Just sayin', a baby Jimmy would look cute in that back seat."

I laughed. "Okay, Cleve. That's a whole other conversation I don't want to have at a car dealership." I got into the driver's seat and ran my hand along the steering wheel. "I think this is the nicest car I've ever seen."

"You like it?" the salesman said. "Only $28,000."

That price sounded cheap after looking at the other car. I looked at Cleve. "What do you think?"

"I think it's sexy."

"Fuck it. Let's do it."

The morning of our trip to see the monuments, I tried convincing Cleve to use his wheelchair. I knew everything would be spread out, and it was a hot July day. I imagined him limping along the sidewalk, sweat pouring down his face. He would get frustrated and then grumpy, would make frequent stops so that he could elevate his blood-pooled leg and take a few extra pain meds. We'd maybe see a couple of things, if we were lucky. I just wanted us to have a good day. Cleve had already made up his mind, though.

"I'm not goin' in that thing," he said, shaking his head. He hopped across the room to his crutches, which were leaning against the dresser. He put one under each arm, then leaned over to grab his wallet and keys.

I nodded and took a deep breath. "Can I have a hug?" I asked.

"Of course," he said. He put his crutches down and hopped back toward me. He wrapped his arms around my shoulders, pressing my cheek into his chest. "You good?"

"Yes," I said. "It's just, sometimes I get so caught up with worrying about what *could* happen that I forget to enjoy what's actually happening. Like, I'm always somewhere in the future, so, really, I just miss . . . everything." I looked up at him. He had that concerned puppy look again, his eyes almost cartoonishly big and head tilted to the side. I wondered if he even knew what I meant. He didn't worry the way I did. He was the opposite of me, always assuming things would turn out okay. "I just get so anxious. Especially after . . . I mean . . ." I gestured toward his leg.

Cleve half-smirked and gave me a squeeze. "You need to stop worrying so much. I mean, okay okay . . . check this out," he said before letting go of me. He backed away and began bouncing in a circle, his arms pumping one after the other into the air. "Happy feet! Happy feet! Happy happy happy feet!" he sang in a high-pitched voice. I started laughing, and he stopped to face me. "See? Everything's fine. Let's have fun today."

I smiled. "Okay."

I brought the wheelchair anyway. I insisted it would help me worry less and promised I would push it around myself. It fit perfectly in our new car.

Our first stop was the Washington Monument. The trek there didn't seem too difficult for him, most of it on sidewalks and under the shade of cherry trees. Still, it was hot, and we were both ready to sit soon after we arrived. I parked the wheelchair in some grass, put the brakes on, and sat in it. I watched Cleve as he balanced on his crutches, looking up at the monument, which pierced a cloudless afternoon sky. In his favorite houndstooth University of Alabama baseball cap, he squinted against the sun.

"Imagine building somethin' that tall," he said.

"Yeah," I said. "Humans."

"Amazing," he said, then swung his legs forward, balancing himself on his crutches, before landing on his good leg. "It's good to be off that base."

"It's good to *see* you off that base."

He dropped his crutches and carefully lowered himself to the grass beside the wheelchair. I sat next to him, rested my head on his shoulder, and people-watched—people passing, people stopping to pose with the monument before passing. A young boy, maybe seven or eight, ran by with a kite, diamond-shaped with a bald eagle on it.

"This is our first date since I was wounded," he said.

"Pretty good first date," I said, smiling.

He nodded and kissed the top of my head.

When we were ready to move on, we headed to the Lincoln Memorial. "I have to get a picture with giant Lincoln!" Cleve said enthusiastically. It was what he wanted to do more than anything. We walked parallel to the reflecting pool, him leading and me following behind with the wheelchair. The foot traffic was overwhelming. People in brightly colored shorts and Tevas with fanny packs around their waists and big cameras around their necks. Kids waving American flags. An older man wearing a U.S. Marines Vietnam vet cap. He looked Cleve in the eye. Nodded.

"Thanks for your service, devil dog," Cleve said.

"Oorah," the man responded.

A man dressed as Abraham Lincoln asked if we wanted to take pictures. We said no thank you. A young girl with pigtails and an ice cream shaped like Mickey Mouse stopped and pointed at Cleve's leg, tugging on her mom's skirt. "Mom, Mom, what happened?" she asked, and her mother, visibly embarrassed, picked her up, apologized, and kept walking.

Cleve stopped near a bench under a cherry tree. "I just need a minute," he said.

"Sure you don't want me to push you?"

"Nah, I'm fine. Just need a minute."

He pulled a bottle of pain pills from his pocket and popped one in his mouth like a piece of candy. He closed his eyes and leaned back in his chair. We sat there for thirty minutes before he was ready to go again.

When we finally made it to the Lincoln Memorial, Cleve stopped at the bottom of the steps, grabbed the hand towel he always carried from his back pocket, and wiped sweat from his face and neck. He sat down.

"Damn, that's a lot of steps," he said.

"I bet there's an elevator. Stay here, and I'll check it out." Elevators seemed to always be hidden around corners or in the back of buildings. After Cleve was wounded, I quickly realized the privilege of being able-bodied. Getting anywhere was so much more difficult now. To me, the inaccessibility of most places sent the message that people with disabilities weren't welcome unless they were willing to adapt. It was infuriating, but this was our world now. Adapt we did.

"No. Just give me a sec. You gotta climb the stairs at the Lincoln Memorial. I'm climbing those stairs."

"Babe, don't push yourself. You've done a lot today," I said. I was starting to get irritated at his stubbornness.

"I'm climbing those stairs," he said matter-of-factly.

One by one, he climbed the damn stairs. I made my way up backward, dragging the wheelchair behind me. I could've taken the elevator myself, but there were so many people. I was afraid of losing him. I'd seen the monument before, so when we reached the top, I parked the wheelchair in a corner and sat in it, watching Cleve admire the giant statue. He turned and waved, pointed toward Lincoln, then made hand gestures suggesting he wanted his picture taken. I took the photo, and we rode the elevator down. We made it to the Vietnam Veterans Memorial before Cleve gave up and agreed to use the wheelchair. Frustrated but still determined, he insisted on wheeling himself. I followed behind him the rest of the day, carrying his crutches over my shoulder.

10

RIDE OR DIE

August 2006

"On a scale of one to ten, how much pain would you say you're in daily?" the pain management doctor asked.

Cleve looked at me and then back at the doctor. "Seven to nine, depending on the day," he answered. The doctor scribbled something on his clipboard.

Cleve had been cleared to leave the hospital and return to Camp Lejeune. The muscle flap on Cleve's calf hadn't fully healed—he was still experiencing some venous congestion and required IV antibiotics—but all we could do was wait. His doctors said we didn't need to be in Maryland to do that. At Camp Lejeune, a nurse would visit weekly in our home to check his vitals and drop off the following week's antibiotics. His pain medication would start being mailed to our home, so we made an appointment with his pain management doctor before we left.

"Are you satisfied with your meds, or do you think you need something stronger?" Cleve's doctor asked.

"Is addiction being considered at all?" I interrupted. Some of Cleve's symptoms were worrisome. He was always sweaty, his face was broken out, and he passed out regularly. "I'm just curious because he's been on these for a while now, and it worries me a little."

Cleve glared at me, and I looked at him like, *Get over it.*

The doctor looked at Cleve. "Are you taking your medication as prescribed?"

"Yes," Cleve said earnestly.

The doctor looked back at me, tapping his pen on his clipboard. The pen stopped before he spoke. "When a patient is in this much pain, taking them off pain medication is unethical, so there isn't much we can do right now. Are you worried he's addicted?"

I shook my head and shrugged. "I don't really know how to know. I just know it's possible," I said, fiddling with my keys. I told the doctor the symptoms I'd noticed, but he didn't look concerned. My cheeks burned. I suddenly felt silly for asking.

"We can keep an eye on it," the doctor said. "If you notice any other symptoms, don't hesitate to let us know."

"Okay," I said, even though I wasn't satisfied with his answer. The wounded veterans were treated like a docile herd of cattle. Go to a pain management appointment, tell the doctor about your pain, get a new pill prescription, pick up a new bottle, repeat. Easy as that. It was just how things were done.

"The meds are fine, Doc," Cleve said.

"Okay then. We'll keep it the same. You should see your medication in the mail in a couple of days."

Before we left, I refiled the TSGLI paperwork. This time, in addition to his injuries, I included the three months he had been bedridden in the hospital. While his leg injury alone was only worth twenty-five thousand dollars, every month he remained inpatient and needed help with basic tasks like using the bathroom, bathing, and dressing was worth twenty-five thousand more. If our request was approved, Cleve would receive another seventy-five thousand dollars, totaling one hundred thousand—the most a Marine can get for a war wound. I was adamant about getting as much money from the military as possible for what he'd lost. He didn't have the energy to deal with it, so I handled it for him. I found out later that most caregiver wives handled these things for their husbands. The work was tedious, but I didn't mind doing it. I was content to be doing something useful with my time.

Finally, we were free. We wouldn't be going back to normal—Cleve still had to fly to Bethesda once a month for checkups with Dr. Gupta—but we didn't care. We were just excited to finally be living outside of the hospital, to be going back to a place that felt like a home. Though our ultimate goal was to move back to Alabama, his doctor insisted the future was unclear until we knew for sure how Cleve's body would react to the muscle transplant. I figured I would try to get a job in the meantime, and we'd just take it day by day.

"Look, it has a porch!" I said the day we got the keys to our new apartment. It was attached by double doors to the dining room at the back of the apartment.

"Hell yeah," Cleve replied from the hallway. He was testing doorways with his wheelchair to make sure they were wide enough.

That style of apartment typically required a yearlong wait. We were allowed to skip the waitlist because Cleve was wounded. Had we not been bumped to the top of the list, we would've been assigned what I called a matchbox house. They were shabby little cinder-block homes, all of them perfect rectangles with two windows at the front and a set of stairs between them leading up to a porch just big enough for one person at a time. From the outside, they were clearly not handicap accessible and looked to be the size of an average living room. I assumed the interior was cramped, too. Getting around in one of those would've been difficult for Cleve.

I opened the double doors and stepped out onto a screened-in concrete slab. It was hot out, and through a large maple tree in the backyard, I could see puffy clouds floating through the sky. I closed my eyes and listened to birds chirping. I took a deep breath as I raised my arms into the air and then exhaled before folding in half and touching the ground. The muscles loosened in my lower back. My spine popped. It felt really good to have our own space again.

After checking the place out, we slept at Brittany's because we didn't have furniture yet. Carson was still deployed, so their house was exactly how I'd left it, all the way down to the picture of Cleve I'd framed in the bedroom I'd been staying in. It was as if everything had been frozen in time, waiting for my return. Laughter filled the house as we made spaghetti and ate it at the dinner table like a family. We spent the rest of the night watching TV and catching up. Though I'd only lived there for a short time, and knew we would eventually leave Jacksonville, I was happy to be back.

Cleve and I met with movers the next morning. The Semper Fi Fund was giving us brand-new furniture. What we were getting had been a mystery to us, so we were delighted as a couch, matching chair, coffee table, matching side tables, dining room set, bed frame, mattress, and box spring were carried off the truck. After the movers left, we sat on our new couch. I ran my hand along the armrest, noting that the dusky brown with a swirling design stitched into it was neutral enough to decorate with almost any color I wanted. I imagined the room with art on the walls.

"I can't decide if we should go with red or teal decorations," I said.

"Why not both?"

"Touché," I said, beaming. "You know what? This is my first new couch. My ex and I always went dumpster diving behind furniture stores when we needed something for the house."

"I think this is my first couch ever," Cleve said. Still seated, he bounced on it to test its sturdiness. "It's comfortable!"

"It is!" I said. Suddenly, I was feeling emotional. "Baby. This is our first couch together." I looked around. "It's our first home. We're about to have so many firsts."

"Come here," Cleve said, caressing my arm. I swung my legs across his and hugged him. We sat for a moment, holding each other and staring at the bare wall in front of us. I wondered if we'd be able to afford a TV.

"Remind me to look at Craigslist tomorrow for a few things," I said.

"Like what?"

"TV, pots and pans, I don't know . . . everything?"

"We could go to Walmart in the mornin' to get a few things."

"Aww. Look how cute we are, playing house," I said, booping his nose.

"We need to get you an apron you can wear with nothin' under it."

"Stop."

"I'll stop when you stop bein' so sexy."

"There's nothing sexy about me right now," I said. I gestured toward the gray hoodie and plaid pajama pants I was wearing. "I need a shower."

"Woman, you're fuckin' beautiful," he said.

I smiled and rolled my eyes. "You're sweet."

"Sweet enough for a kiss?" he asked. I nodded and kissed him, and he grabbed my ass and pulled me closer to him. "You know what else we can do now?" he said. He started taking off my hoodie.

"Mmhmm," I said between kisses, then pulled away. "What about your leg and PICC line? I'm afraid . . ."

"It's fine," he said, untying my pajama pants. "I promise." He leaned over me until I was on my back. His good leg remained on the floor, holding him up, the wounded one propped on the couch's armrest. It didn't look comfortable, but I closed my eyes and gave in. It felt good to be with him again. So much of our connection had been built on lust. But I couldn't stop thinking about the donated couch, the leg, the tiny tube coming out of his chest that led straight to his heart. His skin even felt different. It was clammy and soft, his body much smaller after eating so little over the last few months. I had to keep reminding myself, *This is Cleve, this is Cleve, this is Cleve.*

When we were done, we sat on the cement floor of our back porch, cuddling and smoking cigarettes. We watched birds chase each other in and out of the maple tree's leaves. Kids laughed in the distance, presumably playing at the playground at the center of our little neighborhood. It was one of the most peaceful moments we'd had together since he'd been wounded.

"I'm glad we're here," I said. "Like, I'm glad we're here and together and . . . I don't know. It's weird to think we've only been married seven months. We started dating, what? Ten months ago or something? We've been through so much already. My brain can't keep up." I touched the scar on his thigh where the skin graft had been taken for his calf. It had healed into thin leather, rough and pink and about a foot long, wrapping almost entirely around his right thigh.

"You're my ride or die, girl. Maybe it hasn't been long, but this is the scariest thing that ever happened to me, and who was there? No one will ever understand what I've been through like you." His lip quivered, all the muscles in his face fighting back tears. Imperfect as our relationship was, I'd never believed in someone's love for me more. And something about being in love, despite the impossible circumstances we'd found ourselves in, made me feel invincible, like there was no obstacle in the world we couldn't get through as long as we had each other. Just us against the world.

"I've never loved anyone like this before. It's like . . . I dunno, it sounds weird, but sometimes it feels wrong that we aren't physically attached. Like . . ." I smiled and looked down. ". . . like I wish I could crawl into your chest and live there forever. Like I just can't get close enough to you."

"You can live in my chest," he said. He leaned toward me and brushed his nose on mine before kissing me and whispering, "I love you, too."

Cleve's nurse showed up later that afternoon. She was short and pear-shaped with a gray pixie cut and dimples on both cheeks. She put her bag of supplies on the coffee table and sat next to Cleve. She checked his temperature and blood pressure, and asked him how he was feeling. She took the bloodstained dressing from around his PICC line and replaced it with a new one.

"I'll be back Monday of every week," she said. "Around the same time." She walked out to her car and brought back a box filled with IV bags. "These are his antibiotics and they go in the refrigerator, okay? He gets a new one every four hours." She showed me how to connect a bag to his PICC line and hang it on the IV stand. I set the alarm on my phone for four hours.

"Can he go anywhere while he's attached to one of these?" I held one in my hand, sloshing the liquid around the bag. I tried to imagine what it would be like to do that every four hours every single day. How would I sleep?

"Sure, but the bag needs to be above his head no matter where he's at," she said. "Car included."

That night, Cleve and I slept in our new bed on sheets and pillows we borrowed from Brittany. At two in the morning, my alarm went off. I awoke from a dead sleep. I had the feeling I'd been having nightmares again. I couldn't remember what they were, but I was drenched in sweat and felt uneasy. I turned off my alarm, tiptoed to the kitchen, and got a bag of antibiotics from the bottom drawer of the refrigerator. Cleve was shirtless and asleep on his back, so it was easy to unhook one bag and hook the other without disturbing him. I was nervous twisting the connector and detaching the used bag from Cleve's body. I knew the PICC line led to his heart, and I was terrified of doing some kind of damage. Cleve didn't move. I pulled the empty bag off the pole and threw it on the floor to be dealt with later. I hung a fresh bag on the hook at the top of the pole, then connected it to Cleve's heart. I stood back and looked at my work. Satisfied, I draped the blanket over him, kissed his cheek, and set my alarm for four hours. I crawled into the bed next to him and stared at the ceiling. Wide-awake, I turned my head to look at him and placed my hand on his stomach, so I could feel it rise and fall with each breath. *He looks so peaceful,* I thought. I closed my eyes and counted his breaths, letting myself get lost in the rhythm.

11

JUST KIDS

October 2006

Cleve and I stood in the crowd with Brittany and her baby, waiting. Brittany held a sign we'd made the night before—white poster board with "Welcome home, Daddy!" written in red and blue Sharpie. Young women wore colorful new dresses with high heels and false eyelashes. They clashed against the parking lot backdrop, dust whirling around them. There were babies too young to have ever met their fathers, parents holding each other in anticipation as they waited for their sons and daughters to arrive home from war. Cleve's unit—Third Battalion, Eighth Marines—had been gone seven months. Though everyone was excited to see those who'd survived, we also anticipated the sadness that would inevitably wash over us when the buses emptied too soon.

Cleve was the only one in his unit who'd returned home wounded who could make it to 3/8's homecoming. His injured leg hung under cargo shorts, a mangled mass of flesh oozing blood into his green Converse sneakers. The nurse, like his doctors, advised him not to stand upright too long because it put too much pressure on his already strained veins. While he'd been pretty good about using his wheelchair, he refused to show up to his unit's homecoming in one. His body draped over his crutches like wet clothes on a hanger. He was so sweaty. He was always sweaty. I wondered what his friends would think when they saw him. In the three months since we'd returned to Camp Lejeune, he'd gained back most of the weight he'd lost in the hospital, but he still didn't look quite like himself. His body was softer, dark circles remained under his eyes, and his skin was pallid and covered in pimples and pockmarks. The pain pills also made him hyper-focused on the blemishes. He'd spend hours at the bathroom mirror picking at them, making them worse.

I rubbed the small of his back. "How you doin'?"

He shifted his weight on his crutches and wiped his cheek on his shoulder. "I'm good. I wish they'd hurry up, though."

"I can go to the car and get your wheel—"

"Nope. I'm fine."

I nodded and kissed his arm.

I noticed people staring at his leg. Usually, if I noticed someone staring, I'd try to make them uncomfortable by staring back. I'd become protective of Cleve. But that day, I knew his leg was evidence of the war their family members were arriving home from. I didn't hold their curiosity against them, but I held Cleve close. He always looked straight ahead in large crowds, as if he didn't notice the attention his body attracted. But surely he must have. People weren't discreet about it.

The crowd cheered as the buses appeared in the distance. I thought about Hamilton, who would have been killed by a sniper if he hadn't been wearing his helmet incorrectly. How their battalion had lost seventeen Marines and sailors and suffered 240 casualties. I wondered where *their* families were that day.

"You ready to see Carso . . . I mean, Nick?" I asked Brittany. I felt strange calling him by their last name around her.

"I don't know," she said. "I think so."

Her relationship with Carson had been rocky for a long time, and the deployment didn't help. Their calls often ended in arguments. Brittany was lonely. She'd had Dillon during Carson's first deployment, and when he returned, he didn't seem very interested in getting to know his son. Then, half a year later, he was gone again. The baby could walk now, and Brittany had gotten used to being a single mom. She would have to adjust her life to fit a husband into it again.

"I'm obviously happy he made it home. I just hope he can be a dad this time," she said, looking at Dillon longingly.

The buses parked in front of the crowd, and the doors swung open. One by one, uniformed men and women stepped out. Family and friends had to be patient. The Marines still had things to do before reuniting with everyone. We watched as they unloaded duffle bags from the buses. When they were done, they formed a line and stood at attention. As soon as they were dismissed, the crowd swarmed. Young women leaped into their loved ones' arms, parents hugged their babies-turned-fighters, and fathers met their children for the first time. Cleve's friends found him, sometimes before they found their own families, and took turns hugging him, a few of them with tears in their eyes. When Carson walked up to Brittany he said, awkwardly, "Hello, wife," before giving her a kiss on the cheek and looking at Dillon in his stroller. He pointed at him. "He got huge," he said with wide eyes. Brittany half-smirked. I could tell she was irritated. That was one of the things she disliked the most about her husband—he'd rather crack a joke than shed a tear, even if it was totally inappropriate. She'd spent months worrying about and missing him. She'd imagined, against her better judgment, the kind of homecoming you see in the movies. She was disappointed.

Carson turned to Cleve and his face lit up. "It's good to see you upright, man."

They shook hands, vigorously, jolting both of their bodies. Cleve pulled it in for a hug. "Good to see you back on the home front," he said.

Carson pulled away and looked Cleve's body over. He guffawed when he got to his leg. "That's seen better days."

Cleve laughed. "You ain't wrong, man. You ain't wrong."

Brittany and Carson invited a few friends to their house later that week for a small party. Hamilton, Baker, and a guy I'd never met, Norris, showed up. We all sat by a fire in the backyard, drinking cheap beers and catching up. Cleve had a separate foldout chair for his leg so he could keep it propped up. The guys took turns making fun of it.

"Hey, Kinsey," Baker said. "Your leg looks like shit."

"Don't you think it's about time you cut that fucker off?" Hamilton said.

Cleve reached over the armrest, picked a rock up off the ground, and threw it at Hamilton. "Fuck y'all."

Norris was quietly sipping his beer. He hadn't said much at all since he'd gotten there. He was sitting on the opposite side of Cleve from me. Cleve patted him on the back. "Karie, have you met this guy yet?"

I shook my head. "Not really. Hi." I waved.

Norris had a boyish face, handsome, with chestnut hair and soft, round eyes. He half-waved back.

"I wouldn't be here if it weren't for him," Cleve said, gesturing at Norris. Cleve told me Norris had pulled him from his Humvee after it was bombed and dragged him to safety.

"This motherfucker," Norris said with a subdued chuckle. "Somehow, even with his leg blown to shit, he was making jokes the whole time."

I laughed. "Not surprised," I said, poking the fire with a long stick. I took a sip of my beer.

"He knew he was banged up that day," Norris said, "but he didn't want us to worry as we softened the area so we could get him out. Among all that chaos, ole Cleve kept up that humor of his. He was a true Marine."

I nodded and forced a smile. *True Marine,* I thought. I wasn't sure what that meant. From what I could tell, to be considered a *true Marine,* you had to be tough. And toughness in the Marine Corps, it seemed to me, was determined by how much abuse you could endure with a smile on your face.

The seventy-five thousand dollars I'd applied for showed up a month or so after the guys returned home. I was relieved. When I'd initially said I wanted to reapply, I was told it might be difficult to prove exactly how long he'd needed one-on-one care. The criteria seemed arbitrary to me: *Was he still inpatient? Can the patient clothe himself? Can the patient go to the bathroom by himself? Can the patient bathe himself?* If you answered even one of those questions incorrectly, you no longer qualified. Each month you qualified for was worth twenty-five thousand dollars. If I'd been completely honest, I would have written that he was able to do some of those things himself by the end of the last month he was in the hospital. I claimed the full three months anyway. As far as I was concerned, the war they sent him to had ruined his life and he deserved every penny I could squeeze out of them. I requested Cleve's medical records and highlighted anything I thought was relevant. While at the hospital, I learned quickly that everything in the military that involves paperwork or money is more difficult than it needs to be. You have to be persistent and thorough, and even then, you'll probably be told *no* a few times and be forced to start the process over again. Finding help is nearly impossible. With a disinterested grimace, everyone will tell you that someone else is who you need to talk to, until you realize no one knows the answer to your question or cares enough to find it. At that point, you have two choices: give up or be a pain in the ass. I chose the latter. Squeaky wheel gets the grease.

"Yes!" I yelled. We'd gone to the bank that morning to check for the TSGLI money, something we did every couple of weeks or so. "See? Being annoying pays off sometimes."

"Seventy-five G's, baby!" Cleve cheered as he slapped the steering wheel. He leaned back in his seat and sighed before turning his head toward me. He smiled wide. "I'm getting you a ring," he said.

Caught off guard, I stared at him for a moment, trying to decipher what he meant. "A wedding ring?" I beamed. The thought of having a ring was so exciting to me that it made me feel a little nauseous.

"A wedding ring," he repeated as he started the car. "Let's go to the mall."

"Right now?"

"Yep."

I bounced in my seat. "Oh my God. I'm getting a wedding ring today!"

At Zales, we stood over a case of diamonds in every shape and size. We wore hoodies and jeans and baseball caps—the same clothes we'd worn the day before, having assumed we would only be going to the drive-thru ATM. It reminded me of the day we eloped. We were often so underdressed for special occasions. While I'd been able to find humor in the absurdity of our lives, it was starting to become a little depressing. I envied people who celebrated milestones properly. While I had no desire to be a Cinderella or an Ariel, it would've been nice to have had a ring before the wedding. To have had a wedding with a white dress. To have had some years together in a small rental with thrifted furniture and a couple of houseplants, where our greatest concerns were paying the bills on time and deciding who would be doing the dishes that night.

I tucked my hands in the front pocket of my hoodie and looked at Cleve. "What's the budget?" I asked sheepishly.

He put both of his crutches under one arm and put the other arm around my shoulders, kissing me on the top of my head. "Ten thousand enough?"

I looked at him wide-eyed. "I would think so."

"The wedding sets in that price range are over here," the sales associate said, gesturing toward a case of rings to the right of us.

I looked at her and shook my head. "Five thousand. Maybe." I looked back at Cleve with a goofy grimace and mouthed *Crazy ass*.

The woman continued walking toward the same case and then began pulling out display stands full of engagement rings, the soft light dancing on their diamonds like glitter. I walked over to her and picked each one up, inspecting them, turning them under the light to assess their sparkle. I slipped each of them onto my ring finger, one after the other, holding my hand out to admire them, to feel the weight of them.

"How many carats are you looking for?" the salesperson asked.

I shrugged. "I don't really care. I just want it to feel right."

"What shape would you like the center diamond to be?" she asked.

I thought for a second. "Round, probably. Maybe square. Pear can be pretty, too, though," I said. I hadn't put much thought into diamond shapes, because I wasn't sure if I'd ever get one. While Cleve had mentioned getting me a ring when we were first married, we hadn't talked about it since, and it wasn't a topic I was going to bring up.

She pulled out a white-gold set. It was simple and elegant. The engagement ring had eight round diamonds along the band and a large round one at the center. The wedding band had ten diamonds that matched the ones flanking the larger diamond on the engagement ring. I put them on and smiled.

"How much is this set?" I asked.

"It's $2,999," she said. "I love that one. It looks perfect on you."

"I think I love it, too. A lot." I walked over to a mirror and positioned my hand on my chest so that I could get a full view of my hand with the rings on it.

Cleve walked up behind me. "Are those the ones you want?" he asked, looking at me in the mirror. He reached around me and held my hand in his. "They're sparkly."

"So sparkly," I said. I turned around to look at him. "Are you sure this is okay?"

"Baby," he said, tucking a piece of hair behind my ear, "I want you to have this more than anything."

"I really like these," I said with a teary smile.

"Then it's yours."

A month later, Cleve sent me a listing for an '88 Saleen Mustang, his dream car, and all but begged me to let him buy it for his Christmas gift.

I grimaced. "Huh . . ." I paused. "It looks like that eighties time-travel car in that movie . . . uh. I'm having a brain fart. You know that movie where they go . . . *Back to the Future*! The time-travel car in that . . ." I said.

Cleve looked at me like I had two heads. "This does not look anything like a DeLorean."

"I mean, it kinda does. They're both . . . pointy."

He scoffed. "It's a fox body and it's sexy."

"Whatever you say, sir. If that's what you want, go for it. I'm not gonna tell you how to spend your money. Just keep in mind we don't know how we're gonna make more of it after you medically retire, so . . . ya know."

Seventy-five thousand dollars might as well have been a billion. It was nearly impossible for us to conceive of that much money, and though I was a little more cautious about it than Cleve, we were both spending it like it would be there forever. We needed a financial planner. Unfortunately, we didn't even know those existed.

Cleve squealed and wrapped his arms around me. "Thank you, thank you, thank you!"

The Mustang was white with black trim and had a gray cloth interior.

"The visor's signed by Steve Saleen!" he said. "The tires are from '94!" He was sitting in the front seat, pulling open compartments and pushing buttons.

"Oh! Old tires! Cool!" I said sarcastically. He glared at me. "I'm sorry, babe. I don't get it. But you should definitely get it if it makes you happy."

"Man . . . you suck," he said. He got out of the car and put his hand on the roof to brace himself. He hopped around it on one leg, inspecting every inch. He looked at the guy selling it. "Mind if we test-drive it?"

"Not at all," the guy said, tossing Cleve the keys.

Cleve's biggest concern was whether he could drive a stick shift with his wounded leg. He didn't have great control of his foot, and with the rods in it, his leg took up a lot of space—he wasn't sure it would even fit in such a small car. He was also worried about pain. But none of that stopped him from trying. Cleve got into the driver's seat, and I got into the passenger's. He put the key in the ignition, and the engine roared.

"Yea-ha-ha!" he hollered, pressing the gas over and over. He turned the stereo to a rap station, adjusted his mirrors. We both buckled up, then he sped through the neighborhood. He looked so happy. I suspected that being in the driver's seat of a loud sports car replaced, in his mind, some of the masculinity he felt he'd lost after being disabled. I didn't totally get it, but I supported anything that made him feel more like himself.

"Looks like you can drive a stick shift just fine," I said.

"Yeah. I'm gettin' this car." He pulled into a parking lot and turned around. He drove to his bank just down the street and withdrew eleven thousand dollars, the entire cost of the car. A knot formed in my chest as the banker counted the bills. I scratched Cleve's lower back as if to comfort him, but I was really trying to comfort myself. What I would've given for that much money when I was living in my car. Now, here we were, spending it like it was nothing.

After signing the sales agreement and paying the man, we drove home in separate vehicles. Cleve beat me back, and when I pulled into the driveway he was standing next to his new ride, staring at me. I pulled up beside him.

"What are you doing?"

"I wanna take you somewhere."

"Right now?" I asked. It was starting to get dark out. I was hungry. I needed to shower.

"Yep. I promise it's worth it."

I laughed. "Okay."

He handed me a folded-up piece of paper with directions from MapQuest printed on it. "Tell me where to go," he said.

"This is so weird, Cleve."

"Just trust me."

I read the directions until we were in front of a small brick house in the middle of a large neighborhood. "Now what?"

Cleve got out of the car, so I did too. He pulled his crutches from the back seat and started toward the front door. I stood behind him as he knocked on the door. A blond woman answered.

"We're here for the puppies," Cleve said, and my heart started racing.

I smacked Cleve's arm with the back of my hand and mouthed, *A puppy?*

The woman led us through a cluttered living room to a dining area with a section blocked off by a short gate. Behind it, two brown puppies, so small they squeaked rather than barked, squirmed, one on top of the other. She told us she was pretty sure they were shih tzus, but they were an accident, so they might have been shih tzu and something else. There were eight total, and these were the last two.

"That one's the runt," she said, pointing toward the smaller of the two.

I picked that one up and brought its nose to mine. It was so small it fit in one hand. Its tiny pink paws brushed against my chin.

"Is it a girl or a boy?" I asked.

"A girl."

I looked at Cleve. "I like this one. She's like a tiny little potato."

"Then she's yours," he said, handing the woman a wad of cash.

On Christmas morning, Cleve put a big blue bow on the new puppy's head. We lay on our stomachs on the floor and watched her crawl around.

"We still have to name her," he said.

"I know." I smiled. "I was thinking Sophie."

"That's pretty."

"I thought so, too."

Cleve picked her up and petted her apple head. "Hi, little Sophie."

By March 2007, we were getting bored. Cleve started doing model cars and airplanes and would sit in our spare room on the floor, painting and gluing for hours. I was glad he'd found a hobby besides video games, but he was starting to spend so much time in there that it worried me. Sometimes I'd check on him and find him passed out, cross-legged and folded in half on the floor. This was happening more and more, and anytime I brought it up to him, he got upset. I nudged him awake one day, and he started painting again as if he'd never stopped.

"Cleve. You were passed out. Should I be worried?"

"I'm just tired," he said defensively.

"Tired people don't pass out like that." I was leaning against the doorframe, waiting for him to look at me, but he continued to paint an airplane wing navy blue.

"Look, just worry about yourself. I'm fine," he snapped.

"No. Look at me," I said. He threw the paintbrush and wing onto a piece of cardboard on the floor and looked up at me. I rolled my eyes. "Can you just be honest with me?"

"I am being honest with you," he said through gritted teeth.

"Do you take more than you're supposed to, Cleve?" Since the pills had been coming in the mail, it seemed like he was getting new bottles every other week. I hadn't been keeping track, but something seemed off.

"No, goddamn it!" he yelled. His pupils were tiny, animalistic.

"Quit fucking yelling! I'm just worried about you!" I slammed the door and stomped down the hallway.

"Bitch!" I heard him yell through the door.

I sat on the couch and turned on the TV. "Piece of shit!" I yelled back. He hated being called that more than anything, and I knew it.

His door swung open, and he hopped down the hall, bracing himself on the wall. "What the fuck did you just say?"

"Nothing," I said, suddenly scared. We'd had arguments before, and sometimes they got nasty, but this was different. He'd never come at me like this before. Charging down the hallway, he looked like an irate gorilla.

He stood in front of me, all puffed up. "You sure about that?"

"I can't see the TV," I said. My muscles were tense, but I tried to look unbothered.

"That's what I fuckin' thought." He turned around, hopped back to the spare room, and slammed the door behind him. I looked down at my rings and spun them backward so that the diamonds were hidden in my fist.

After that, it became more common for our squabbles to become brawls, often ending in us calling each other names and sometimes Cleve threatening to kick me out. It was dizzying trying to keep up with his moods, which rapidly swung from one extreme of a pendulum to the other on any given day. I'd wake up each morning unsure of which version of him I was going to get. I hadn't noticed this side of Cleve before, but there hadn't been many reasons to argue at the hospital. Now that we were navigating life in the real world, it seemed like any small thing could turn into a full-on fight. After the worst ones, Cleve would go to our room and loudly clean his guns, something he'd done neurotically since returning from Iraq. It seemed almost meditative for him, a way he self-soothed. But sometimes I wondered if it was meant as a threat, the clinks and clangs a reminder to me that I probably shouldn't push a man who's been to war. In those moments, I would remember that I didn't have my own income, that I was—once again—completely dependent on him to survive. I was usually the one to defuse the situation. I'd apologize—even if I didn't think I was wrong—give him a hug, tell him I loved him, lay low.

During one such argument, we had reached the point of yelling and name-calling, and Cleve decided he'd had enough. He left the room, and I followed behind him to our bedroom. I had a difficult time stopping once a fight got going. The urge to fix the problem then and there was too strong.

"I just wanna talk," I said, standing in the doorway so he couldn't leave.

"I'm too pissed to talk. I need some space." Cleve paced on the other side of our bed.

"I'm not going anywhere until we figure this out," I said, crossing my arms.

Cleve walked up to me. "Then *I'll* leave. Let me through."

"No."

Cleve's jaw quivered, and his eyes closed. He clenched his fist around his IV pole, a bag of antibiotics dangling from it, and put his nose next to mine. "I'm going to hurt you if you don't fucking move right now. I don't want to hurt you."

"No," I repeated.

His pupils were tiny again, and beads of sweat collected on his forehead and upper lip. Suddenly, he was ramming his skull into my chest over and over like an angry buck. I was enraged. In a tunnel, a blackness, an urge to fight back so strong I couldn't see straight.

"Get the fuck off me!" I screamed as I grabbed his IV pole and threw it across the room.

I regretted it before the pole hit the floor. I immediately felt sick.

"You stupid bitch! You stupid fucking bitch!" he yelled, checking his PICC line site to make sure it was okay as I scrambled to pick up his IV bag.

"I'm sorry! I don't know what I was thinking! I'm so sorry!" I sobbed.

I don't remember how we made up, but I imagine it involved both of us crying and hugging and apologizing for being assholes, because that's how most of our fights ended. We'd become volatile, and we were afraid to tell anyone about it, both of us ashamed to admit that all the stress had unleashed monsters in us. We were supposed to be heroes. Or, at least, that's what everyone was calling us. But not knowing what our futures held—*Would he be disabled forever? Would he be able to work?*

Would I? Where would we live? How long would he need pain medication? Was he becoming addicted?—left us feeling powerless and afraid. Sometimes those feelings brought us together. Other times, like desperate animals who'd been cornered, all we knew to do was fight.

We'd fight, and then hours later, when everything settled, we'd forgive each other. We'd sit side by side in our chaotic world knowing that, as shitty as our monsters were to each other, they were also connected. They understood each other. They were just as comforted by each other as they were triggered. We'd become enmeshed. Codependent. We also hadn't told anyone what was happening because we were afraid we'd be told to separate. We could deal with a lot, but we couldn't bear being without each other.

I decided I needed something to occupy my time. I also wanted to get some independence back, but I didn't mention that part to Cleve. I applied for college again and got a job at a call center working for AARP. It was only a few days a week, but I was still nervous about leaving Cleve alone. I'd been his full-time caregiver for nine months. I was all he had now. He insisted he'd be fine and encouraged me to go, so I did.

"Call me if anything at all happens," I said before leaving for my first day at work.

"I will."

"I'll have my cell on no matter what."

"Okay."

"It doesn't matter what my hours are. If you need me, I'll leave immediately."

"Karie, I'm goin' to be fine." He hugged me and kissed me on the head. "Have a good day."

My job was to sit in a cubicle with a headset, calming down angry older men who insisted eight Cialis a month was simply not enough for their very active and youthful lifestyles. I'd come home in the evenings to a trashed house and Cleve waiting for me to cook dinner. I wondered if getting a job had been the right decision. Coming home from the call center only to begin my second job as Cleve's caregiver quickly began to wear me out.

I'd been working at the call center for a month when Cleve came to my office looking for me. On days he drove me, I waited for him to pick me up, but on this day I was stuck on the phone with a customer. I could tell he was upset when I found him in the lobby. When I asked what was wrong, he told me that as he was walking toward my office, a woman had approached him and asked to take a selfie with his leg.

"She fuckin' had her phone out and everything with a shit-eatin' grin on her face," he said.

I was appalled. Livid. I wanted to know who it was, but he didn't know. When I asked him about his reaction, he said he let her take it but made sure to get his middle finger in the photo. I smacked him on the butt, said "Good for you," and we went on our way.

We hadn't anticipated the culture shock. Yes, we had lived in Camp Lejeune before, but never as a disabled person and his caregiver. At the hospital in Bethesda, wounds were the norm. We never had to worry about people staring or asking inappropriate questions. It was a safe space that we'd taken for granted. Out in the world, people could be cruel. A woman at the mall said Cleve looked like he had elephantiasis. He took it well. He smiled, lifted his hand, gave her the middle finger, and didn't talk about it again. I, on the other hand, was pissed.

"Some people need to keep their bullshit thoughts to themselves!" I said in her direction as she walked away. I talked about it for weeks.

At a restaurant we frequented, as the host was showing us to our seats, we passed by a seated couple and the woman dropped her silver-ware emphatically on her plate, the clang echoing through the room. I turned to look, and she was staring directly at Cleve's leg, her face twisted the way you'd expect a face to do after seeing someone being murdered.

"Well, I can't eat now," she whispered to her date. He turned to see what she was looking at, gave Cleve's body a once-over, then looked away.

"I'm gonna fucking say something," I said, but Cleve grabbed my arm and shook his head.

"It's not worth it. Fuck 'em. We came to eat crab legs. We're goin' to eat some fuckin' crab legs."

When we sat down, Cleve pulled another chair over and propped his leg on it, so it sat directly in the woman's line of vision. "Can we get a bread basket, please?" he asked the waiter. He looked at me and grinned.

Cleve's health was declining. I'd often find him on the porch, passed out with a lit cigarette in his hand, the ashes an inch long. This had all snuck up on me. I was with him every day; it was difficult to pinpoint the exact moment he'd changed. I convinced myself he was fine. The symptoms probably weren't as serious as they seemed. Besides, the nurse was supposed to be on top of his health. Though she told us to let her know of any odd symptoms that might signal his leg was infected, I wasn't sure what to look for. The symptoms I did observe—lack of appetite, drowsiness, constricted pupils—seemed to me like normal side effects of taking painkillers. I wasn't even sure what opioid side effects were considered problematic. I also knew that if I mentioned any of this to the nurse, Cleve would be pissed. I kept my mouth shut.

At the end of June, Cleve celebrated his twenty-third birthday, and I was a month and a half shy of turning twenty-two. We had been back at Camp Lejeune for nearly a year. Every month or so, Cleve would return to Bethesda—usually alone because the military didn't think it was necessary for me to go—so that his surgeon could make sure his leg was healing properly. While on one of his trips, Cleve called me crying. I pictured him as he wept. He sat on his hospital bed, his right leg folded under his left thigh, his left leg dangling from the side of the bed, dripping blood into a growing puddle on the floor, his tears streaming down the hand that held his cellphone to his ear. A dark figure, alone in a fluorescent white, antiseptic room.

"They're gonna take my leg," he sobbed. "They have to fucking cut off my leg." His voice cracked with wet, heavy breaths.

"Breathe, baby. Breathe," I said.

The news was a punch to the gut and came with a lot of uncertainty. But as scary as it was, and as much as I hated hearing Cleve in so much emotional pain, part of me was relieved. Keeping his leg had always been his choice. Doctors reminded him often that if he ever grew tired of fighting to keep it, amputation was always an option. They told him it might even be an easier option. We'd seen plenty of men and women with missing limbs, fancy robotic ones in their place. They rock climbed and walked without crutches. They ran and swam and drove and fucked like regular human beings. They were also free of pain, many of them totally off medication. Secretly, I'd been rooting for Cleve to choose to amputate, to get a fancy metal leg for himself. What hung below his knee hardly resembled what was once his leg anyway. Much of the leg he was born with was left in Iraq, and what came back was in shreds. Now, he had an ugly hunk of meat that did not function as a limb. It was deadweight. It was pain. It was a constant reminder of everything he'd been through. I didn't understand why he fought so desperately for it. But Cleve saw himself as a fighter and he was adamant. Amputation, in his mind, was giving up.

The sound of him crying made me feel evil for not being more upset about the leg. I began to cry, too, but not because of the amputation. I cried because he was crying. His grief was my grief. I cried because I wasn't there to comfort him.

"I'm coming," I said. "We'll get through this together like we always do."

I drove through the night and arrived early in the morning. We discovered they had to amputate because his bone had become infected—osteomyelitis—and it was spreading. His doctors said that if it spread past his knee, they'd have to amputate that, too, and mobility without a knee is much more difficult. He had no choice. Two days after he called, he went into surgery.

When his surgery was complete, I walked to his room and stood in the doorway, staring at the sheet covering his legs. He was sleeping, and I found myself afraid to walk up to him, to see him cut in two, to be forced to accept that all of it—the war, the wounds, the hospital—had been real and would continue to be real. The nurse walked past me into his room and began taking his vitals. As she checked his blood pressure, his left leg shimmied from beneath the sheet, peeking into the summer afternoon light that filled the room from the windows. The unfamiliar body part—I was afraid to name it—was out in the open, his foot nowhere to be found. I was later told to call it a "stump," a word I would never feel comfortable saying. The empty space below his knee sucked the air out of my body until I was empty, too. And then I was running in the opposite direction. It was too permanent, too real. His foot was gone. It was just fucking gone.

I grasped at the hospital's beige walls to keep myself upright as tears clouded my vision. Posters and well-wishes from people around the country covered the walls and rushed past in a red, white, and blue blur. I made it back to the waiting room, where I cried in a ball on the floor until my body couldn't spare any more tears. I don't remember how long it took—five minutes, an hour—but I finally pulled myself together and returned to his room. This time, I went straight to his bed and put my hand on his. He squeezed my hand and opened his eyes.

"Hi," I said. "How ya doing?"

"All right." He looked down and pulled his new leg from the sheet. What was left of it was wrapped in gauze like a hat. "It's not as bad as I thought it would be." He wiggled it in the air. Unexpectedly, we laughed.

"It's kinda cute," I said. "Is that weird?"

"Kinda." We were silent for a moment, surveying the new shape of his body.

"Hey. Did you see me in here earlier by any chance?"

"No. I've been dozing in and out. They have me on the good stuff." Relief.

"Lay with me." He motioned with both arms for me to come to him.

Carefully, he moved to the side and pulled down the sheet. I crawled in next to him.

I combed my fingers through his hair and studied his face. "Does it hurt?"

He shook his head. "You know what's weird?" he said, closing his eyes to focus. "I swear I can still feel it. Like right now." He scrunched his face. "Feels just like I'm wigglin' my toes. Like I could reach down and scratch 'em." It was phantom pain, a phenomenon commonly experienced by amputees, their limbs turned ghosts refusing to be forgotten. He opened his eyes and looked at the space where his foot should have been. "But it's definitely gone."

"Yeah," I said, moving my hand from his hair to his ear. I rubbed his earlobe in circles with my thumb. "I'm so sorry you have to go through this."

Cleve pulled my hand from his ear and kissed it before holding it to his cheek. "I know," he whispered. His eyelids were getting heavy again. "No turning back now."

His breathing became heavy and rhythmic. I listened to his heartbeat. I imagined what cutting off a leg entailed, what it must have looked like lying beside the rest of his body. *What does one do with a severed leg?* I wondered. I wondered where all the body parts left over from the war ended up. The more I thought about it, the more upset it made me. Why were we here? Why was all of this necessary? Why did people like us have to fight on the opposite side of the planet while the president got to sit stateside in the safety of his white mansion? I didn't know much about politics or our history with the Middle East, or even about this particular war. I'd always been taught to accept anything people in power told me. I did what I was told without asking why. But, looking around, I knew something was wrong and I was sick of accepting it. The sight of Cleve's body, forever broken, roused an anger that I hadn't felt since my dad attacked me. I imagined a pile of amputated limbs on the White House lawn. I imagined picking Cleve's leg up, setting it on fire, and throwing it on the top of the pile: black smoke billowing, an unfathomable stench, and the look on the president's face when he found it.

III

Oh God, I pray. *Nolite te bastardes carborundorum.*
—MARGARET ATWOOD, *The Handmaid's Tale*

12

WELCOME TO THE CLUB

September 2007

The prosthetist's office was small and white and cold. I sat in a stiff chair across from Cleve, whose nub hung over the edge of the treatment table. He wiggled it up and down, as if he was using it to try to tell me something. I giggled

"Your nub looks like a little shrimp."

Cleve scoffed. "No way. This here's a shark," he said, patting the end of it.

"Oh my God," I said. "It does kinda look like a shark!" The skin that had been wrapped around what was left of his tibia had a large scar that reached from one side of his leg to the other where the pieces of flesh had been sewn together. When he held his leg in the air, his tibia pointed straight ahead while the piece of calf muscle that remained hung from the bone, creating what looked like a chubby, smiling shark.

The surgeon who amputated Cleve's leg had saved as much of it as possible. Because the infection was spreading rapidly, his doctor had to be certain he took enough that the infection wouldn't reach above Cleve's knee. Anything it spread to couldn't be saved. His surgeon explained that prosthetic knees had come a long way—they even had ones specifically for skiing—but nothing was as good as the real thing. Cleve still had his knee and around six inches of calf, which was lucky.

We'd been anxiously awaiting this day. It had been a year and five months since the bomb, and Cleve hoped he would finally be able to walk without crutches again. I hoped the prosthetic leg would offer him more independence, and I hoped that independence would give him his confidence back. I missed how energetic he'd been when we got married, his quick and silly humor, the way he'd strut, carefree, through any room as if he knew he belonged there. Though there were still glimpses of the Cleve I'd fallen in love with, he'd become a faded, fragile version of himself. Whereas he had once made me feel protected, wrapped in his muscular arms, I was now the one doing the protecting. It left me feeling vulnerable, and I selfishly wished he would get better so I could curl into the safety of him again.

The door opened, and a stout man with a crew cut and a short-sleeved plaid shirt tucked into khakis walked through. He was carrying a footless prosthetic leg under his left armpit, a clipboard in his right hand. He looked at Cleve and then at me and then at Cleve again with squirrel-like movements. He was out of breath, sweat saturating the fabric under his armpits. It was late afternoon, and it was apparent he'd seen a lot of patients that day.

"Hey, guys! How's it going?" he said. He looked down at his clipboard and flipped through a few pages before his eyes shot up to meet Cleve's. "Jimmy Kinsey?"

"That's me," Cleve said. He shifted his weight from one side to the other and dabbed sweat from his forehead with the small towel he always carried.

"Hey there. I'm Dan. I'll be your prosthetist."

"Dan the man!" Cleve said. "You goin' to get me walkin' again?"

Dan nodded. "That's my job," he said, lifting the prosthetic in the air. "I got this right here for you to try out. How's that sound?"

"Sounds like I'll be an Olympic runner in no time."

I snorted. "Yeah, right. You didn't like running even before you were wounded."

"You never know!" he huffed. I pursed my lips, mouthed *okay,* and took a sip of my water.

"Well, let's start with walking," Dan said. "What color foot you want?"

Cleve laughed. "Really?"

"Yes, really. Gotta ask."

"It's not obvious?" Cleve held his arms out in front of him, looked at them and then up at Dan with a confused expression.

"You'd be surprised." Dan shrugged.

"So, a white dude could walk out of here with a Black foot if he asked for it?"

"Sure. Why not?"

I cringed.

"Let's just stick with what the Lord gave me," Cleve said.

"White foot it is," Dan said as he walked toward the door. "What size shoe do you wear again?"

"Twelve," Cleve said.

Dan left the room. When he came back, he had a plastic foot in his hand.

"Alrighty. Come sit in this chair over here, and let's see how your new leg fits." Dan sat directly in front of Cleve. He patted his own lap. "Go ahead and put your leg here."

Cleve did as he was told, and Dan put what looked like a thick, gel-lined swim cap on the end of his nub.

"Aw, it gets a little hat!" I said.

"Nice. Does it come in Gucci?" Cleve joked.

Dan laughed. "Unfortunately, no. This is the liner. You always put this on first. It'll make it much more comfortable. Then you put this over it," he said as he pulled out what looked like a long white beanie. "This is the sock. It goes on top of the liner." Dan slid the sock on. "Alrighty!" he said again as he reached behind him for the prosthetic. "We're ready for the leg."

"Oooh! Exciting!" I said, clapping. Cleve shifted from side to side as Dan placed the leg on his nub.

"Stand on it and see if anything feels uncomfortable," Dan said.

Cleve stood up and slowly spun in a circle, putting more weight on his left leg each time he stepped on it. He had a big grin on his face. "Not bad," he said. "Not as heavy as I thought it would be."

"Are there any areas with too much pressure? If so, let me know now, and we can adjust the socket," Dan said.

Cleve didn't look up from his new leg. "No, I don't think so. It's not bad at all."

Dan instructed Cleve to practice walking with the assistance of parallel bars that ran the length of the far wall. Cleve held on to the bars and walked slowly. Every time the prosthetic hit the ground, he'd bounce on it a little, lean back, lean forward, and bounce on it again.

"Looking good, babe," I said. It was a big moment for him, for us. I hoped with everything in me that this wasn't just his first step in a prosthetic, but his first step toward recovery. "How does it feel?"

"Real good," he said with a huge smile on his face. He turned to Dan. "How long before I get my machine-gun leg?"

"Well, that's a first." Dan laughed. "I'll see what I can do."

Once Cleve had a prosthetic, we were transferred to Walter Reed Army Medical Center, where a thirty-one-thousand-square-foot state-of-the-art rehab facility that cost nearly nine million dollars to build was scheduled to open a few weeks after we arrived. Walter Reed had been in the news a lot that year, and none of it was good. *The Washington Post* had reported that patients were recovering from war wounds in facilities covered in mouse feces, roaches, and mold. As those in charge scrambled to keep things under wraps, the rumor was that anyone who spoke to the press would get in some kind of trouble. What kind, nobody was certain.

By the time we arrived—seven months after the *Post* ran their scathing articles—Walter Reed seemed to have improved. I was glad. Rodent feces and mold? Fine. But roaches? I had an irrational fear of them. When I was growing up, they were in our shoes, in our kitchen cabinets, crawling across our faces at night. I could hardly be in the same room with one without screaming. That was the last thing I wanted to deal with at the hospital.

Cleve and I were given a room at the Mologne House Hotel on base. The hotel was much larger than the Navy Lodge. After entering the four-story brick building through automatic doors, patients were greeted by a grand staircase. The decor was crimson and beige, the walls wainscoted and adorned with oil paintings. To the left of the main lobby was a cafeteria that served things like paninis and chicken tenders. To the back, through double doors, was a dining room that looked like a fancy-in-its-day restaurant. It was now outdated, with beige wallpaper, red and black carpet with a dizzying geometric pattern, small tables each with four upholstered aluminum chairs, and an oversized epoxied bar that looked like it belonged in an Irish pub. My understanding was that the hotel had originally been built for higher-ranked Walter Reed patients and their families. But after the wars in Iraq and Afghanistan began, generals recovering from routine surgeries were replaced with corporals with missing limbs. The Mologne House was much nicer than what a family of our rank was used to. Living that luxuriously was exciting, even under the circumstances.

On days I was bored, I'd wander to the bar and order a watered-down vodka cranberry, then sip it on the back patio next to the koi pond. I'd watch the fish swim, pretending not to notice a woman in the gazebo across the way. *Was she crying?* Or a young man with a below-the-knee amputation circling a picnic table on his Segway, laughing hysterically as he told his friends a story with a beer in his hand. *Is he drunk? He's definitely drunk.* I was suddenly struck by how odd it was that we were provided alcohol. Seemed counterproductive, but that wasn't going to stop us from drinking it. Anything to take the edge off.

Our room at the Mologne House wasn't much different from the one I'd stayed in at the Navy Lodge. The decor was that of a cheap hotel: blue carpet, outdated beige wallpaper, blackout curtains made of cheap-looking floral material, and itchy filigree bedspreads. The difference that stood out to me was that, instead of a kitchenette, we had a brand-new, fancy-as-hell-to-me Mac desktop. It was unlike anything I'd ever seen. All I'd ever had was the bulky desktop my dad had stolen for me and the clunky Dell laptop we'd purchased when I first arrived at Bethesda. This computer was contained within a sleek silver monitor. I squealed with delight when I first saw it.

"I wonder if we get to keep it?" I exclaimed to Cleve. I went to the room's only window, located on the wall farthest from the door. Forgetting that we were still on base and not on vacation, I pulled the thick curtains aside to check for a view.

"Well." I paused. "We'll be able to see when new people arrive!" I said, attempting to put a positive spin on our view of the parking lot.

"Yeah, right," he said as he dropped his duffle bag on the bed. "No way we get to keep that computer. Looks expensive. I'm afraid I'll break it."

While Bethesda Naval Hospital was full of men and women with severe wounds that would require multiple surgeries, Walter Reed was full of people on the mend. Almost all the patients at Walter Reed were amputees, which was a relatively easy war wound to address. Once the leg was gone, the healing process could begin, and the injured could learn to walk again.

In some ways, life at Walter Reed was more structured than life had been in our duplex at Camp Lejeune. Now that Cleve had a prosthetic, he needed to strengthen his body. Because he had been healing from an experimental surgery, it had been unclear how long it would take before he would be cleared to retire from the military. But an amputation was much more common and, therefore, more predictable. We were told Cleve should be ready to medically retire from the Marine Corps within the next two years. Upon retirement, he'd be given Tricare health insurance and a monthly stipend and would be seen, from then on, by doctors at the Department of Veterans Affairs. Though retirement was still a ways off, and we still didn't have an exact date, it was a relief to imagine a new beginning.

At Walter Reed, Cleve was given a schedule he was expected to adhere to during the workweek. Every morning he had to be up early for formation before heading to the main hospital, where he worked as an events coordinator. I never saw formation, but I imagined all the amputees standing in a line at attention in the bar downstairs. I asked Cleve about it once, but he shrugged and said, "Just somethin' we have to do." When I asked why, he said, "Just 'cause I lost a leg doesn't mean I'm not still a Marine." His chest puffed a bit when he said the word *Marine*. Even after all of this—or maybe because of it—his status as a Marine was his purpose and sense of pride. It worried me. When I asked him what he wanted to do after retirement, he said, "Move back home," in a tone that suggested my question was dumb.

"Alabama is fine, but that's not what I mean. Like, what will we *do*?"

"Go back to school, I guess. Maybe use the GI Bill to get a history degree. I could be a history teacher, maybe. Or a crop duster." He smirked. I remembered him saying the same when we were in high school. I was skeptical. Because of his pain medication, he struggled to even show up for formation. He passed out early and woke up late. Sometimes he'd cry when talking about his leg, as if he'd just remembered he was an amputee and always would be. He'd lost the motivation to do anything besides watch TV. It was hard to imagine him showing up to classes, doing the homework, graduating, and eventually applying for jobs. The idea of him flying a plane, high on his meds, made me shudder.

Walter Reed also allowed us more freedom, which often led to chaos. In the evenings after work, Cleve would return along with the other patients living at the Mologne House, all of them pouring into the lobby on their Segways, crutches, and wheelchairs. As the sun set, the slow, quiet vibe of the place shifted. At first glance, it seemed innocent: patients and their families in line at the cafeteria or playing bingo in one of the community rooms, with a USO volunteer at the door trying to convince passersby to play. But if you lived there, you knew there was probably a party somewhere where people were doing things they shouldn't be.

One night, we met Jenna and Walker at a party in their room down the hall from ours. Walker had a below-the-knee amputation similar to Cleve's, and Jenna was his girlfriend and non-medical attendant. Jenna greeted us at the door. When we walked in, I noticed Walker had a mirror in his lap with white powder in a line across it, a rolled-up twenty-dollar bill in his hand.

"It's that kinda party, huh?" Cleve said.

"Only if you brought your own, man," Walker said before putting the twenty in his nose, bending over the mirror, and snorting the powder in one exaggerated inhale.

"What's on the menu tonight?" Cleve asked Walker as he sat on the bed.

"Oxy, my man," he said as he put the mirror on the bed. Jenna picked it up, put a small pill onto it, covered it with a credit card, and put all her weight into it. "You can use that next if you want it," he said, gesturing toward the mirror.

"Nah, man. Too much trouble. I take mine the old-fashioned way," Cleve said.

Jenna looked at me and held out the mirror with the crushed pill on it. "I'll share. You want some?"

"No, thanks," I said. Cleve had given me one earlier that evening, and I was already feeling so high my stomach ached. I didn't tell Jenna that, though. It was rare that I took one of Cleve's pills, though he offered them to me often. The few times I did accept, it was usually due to a mix of boredom and peer pressure. I struggled to say *no* to people, even Cleve. If someone wanted me to do something, all they had to be was persistent. As long as it wasn't hurting someone else, there was a good chance I'd eventually give in.

I'm not sure why Cleve wanted to share his pills with me, but I suspected, at some level, he must have felt that my taking pills with him meant what he was doing, what he had to do to live without pain, was normal. And I was probably more fun high. My mind was always switched on, thinking about appointments, or paperwork, or our future after the military. I didn't know how to turn the worry off anymore. OxyContin did the job for me. It made my body feel weightless, my mind feel like it was stuffed full of cotton, so much so that it was impossible to focus on any one thing to worry about it. When I'd take a pill, nothing outside the hotel mattered. I was comfortably numb. But as the high faded, shame for succumbing to the very thing I suspected was hurting Cleve would take its place.

Jenna and Walker's party wasn't anything special. We watched Cartoon Network, played card games, and listened to music. Jenna and I pulled up the CamWow feature on their Mac and took pictures of ourselves making silly faces while Cleve and Walker talked shit about some guy I didn't know. Cleve and I went back to our room just before midnight. We were getting ready for bed when we heard screaming. We suspected that a Marine who lived down the hall had been hitting his girlfriend. People had been whispering about him, but no one took the rumors of his abuse seriously because he had no legs.

"How does he even reach her?" I remember someone saying.

I admit, I'd wondered the same. I wish I'd done something, but I felt helpless. I wasn't sure who to talk to about them, and even if I did, I was afraid of backlash if I reported it. Since marrying into the military, I'd learned that there were certain things wives shouldn't meddle in—that translated to almost anything that happened on base. I got the sense the military liked to keep what happened on base away from the eyes of the civilian world. I was so afraid of upsetting Cleve, his friends, or even the higher-ups that I thought it best to pretend I didn't notice any of it. But that night, after Walker and Jenna's party, I couldn't take it anymore. I called the cops.

"I didn't tell them who I was," I told Cleve.

"I wish you'd just stay out of it. How hard could he even hit her, anyway?"

"Well, it sounds bad. The cops can decide if it's worth breaking up. Just play stupid if it comes up."

From our room, we heard the cops knock on the door down the hall and then we heard some mumbling, then a door slammed shut, then . . . silence. I peeked into the hallway and watched as cops escorted the woman toward the exit.

"Oh, man. Do you think she was the one hitting *him*?" I asked Cleve.

"No question she could take 'im," he responded, his eyes glued to *Squidbillies* playing on the TV.

Anyone who had a room facing the front of the hotel could see the blue lights flashing from the parking lot and the cop car whisking her away. The next day, everyone was talking about it. The other amputees grilled the Marine about what had happened until he finally admitted she'd pissed him off and he'd hit her. When she defended herself, she knocked him out of his wheelchair. I tried to imagine how that must have looked. Neither of them were big. I imagined him standing on his nubs in his wheelchair so he could be level with her eyes, his wheelchair brakes on so that she couldn't roll him away. I imagined her pinned against a wall, protecting her body from his blows, afraid to fight back because he was wounded. I imagined her allowing him to take his anger out on her because part of her felt bad for him. And then I imagined something in her igniting and her pushing his ass out of the way before she could think it through. I wondered if she had tried to help him off the ground after he fell or if she had let him drag himself back to his wheelchair. I know I would have tried to help Cleve up. But then what? The thought of Cleve writhing on the floor with no legs made me wince.

A month after we arrived at Walter Reed, Cleve was missing formation more than he was going to it. On the worst mornings, Staff Sergeant Farris would come to our room and bang on the door—I mean really pound on it—until we let him in. Farris was a Marine with invisible war wounds—post-traumatic stress and traumatic brain injury—who seemed to have his shit together compared to most of the other guys. He was tasked with overseeing the more severely wounded who were ranked below him, a job that was more difficult than it sounded. Walter Reed wasn't as clearly hierarchical as the military usually was. Though Cleve and his friends still respected folks with higher ranks, it was often unclear who was considered their direct superior, which created a lot of confusion. It was like working at a job with multiple poorly trained managers. Some people seemed to have some authority, but their roles were unclear, and they were often just as confused as everyone else. Nobody knew who to go to when they needed something. It was clear that this whole setup—a hotel of severely injured Marines, recently returned from war and working to recover from injuries—was new to everyone. The military was figuring it out as they went. This left the wounded with a lot more power than they'd had before. There was ample room to push boundaries, and they took advantage of it.

Farris seemed stressed. When he'd bang on our door in the morning, if we ignored him long enough, he had a key and he would use it, flinging the curtains open like a cartoon character. "Kinsey, get the fuck up!" he'd yell. One morning, Farris went into the wrong room. The only person there was Kristin, the girlfriend of Scott, a double amputee Cleve had befriended during formation. She was in bed, completely naked, scrambling to cover herself with the blanket. She asked Farris what the fuck he was doing, to which he responded, "You're not Kinsey's wife . . ." with a confused look on his face. This is how rumors started at the Mologne House.

"Giiiiirl, I'm starting to get sick of them acting like these guys are just normal and healthy like the rest of us," Kristin said that night, pacing next to the koi pond. Cleve and Scott had become close, and I was relieved to learn Kristin was great. Though Jenna was nice, we didn't have a lot in common. Kristin was a firefighter and college student, a straight talker with a grit I recognized from many of the southern women I'd grown up with. We had a similar sense of humor. She was quickly becoming my closest friend at the hospital. "I mean, yeah, they sleep in! They're all on pill cocktails!"

She was right. We'd been so hyper-focused on Cleve's leg that we still hadn't addressed the fact that he'd been taking prescribed painkillers for a year and a half. The night before, he'd been so high he was talking to himself. With slits for eyes, he sat upright in the bed, his head drooping slightly to one side. His arms were limp, the remote control lying in the palm of his open hand.

"Cleve," I said before walking over to him and snapping my fingers in front of his face. "Cleve, you good?" He snapped out of whatever alternate reality I'd lost him to, and he started changing the TV channel as if he'd been doing it all along.

"I'm fine," he barked. He still hated when I questioned how high he was.

I wasn't sure if the prescribed dose was doing this to him, or if he was abusing the pills. Whenever I tried to bring it up, he'd go on and on about his pain. If I pushed too hard, we'd end up in a fight, so I usually let it go. It was easy to pretend that whatever was happening to Cleve was normal, because it seemed like everyone at Walter Reed was struggling with dependence on their medications. Cleve's friends talked casually about swapping their pills, snorting them, and giving them to their spouses. Though the drugs were prescribed to treat the pain of physical wounds, the guys also used them to bury the emotional ones that doctors largely neglected. What these guys needed—what we all did—was therapy. Jobs, formation, visits from celebrities—it all felt like a distraction. But as easy as it was for us to acquire substances to bury our various forms of pain, it was just as difficult to get proper therapy.

"Yeah, it's fucked," I said to Kristin. "The thing that really trips me out, though, is that Farris has a key to our rooms. This isn't the barracks. Civilians live here."

"Right?" Kristin said, throwing her hands in the air. She shook her head. "Girl, I'm just glad I put a blanket over the chinchilla cage."

"Dude, can you imagine?" I laughed.

"It's kinda funny, but I'd be pissed if we had to find someone to keep them! They make us happy. There's not always a lot to be happy about around here."

"Yeah. Well, chinchillas one, Farris zero," I said. I kicked a rock across the concrete. I knew Kristin's beloved chinchillas would be found eventually. Cleve's parents had been watching Sophie for us. We'd considered sneaking her in, but we were sure she'd bark too much. I hadn't had her long, but I'd become very attached to her. At Camp Lejeune, after Cleve and I would fight, I'd sit in the shower and cry with her held to my chest. Sometimes we'd hold eye contact, and I swore she could tell what I was thinking. I missed her fluffy brown ears, giant brown eyes, and goofy underbite.

Cleve had physical therapy in the mornings just after formation. He met with his PT, a white-haired woman named Sunny who looked as sweet as her name but who, you learned quickly, took no shit.

"Where have you been, Kinsey?" she said one morning, pointing to her watch. Lips pursed and eyebrows raised, she waited for his excuse. Cleve was almost always late to physical therapy. It gave me anxiety— I hated being late to things—but Cleve seemed perfectly fine with it. Well over a year after his injury, he was starting to use the wounded warrior thing and his Purple Heart status to push as many boundaries as he could, all the way down to shaving his face. He rarely did it. Higher-ups complained a couple of times. On those days, Cleve came home and shaved, cursing the entire time. I didn't get it. He wasn't exactly blessed with bountiful facial hair. His beard was a patchy mess. But maybe that wasn't the point. Autonomy was hard to come by in the military. Perhaps keeping his beard was a way of saying, *This is still* my *body. You can't take it* all *away.*

I looked at Sunny with eyes of disapproval, because that was what was expected of me, and gestured *sleep* with my hands at my cheek. Cleve was never late because he had important things to do. The OxyContin made him queasy and tired.

"Well?" Sunny said with her hand on her hip.

Cleve shrugged. "I know, I know. I'm sorry, Miss Sunny. I didn't hear the alarm."

"Sorry, Sunny. I tried," I said. There was an unspoken expectation that caregivers were supposed to keep their family members on track. On paper, we were there to support. We helped change bedpans, wrapped wounds, assisted with showering, pushed wheelchairs, and did whatever else was necessary to keep our wounded loved ones healthy and comfortable. It seemed easy enough at first, but with time it became apparent that we were also expected to make sure the guys adhered to their schedules and behaved appropriately. If Cleve fucked up, eyes were on me. Forcing a grown adult to do things he didn't want to was, it turned out, difficult. In fact, it was the source of many of our arguments. A mother/son dynamic had developed between us. Cleve would push a boundary, I would remind him of the consequences, then he'd lash out, and then I'd lash out. It was the opposite of sexy or fun.

"Sounds like maybe you need a louder alarm," Sunny said. "What am I gonna do with you?"

Cleve responded with a toothy smile and exaggerated shrug, his hands in the air. She rolled her eyes and smiled back. "Come on. We have twenty minutes. Let's do some laps around the track."

Officially, the new PT facility was called the Military Advanced Training Center. But the guys called it the fishbowl. Inside, it shined silver like the entire thing was made of cool metal. It felt like something from a sci-fi movie, maybe a gym on a spaceship. The Army spared no expense, packing it with cutting-edge equipment. It included a rock-climbing wall that started on the first floor and stretched to the second, where a track complete with a Solo-Step harness system above it lined the perimeter. There was a driving simulator—which looked like the front end of a white Chevy truck—used to help amputees learn to drive with their modified bodies. A 3D virtual reality treadmill that looked like a fancy arcade game sat at one end of the first floor. Cleve used it from time to time, and I wondered if the VR component had a purpose beyond making workouts more exciting. Half of the facility—the half with the rock-climbing wall—was kept exposed between the first and second levels.

Often, while Cleve was working out on the first floor, I'd watch in awe as patients—usually men with more than one amputation—learned to walk again, one step at a time. Men with multiple amputations or severe facial injuries were known as "The Token Broken." They were the ones nonprofits wanted for their commercials and pamphlets. Celebrities wanted to be seen with them. Coordinators of fancy events wanted them sitting in the first row. They were usually the first to be offered extravagant trips and gifts—things like Bose headphones and iPods. The general consensus among the rest of the wounded was that the Tokens deserved anything they could get. After all, they'd sacrificed so much. But it was hard to tell sometimes where the altruism of those offering the "perks" ended and where exploitation began.

It wasn't just the Tokens who were exploited, either. Anyone with an obvious physical war wound experienced it at some point. Some days at the training center, I'd notice tours of celebrities and doctors peering through the windows that lined the wall connecting us to the main hospital. They'd stand, staring, as if we couldn't see them wide-eyed, looking directly at us. "Inspiring," they would say if you asked—observing us like fish in a big, shiny, state-of-the-art bowl. Should we wave? Dance? Get on all fours and throw feces at each other? I wasn't sure what they wanted, but when I noticed them, I'd put my hoodie up and stand between them and Cleve so he could work out in peace.

After physical therapy, Cleve and I went our separate ways. I returned to the Mologne House while Cleve worked as an events coordinator in a shared office down the hall from the fishbowl. His new title was just a fancy way of saying he walked around the hospital with a clipboard, trying to convince wounded folks and their caregivers to go on free trips offered by nonprofits. The guys were expected not only to wake up for formation every morning and then attend physical therapy, but also to hold jobs. It wasn't clear to me whether the jobs were meant to keep them motivated or to squeeze every last penny out of them before they medically retired.

"Jobs! Are they serious?" Kristin said one night. Apparently, Scott had gotten smart about evading work and appointments. He'd show up and check in, so that on paper it looked like he'd been there, then he'd leave when no one was around. He'd spend the day rolling around the hospital, showing his face where he needed to so that people would say he was accounted for, ultimately doing nothing. Sometimes, he'd even sit in the waiting area near the pharmacy and take a nap in his wheelchair. Because why not? Eventually someone noticed and called him out on it. Farris tried to force him to adhere to his schedule. "I mean, it's one thing to give them the opportunity—it's good to feel like you have a purpose or whatever—but they shouldn't get in trouble if they can't keep up." Kristin took a drag of her cigarette and shook her head, smoke billowing out of her nose. Our husbands were constantly being ragged on by Farris for being lazy. "I just don't get the military sometimes. They were blown up, ya know? At *war*. They did what they signed up to do. Give 'em a break."

"You're right, you're right," I said. "Farris keeps telling Cleve to shave. Addair used to do it when he was at Bethesda. Straight up, Cleve would be chillin' in his bed with his balls out after surgery and Addair would have the audacity to tell him to shave. I'm just like, really? *Really?*"

"Okay, that's bullshit, but also I really didn't need a mental image of Cleve's balls."

We both laughed. I almost always agreed with Kristin's critiques, but I didn't have the same fight in me that she did. When she didn't like something, she'd immediately jump rank and complain. I was too afraid to. At Walter Reed, I felt like the child of a parent who swung between overbearing and neglectful. While Farris was barging into our room or forcing Cleve to shave his beard, we had little support filing paperwork for things like insurance and retirement, and pain meds were being prescribed to Cleve with what seemed like little regard. Rather than push back, I backed down. It was the safer option. Cleve and I were specks in a complex universe full of powerful men with uniforms, guns, money, and secrets. The military controlled nearly every aspect of our lives because it could. We needed it. Without it, we had nothing: no paycheck, no housing, no healthcare, no purpose. That hand fed us, and I wasn't about to bite it. I was drawn to women like Kristin: confident women who demanded respect and knew their worth.

"You might be my favorite person," I said.

Cleve and I were settling into our life at Walter Reed. It wasn't perfect, but we were comfortable. We got to sleep in the same bed. We had friends. We were free to leave the hospital as we wished. We were content, more so even than we had been at Camp Lejeune. While we had thought going home meant going back to a normal life, we had quickly realized there was no normal. Maybe, even, there was no home. We'd struggled to integrate into the world outside of the hospital. Sharing a home for the first time, romantic as I thought it sounded, had only added more stress to our lives. As the infection took over Cleve's body, it became clearer that his injury was the center of our universe and would continue to be, no matter where we lived. All of our belongings remained in that duplex apartment while he received treatment at Walter Reed. We hadn't been back to Camp Lejeune in months. I imagined everything layered in dust. That apartment didn't feel like home any more than the hospital did. At least Walter Reed had a community of people like us who had an intimate understanding of what we were going through. Though we liked to complain, the truth was, chaos and all, Walter Reed was the closest thing to home we had.

By November, the hot topic was the Marine Corps' birthday. That year, we were free to attend any of the many Marine Corps balls held in the area. Cleve was finally healthy enough to go. I'd never been to one. When I asked him what they were, he chuckled and said they were parties where everyone dresses up, eats cake, and gets drunk to celebrate the Marines. Some are big, like the Commandant's Ball, which has an elite guest list, is invite only, and hosts up to three thousand guests. Most of the parties, however, are much smaller. Each company or battalion throws its own each year at venues on or near the base where they're stationed. Everything is paid for by the Marine Corps.

The night of the ball, we drove to downtown D.C., where we arrived at an upscale pub with a thick, rectangular wooden bar at the center. Cleve wore his dress blues, and I wore a long, navy blue gown I'd purchased at Dillard's the weekend before. The neckline was cut in a low V, and the slinky material shimmered when the light hit it just right. I felt beautiful.

We arrived just in time for a prayer, followed by the cake-cutting and a collective *Oorah!* Afterward, we pushed our way through the sea of blue uniforms to the front of the bar and ordered two drinks each—a redheaded slut shot for each of us, a vodka cranberry for me, and a scotch on the rocks for Cleve. Two drinks turned into so many I lost count. Hip-hop music played on a speaker in the corner. I was grinding on a woman wearing a red dress; Cleve was grinding on me from behind. Everyone was grinding on everyone. Then, before I could really register what was happening, a prosthetic leg with tawny liquid in it was being handed to me.

"Drink up!" a man next to me said, passing me the leg. I looked at Cleve, making sure the leg wasn't his—it wasn't. I peered into the prosthetic's socket and, still dancing, smelled it before bringing it to my mouth and taking a sip. The cheap beer's bitter carbonation burned the back of my throat as I chugged. I raised the leg in the air, and the group cheered. When I passed it along, someone nudged my shoulder. I turned to look, and Cleve handed me a glass eyeball.

"What the fuck do I do with that?" I yelled over the music.

"Ya lick it, goddamn it!" Cleve's face was red and sweaty, glowing under the strobe lights. I took the eye from his hand. Everyone was still grinding, and the little glass ball that had presumably just been in someone's face looked up at me, waiting. I looked back at Cleve, then scanned the people around us for someone missing an eye. I couldn't figure out who it belonged to.

"We're really doing this right now?" I yelled.

"Yeah, baby! Welcome to the club!"

The eye was smooth and cool on my tongue.

13

CHICKEN

Christmas 2007

I put my suitcase on the bed and pulled the notepad with my packing list from my back pocket. "Do you want me to pull your suitcase out, too?" I asked Cleve, who was lying on one of the beds, watching cartoons. He reached for the remote and turned the TV off.

"Nah, I got it," he said as he got out of the bed and hopped to the closet. He opened the sliding doors and pulled his prosthetic from a shelf before throwing it onto the bed. He pulled out his suitcase and threw that, too, before hopping back to the bed and sitting down.

We were packing for a trip to Foley to spend Christmas with his family. I was nervous. Though his family and I were in an okay place by then, that hadn't been the case for long. Soon after we moved to Camp Lejeune, Cleve had stopped talking to his mom because she refused to respect our relationship. After months of the silent treatment, she finally apologized. All I wanted was for her to accept me as part of the family. And maybe to acknowledge how hard I was trying to make things work in an impossible situation. From then on, she called me names like *sweetie, honey, baby*. I didn't trust it, but it was better than nothing.

We packed in the morning, loading our bags into both cars. We needed the Escalade to fit the bulk of our things, but Cleve also wanted to show off his Saleen. Cleve went to morning formation and then to physical therapy while I stayed back to clean our room. I pulled the sheets and linens from the bed so they could be washed. I started emptying the trash can under the desk, then remembered I could play music on the computer. I wiggled the mouse to bring the screen to life and clicked on Safari, and Cleve's email appeared. He was the last person to use the computer and he must have left it open. I stared at the screen, interlocking my fingers at the top of my head. I bit the dry skin on my lip, trying to avoid the temptation.

"Fuck," I said. I'd been tempted to check his phone before, but I'd resisted the urge. I wanted to prove to him and myself that I trusted him, despite what had happened with Lisa. But his email was *right there*. I stood up and went to the bathroom. I sat on the toilet longer than I needed to, with my head in my hands. *I could just look at a few subject lines,* I thought. *I won't even click on them!*

I went back to the computer and scanned what could be seen without scrolling. Nothing. I walked away and paced, considering my options. If I looked, even if I didn't find anything, I wouldn't be able to take back the fact that I'd betrayed his trust. He might not ever know, but I would. But what if there was something? I had to know. I went back to the computer and started scrolling through his emails. There were some from his mom that were difficult to ignore, but I did anyway. A bunch of emails from his higher-ups. Emails about upcoming trips for wounded service members and their families. Some junk mail. And then I froze. An email from AmateurMatch.com that read *wannaeaturpussy, we have 1 member near Jacksonville that you're looking for!* I immediately felt rage boil in my stomach. I no longer cared about respecting his boundaries. I clicked on the email, then clicked on the link to the website. Where it asked for login information, I chose *Forgot Password*. A prompt to change the password was sent to his email. I followed it, changed it to something I would remember, then logged in.

His profile picture was a photo of his dick. The headline: *My Wife's a Bitch, Just Wanna Eat Some Pussy*. I imagined Cleve creating the profile on the floor of the spare room in our Camp Lejeune home, attached to his IV and surrounded by his model airplanes. I must have been at work when he did it. *Pathetic,* I thought. In his inbox were multiple messages from women around Jacksonville who, I assumed, wanted their pussies eaten.

He hadn't responded to any of them. I wondered if he'd made his profile after one of our fights. Maybe he regretted it later and never used it. But if that was the case, why didn't he shut down the account?

"Bitch?" I whispered to myself. How could he call me a bitch when I'd put my entire life on hold for him? I remembered the night he told me about Lisa, how he swore he'd never do that to me again. "I'll show you a bitch."

I changed his profile picture to an image of the smallest penis I could find on the internet. I changed the details on his profile, too. Now he was short, fat, and bald, and his headline read *Married Piece of Shit.* I logged out of the Amateur Match profile and stared at his email for a moment before logging out of it, too. I didn't need to know anything else. We had a long drive ahead of us. I wanted to calm down before he got back from PT, so he wouldn't know anything was up. I'd decide on the drive what to do from there.

Cleve came back in a chipper mood. "You ready to get on the road?" he asked as he glided through the door. He looked around the room. "Didn't feel like cleaning?"

"My mom called," I said. "We talked longer than I realized. Sorry."

"It's fine!" He went to the bathroom and stood in the mirror fixing his hair. "Do we need anything else, or can we get outta here?"

"I think we're good." I grabbed my keys off of the dresser and started turning the lights off. "You have your wallet?"

He turned the bathroom light off and stood beside the door. "Check."

"Keys?"

"Check."

"Sunglasses?"

"Shit. I think they're in the drawer over there," he said, pointing to the table on his side of the bed.

"Got 'em," I said. "What else? Did you pack underwear? Toothbrush?"

"Yep."

"Your wheelchair is already in the car, you have your crutches and prosthetic . . ." I thought for a moment. "I think we're good?"

"I'm so happy we get to go home this Christmas," he said.

I wanted to say, "I hate you right now and I hate Foley, too." Instead, I said, "Yeah, it'll be fun."

We planned to drive all the way to Alabama without stopping to sleep. As long as we didn't run into any issues, we hoped to get there between one and two in the morning. At first, I was glad we were driving separate cars. I didn't want to be near him. I started the trip off listening to burned CDs and talking to friends on the phone. *Everything's fiiiine,* I told myself. But by the time we got to Georgia, I was tired and had had too much time to think. I tried playing loud music to drown out the noise in my head. I chain-smoked cigarettes. I rolled the window down, letting the cold air hit my face. But it wasn't enough. Our life played over and over in my head. The note. Our first kiss. Myspace. The elopement. The injury. So many days at the hospital. Fucking *Lisa.* The amputation. I'd put so much of my time and energy into him. I loved him so damn much. Everything I had, as little as it was, I'd given to him. And for what?

With every hour that passed, I became more and more upset. It was just past ten P.M. when Cleve's blinker flickered on. We both merged into the right lane and turned onto a dark exit that had nothing but a run-down gas station hugged by woods.

As we pumped gas, I decided to log in to Cleve's Amateur Match account again from my phone. By then, I was obsessing. I had to be absolutely sure he hadn't responded to anyone. I looked up and saw Cleve walking into the gas station. The gas hose clicked. I got out and hung it back up, then closed the gas tank. I climbed back into the SUV and lowered myself into the seat. I clicked on the inbox I'd already looked at. Still no responses. I clicked on *Trash,* then looked up to see if Cleve was coming back yet. He was still inside. I looked back at my phone and there it was. Three conversations between him and random chicks near Camp Lejeune. The conversations were short. "You look tasty," he said to one woman. To another, "I bet you taste sweet." None of them talked about actually meeting, but it didn't matter. I was fucking fuming. Seeing red.

Cleve came out of the gas station with a bag of something, probably snacks or cigarettes. He opened the door to his car, then looked at me and gave me a thumbs-up. I gave him one in return. When we got back onto the road, my head was spinning. The road was long and dark, without a single streetlamp. I slammed my foot onto the pedal until I was riding just behind him, jerked into the opposite lane, then cut him off before speeding away. I was going 80, then 90, then 100. His car shrank in my rearview mirror. I flew past the highway exit, continuing down the dark road. No houses. No lights. No stop signs. 105, 110. My phone rang. I picked up, said, "Nope, motherfucker," before Cleve could respond, and then hung up. I looked in my rearview. Either he'd stopped or I'd lost him. I slowed down and pulled into a parking lot. My phone rang again. This time, I picked up and listened.

"What the fuck!" he yelled. "What the fuck is wrong with you?"

"Fuck you, Cleve! Or should I say *Wannaeaturpussy?*"

Cleve was silent. "What are you talking about?"

"You know what the fuck I'm talking about! You want to eat a bunch of pussy, go for it! I'm not fucking going to Alabama. Fuck this. Fuck you!"

"You need to calm the fuck down!" he said.

I could see his headlights in the distance. I hung up the phone and gunned it, pulling into the street from the parking lot. I swerved into the left lane, where he was headed straight toward me. I kept my foot on the pedal. *40, 50, 60, 70, 80 . . .*

"I'm not moving, motherfucker!" I yelled. The last two years raced through my mind. "I've given everything to you!"

His headlights grew brighter and brighter and then we both swerved—him onto the grass at the side of the road and me into the right lane—at the last second. I began sobbing. I slowed down and went back to the gas station where we'd originally stopped. I parked in a space hidden from the lights and began hyperventilating. I couldn't breathe. I couldn't think. I was hot. I was suffocating. I pulled my sweater off and then my T-shirt so that I only had a tank top on. I got out of the car and ran to a patch of grass. I fell into it, crying uncontrollably. At some point Cleve pulled up next to me and got out of his car. He knelt down and put his hand on my back.

"Breathe," he said. "Deep breaths."

I pushed his hand away. "You did this!" I gasped. "This is because of you!"

"I'm sorry," he said. "I don't know what else to say. I'm just sorry."

"Are you? I don't even know who the fuck you are. A dick pic, Cleve? What the fuck is wrong with you?"

"I'm an idiot," he said. "I get mad and I do dumb shit."

I was still on all fours in the grass, snot and tears falling to the ground. I shook my head. "There's nothing to even say. Two years of my life fucking wasted. I could've been done with school by now. I'm the idiot. I'm the fucking idiot."

"You're not an idiot." He tried to put his hand on my back again, and I didn't have the energy to swat it away.

"I love you. I love you so much," I sobbed.

"Can you get up?" he said. He pulled on my arm and I lifted myself to my knees, my head and shoulders limp. "Can you look at me for a second?"

"No," I gasped.

"Please?" I looked up and glared at him. I was sure I looked insane. "I made that after our last big fight."

"Oh! In that case!" I threw my hands in the air.

"I know it's not an excuse! I'm not sayin' it's a good excuse, but I was mad for a few days and I was stupid. I never met anyone, though, I promise."

"You *talked* to them! You said they looked like they *tasted* good!"

Cleve's face twisted as if he were in pain. "I know. I was mad at you. I don't know. I don't know what I was thinkin', but I thought I trashed those. I never met anyone, I swear."

"How do I know you aren't lying?"

Cleve shook his head. "I don't know. You just have to trust me, I guess."

"Oh, right," I sneered. My tears were starting to dry but my face was still wet. "Because that has really worked out for me so far." I wiped my cheeks with the palms of my hands and dried my hands on my shirt.

"Look, I fucked up. I know I fucked up. I know I have to make it up to you and earn your trust back, but it's not goin' to happen in this parkin' lot," he said.

I crossed my arms. "Where the fuck are we even?"

"I have no fuckin' clue," he said. "Bumfuck Georgia."

We looked at each other for a moment. Cleve's eyes were large and sad. I wondered if he was upset because he'd been caught or because he actually regretted hurting me.

"I don't think I can drive another five hours like this," I said. "I just wanna lay down."

Cleve pulled the towel from his back pocket. He wiped his face with it. "I'm gonna go inside and get some Cokes and snacks and let's sit here for a bit."

"Yeah," I said. I sat down on the curb and laid my head on my knees. "What am I doing?" I whispered. I closed my eyes and breathed deep, paying close attention to my heartbeat. As it settled, my thoughts made sense again. I was starting to feel bad for being so reckless. I wasn't even sure where that had come from. It was as if the rage had swallowed all other emotion, all logic, like a pressure that had been building for so long and could no longer be contained, and the only way to relieve some of it was to destroy something, so why not myself?

The door dinged as Cleve came back out with a plastic bag full of snacks. He sat down beside me and opened a Barq's root beer and a Heath bar. He handed them to me. "Your favorites."

"Thanks," I said. "I'm sorry I almost killed both of us." I took a sip of the root beer.

"I'm sorry I keep fuckin' up when I'm angry," he said. "I think the meds turn me into someone I'm not sometimes. It's like I lose control. Or just . . . things get away from me sometimes."

"You do seem like someone else sometimes. You get this look in your eye that seems almost evil. It's like I don't even know who you are anymore. I can't talk to you about it, though. You get so mad. Although I guess I'm not any better."

"I'm stubborn," he said.

"You are." I paused to take a bite of my candy bar. "Can I ask you something without you getting upset?"

"Yeah."

"Do you think you're addicted to them?"

He looked at his prosthetic leg and shrugged. "I'm just still in so much pain. I think I could stop taking them, but I'm afraid to."

"Right. There's no way to know, then, I guess." It felt hopeless. There was no good answer. I resigned myself to the fact that we were not in control and would simply have to wait it out. "But, like, do you ever take more than you're prescribed?"

Cleve hung his head. "Sometimes."

"Why?"

"Usually pain. It never stops, just always there. It makes me feel crazy."

"That's not good, Cleve."

"I know."

Cleve stood up in front of me. It still startled me how easily he was able to move around now that he had a prosthetic leg. He held his hands out toward me. I screwed the cap back onto the root beer, rewrapped the candy bar, and handed them to him. He put them in the bag around his wrist, then held his hands toward me again. I took them and stood up.

"I don't expect you to forgive me right now, but I hope you know I love you," he said.

I nodded. "I think I do."

"Can I have a hug?"

"Yeah," I said, and we melted into each other.

14

HERO TREATMENT

March 2008

"Welp. I guess I'm goin' to have to drive to the hospital now," Cleve said in a melancholy tone. His body was hunched, his arms folded in his lap.

"And we'll never go back to Camp Lejeune," I said. I stared off into the distance, my vision blurring as I thought about how huge a part Camp Lejeune had played in my life, despite how brief my time there had been. "Weird."

I looked around at the mess that had accumulated in our hotel room. It was hard to stay tidy in such a small space. We had books and suitcases and other belongings crammed under the beds, cans and boxes of food lining the windowsill, and clothes draped over the chair in the corner. We'd just been issued a Permanent Change of Station without any notice. That meant the military was changing our home base from Camp Lejeune to Fort Meade, a small base in Maryland within driving distance of Walter Reed. Nobody knew how long Cleve would need care at Walter Reed, but now that he could walk, he didn't need to be there every day. We were taking up space at the Mologne House, and I was still being paid non-medical attendant pay. I would continue to get it as long as Cleve and I were living at the hospital, away from our home base. The military didn't want that; it was cheaper for them to officially change our home base to Maryland and let us commute to appointments until Cleve no longer needed the facilities at Walter Reed and qualified for medical retirement. Just another stepping stone on our way to . . . I wasn't sure. We assumed Alabama, but the details were still murky in our minds.

"We could still visit Jacksonville," Cleve said.

I shook my head. "But why? Everyone we know'll be gone by the time you're retired."

"Oh, yeah." Cleve hung his head. "Damn. I feel like I missed out on so much."

I put my hand on Cleve's back. "I know. But hey," I said with a smirk. I leaned in front of him until our eyes met. "Let's look at the bright side. Camp Lejeune is kind of a shithole."

Cleve frowned and glared at me. "It's not that. It's my friends. I have a lot of good memories from that place."

My face dropped. "I know. I'm sorry." I turned toward him, wrapping my arms around his shoulders. I kissed him on the cheek before laying my head on his chest. "I still think it's pretty great that you have all those good memories to hold on to forever. Nobody can take those away. And, baby?"

"Yeah."

"You're alive," I said.

Cleve nodded, straightening his posture. He pulled away for a moment, looking at me with a half smile. "You're right. And I got you," he said. He pulled me back in and touched his nose to mine before curling into my arms and letting out a heavy sigh. Severing ties with Camp Lejeune was a big step, a signal that his medical retirement was coming and that our time in the military would soon be over.

Our new home was a one-story apartment attached on one side to seven identical homes, all lined up. It was located at the curve of a cul-de-sac, and we had one of the larger yards on our street, which gave us the illusion of privacy. I stocked the kitchen with cookbooks and taught myself to cook things like apple pie and fried pickles, some of my favorite comfort foods. Sophie could live with us again, too. As soon as we had the chance, we made a quick trip to Foley to pick her up.

Now that I didn't qualify for the non-medical attendant pay, I had to get a job. I stopped going with Cleve to his physical therapy appointments and started working as a veterinarian's assistant, which, to my surprise, required no experience and very little training.

I liked my job. When I'd played MASH as a kid, I always hoped I'd land on veterinarian as my career. I knew I'd never go to school to become a real one, so being an assistant was close enough for me. When I was hired, I was told I would eventually be trained to do anesthesia, and on my first day, I shadowed another assistant who taught me how to administer shots. By the end of day two, I was alone in a room with a stranger who helped me hold down her four-year-old puggle while I stuck a needle in its thigh. The woman had come for her dog's regular checkup and rabies vaccination. She carried an oversized Coach bag, had freshly highlighted hair and manicured nails, and wore a giant diamond on her ring finger. I wondered how she'd react if she knew it was only my second day and I'd never done this before. Part of me was uncomfortable with being given such responsibility, like I was complicit in endangering every animal I was put in charge of. But another part of me loved it. The role was a crucial one. I was someone who *administered vaccinations*. People trusted me with their pets' lives. They came to me for answers. They *needed* me.

Cleve and I were feeling pretty good about our new setup. It was nice having our own space again and being the only ones who had a key to it. It helped me to feel more secure knowing Walter Reed and our war-wounded friends were close by. Cleve continued working as an events coordinator, so he was occupied for most of the week, which made it easier for me to work than it had been at Camp Lejeune. On weekends, we would invite Scott and Kristin over for BBQ and beers. We had the best of both worlds: our own home and access to our friends from Walter Reed. I was hopeful.

Back at the Mologne House, we met up with a big group that was being given a trip to Vegas for Memorial Day weekend. More than fifty of us were waiting in the lobby when a parade of blue vans pulled up.

"Shotgun!" Cleve yelled over the chatter. It had been two months since our move and we were excited to be with our friends for the entire weekend.

"Are we gonna miss our flight?" I asked Staff Sergeant Lopez. The vans had been more than fifteen minutes late.

He laughed. "Nah. These planes leave when we're ready to leave. No worries."

Staff Sargeant Lopez had also been wounded in Iraq, but his wounds were less noticeable than Cleve's. He was stationed at Walter Reed to act as the lead events coordinator and liaison ahead of the patients who were almost always ranked below him. Lopez was a stocky thirty-something man from Southern California. Cleve and I liked to joke with him about how he manscaped—his eyebrows and hair were always perfectly shaped. In his off time, he played guitar and sang and dreamed of the day he could retire and focus more on his music. He oozed confidence, sometimes coming off as a little cocky, but usually managing to do it endearingly. Because he was Cleve's boss, they became close. We loved him. He loved us. With time, we thought of him as family.

We skipped the drop-off line at the airport and drove onto the tarmac, where we stopped in front of a lone 747 with its airstairs down.

"Wait a fucking second. Is that for us?" I asked as I leaned over the seat in front of me to get a better view.

"Lopez did say private jet," Cleve said. Lopez was riding in another van, so he wasn't there to confirm. "But he didn't say anything about this big boy."

"Okay, look, my dudes. We *have* to get a spot upstairs. That's all I care about right now," I said.

"Girl, don't worry, I'm runnin'," Kristin said.

When we exited the vans, we were instructed to wait before boarding. A flight attendant gave us a quick rundown of how the plane worked. There were rooms with beds throughout the center of the aircraft, upstairs was a lounge, and the front of the plane was the smoking area. There would be fruit and veggie trays, nonalcoholic drinks, and one meal.

"Hell, we can smoke on it?" Scott said excitedly. He towered over me and had a toothpick hanging from his mouth. "You know where I'll be."

The flight attendant continued to talk, but I stopped listening. I was too giddy.

"Cleve, Scott," I said, waving my hand from side to side. "Get closer so I can get a picture." They were standing in front of the plane, and I wanted to get a picture of it for the scrapbook I hoped to make. Cleve put his arm around Scott and they posed with their hands signing the shocker—just guys being guys or whatever, but still gross.

"Y'all are so immature," Kristin said, shaking her head. She looked at me and stuck her tongue out as if she were gagging, before something caught her attention. "Hey, I think they're about to let us board. Get ready!"

"Don't wait for anyone. Just one person needs to get up there to hold everyone else's seats," I said.

When we were given the go-ahead, we all took off like a bunch of kids racing to the front seat of a car. Scott, an above-the-knee amputee, was last, but I was surprised by how quickly Cleve got up the stairs.

"Oh shiiiiit," Kristin exclaimed as we walked through the door of the second floor. Even though they called it a lounge, I had imagined upright seats. What we found was floor seating that looked more like beds than chairs. Each one was wide and meant for more than one person to share. They still had seatbelts, but the only way to buckle them was to lie back and strap yourself in at your midsection.

"What is this, a sex room?" I said, laughing.

"Riding to Vegas in the sex room!" Cleve announced as he fell onto one of the bed chairs. He rolled onto his back and kicked his legs like a baby. I collapsed next to him, and we held on to each other, rolling around and squealing.

After takeoff, flight attendants offered us fruit and spaghetti that we ate on our bed seats. When we were finished, we toured the plane. Though they'd told us there were bedrooms through the center of the aircraft, it hadn't occurred to us that the plane was big enough to contain bedrooms the same size as you'd find in a middle-class home. Some rooms had queen-sized beds, some had multiple oversized seats with ample space, and many were attached to large bathrooms.

"We need to get one of those next time," Kristin said.

"Yeah. We chose wrong," I said, half-joking.

We spent much of our time at the nose of the plane, smoking. That area looked the same as any plane's coach section—dated, grayish seats in rows, all facing forward. Even though our sex room was unlike anything we'd ever seen on a plane, there was something even more exciting about doing a typically forbidden thing—smoking on a plane. Before long, the entire cabin was filled with smoke. Kristin lay across multiple seats with her feet hanging into the aisle while I pranced through each row just because I could.

"I can't believe there are people out there who always fly like this," I said.

"Bitches," she coughed, smoke billowing above the seats where she lay.

When we landed and the plane's doors opened, we were in a giant hangar, and an older man with exaggerated facial features and slicked black hair stood at the end of the stairs, smiling.

"Is that supposed to be Elvis?" I whispered to Cleve.

"No, girl, that's Wayne Newton," he said. I'd heard the name, but I still didn't know who he was.

"Oh, okay," I responded. "Does anyone know what that is?" I asked, pointing at an expensive-looking powder-blue car.

"A fuckin' Rolls-Royce is what that is," Scott said, reaching down to adjust his prosthetic.

Born and raised in North Carolina, Scott had a southern accent, too. When he and Cleve got going, their accents got thicker and thicker. I joked once that they sounded like Hank and Dale from *King of the Hill*. I think Cleve took it as a compliment. Though Scott's family had more money than Cleve's and mine, both he and Cleve had been raised in the country and had enough in common to keep a solid friendship going: a love of guns, hunting, their hometowns, and their mamas. Scott, however, had a much calmer demeanor. He didn't enjoy attention the way Cleve did. Kristin gave him all the attention he wanted. Of all the guys we'd met at Walter Reed, he seemed exceptionally grounded. He didn't want for much. He was looking forward to retiring, buying a house near his family, and living the rest of his life with Kristin. He was also the only guy we knew who didn't seem to struggle with pill addiction.

"Wow. Okay, then," I said. I wondered what the car looked like on the inside.

"Welcome to Vegas!" Wayne Newton called. He shook everyone's hands as we descended the stairs.

Once all fifty of us made it off the plane, an employee with the Armed Forces Foundation briefed us on what to expect. We were given itineraries and told it was Sheldon Adelson, one of the wealthiest men in the world, who had funded the trip.

That explains this hoss, I thought, thinking of the 747.

"You'll be staying at one of his hotels, the Palazzo, in penthouse suites," the man said. "Some of you will need to room together. Some of the suites have more than one room."

Kristin and I looked at each other and squealed, "Roomies!"

Mr. Adelson stepped forward and welcomed us. He said it was an honor to have us there and that anything in the hotel was ours, free of charge. *I bet that's his car,* I thought to myself. I struggled to focus on what he was saying, too distracted by the silver figure on the hood. *Is it an angel?*

"He said we can have anything," Cleve said, nudging me. I don't think Mr. Adelson understood what he was getting himself into by not being more specific.

"That's cool," I said. "We're some expensive-ass charity cases."

A row of commercial buses pulled up to the hangar. After Mr. Adelson finished his welcome speech, we boarded the buses, and cops escorted us to the hotel, where hundreds of cheering and clapping people greeted us. They'd decorated the casino in red, white, and blue for the holiday. We were told that all the casino's employees had stopped what they were doing to express gratitude for our service to the country. It felt like the parting of the Red Sea—countless people on either side of us—as we made our way through the casino. We must have looked shocked, because we were definitely not expecting to be paraded through a casino that day.

The scene was overwhelming. Though I appreciated the gesture and knew all the onlookers meant well, I hated being the center of attention. I considered the wounded vets, wondering if the crowd was triggering anyone with PTSD. It was well known in the military that big crowds and loud noises were no-nos around people who'd deployed to war. As we walked, I put my hand on Cleve's back and whispered, "You all right?"

"I can't believe they're all here for us," he said.

"Yeah, that's a lot of people. Is it too much?"

"It's kinda loud, but it's cool."

"I have some earplugs in my bag. If you need them, just let me know."

I knew it bothered him, even if he wouldn't admit it. When he wasn't staring at the ground, his eyes darted from one side of the room to the other. It reminded me of something that had happened just after we started dating. A few weeks before Cleve's second deployment to Ramadi, we were driving to a friend's house after dark when he noticed a water bottle standing upright in the middle of the street. He slammed on the brakes.

"That don't look right," he'd said.

"What doesn't?"

"That bottle. Why's it in the street like that? And how's it standing like that?"

"I don't . . . know?" I was confused by his behavior. The sudden stop had jerked us forward, and Cleve was scaring me. "I'm sure it's fine . . ."

He drove slowly around the bottle, giving it a wide berth. Later, he told me he had thought it was a bomb.

Now, watching Cleve mop his sweaty face in this crowded lobby, I knew he was mapping out emergency exits and planning what he'd do if someone spotted a bomb or pulled a gun. Eventually we made it to the elevator. When we got on, Cleve took a deep breath.

When we opened the door to our suite, we gasped. It was huge. There was a piano. A full bar. A sauna. Two bedrooms, each with its own bathroom attached. A living room. A wall of floor-to-ceiling windows with a view of the strip. We chose our rooms, dropped our bags on our beds, then found the room service menu.

"We need to toast," Cleve said.

"Holy shit, they have Cristal!" I said. It was the only expensive champagne I knew about.

"Should we get it?" Kristin asked, joking.

"That Sheldon dude said we could get whatever we wanted," I reminded everyone. "He literally said anything in the hotel."

"Yeah, fuck it," Scott agreed. "If they didn't want us ordering somethin' off the menu they shoulda said so."

"Okay, but who's gonna make *that* call?" Kristin said.

Cleve raised his hand. "I got this."

When the champagne arrived, Kristin, Scott, and I held the glasses as Cleve popped the cork.

"Heyyyyy," we said in unison.

Cleve filled our glasses, then his own.

"Is that the whole bottle?" I asked.

"Yep, that's it," Cleve said.

My jaw dropped. "Seven hundred and eighty dollars for four small glasses of booze. This better be the best champagne I've ever tasted."

"Cheers to Sheldon!" Cleve said.

"To Sheldon!" we echoed before clinking glasses.

I sipped my champagne in front of the toilet, watching water from the bidet shoot into the air. "People really squirt toilet water on their butts? Do they wipe too? Or do they just have a wet butt?"

"I have no idea," Kristin said. "Do you think we could both fit in that tub?"

"I don't know. Let's try it out," I said.

We both crawled in and sat across from each other.

"This champagne isn't even that good," I said, looking at my nearly empty glass. "You would think there'd be something special about it, but it just tastes like regular champagne."

"I don't even want to think about how much regular alcohol we could have gotten for seven hundred dollars," she said.

"I guess we'll just have to order that, too. We ain't payin'." We both laughed.

That night, we met Mr. Adelson and the rest of our group for dinner at an upscale steak house in the Venetian. Scott and Kristin sat at Mr. Adelson's table, while Cleve and I had one across the room. I ordered the filet mignon because it sounded fancy. We all got drunk on expensive cocktails. The food was good but, once again, I didn't understand the prices. Someone said a live turkey was walking around the restaurant at one point, but I missed it.

On our way back to our room, Kristin told me Scott had told Mr. Adelson they wanted to elope at one of the chapels on the strip. Without hesitation, Mr. Adelson insisted on throwing Scott and Kristin a proper wedding at the hotel.

"He said he's sending a wedding planner to our room in the morning," she said.

"Are you serious right now?"

"Dead. He's even willing to fly in our family if they can make it."

"You gonna do it?"

"I mean, yeah. I don't think I have a choice, anyway. He's already setting it up. Wanna be my maid of honor?"

"Aww. Of course!" I squealed, excited.

When we entered our room, we were greeted by two electric wheelchairs. We'd ordered them before dinner, not because the boys needed them, but because they sounded fun. Steam had also filled the room while we were gone. Kristin and I had forgotten to turn off the steam shower.

"Shit!" I said as I ran to the bathroom to turn it off.

"It's kinda like the club in here!" Cleve said. "Let's get some music going!"

Cleve ordered room service again. He was the only one brave enough to say our outrageous order out loud. "A bottle of Crown Royal, a bottle of Captain Morgan, umm, four cigars . . . hold on one sec." He covered the phone with his hand and looked toward us. "Anyone else want crab legs?"

"If it's free, it's for me," I said as I flipped through a local magazine.

When the booze arrived, things got weird. We figured out how to make the piano play itself. We were so delighted that we decided to let that be the night's background music. Kristin and Cleve each claimed an electric wheelchair and rode around the room in wide circles, Cleve wearing nothing but one of the white robes the hotel provided. We all smoked our cigars, tapping the ashes into heavy crystal ashtrays. We poured drink after drink after drink. Someone turned the shower back on, so the room started to fill with steam again. And then I heard a crash.

"My bad!" Kristin shouted. She'd collided with one of the end tables, breaking the lamp.

"Uh-oh. Party's over," Scott said. We all laughed.

The next morning, a petite woman with blond hair slicked into a bun and a clipboard showed up at our door.

"I'm here for Kristin and Karie," she said. "Do you have time today to come by my office and plan this wedding?"

Kristin looked at me and shrugged. I was a little hungover, but it wasn't anything I couldn't push through. I nodded. "Can we come now?" Kristin asked. "We still have to go dress shopping later."

"Of course," the woman said. "I'll wait for you two in the hallway."

In the woman's office, Kristin flipped through books full of flowers and extravagant cakes. The wedding planner said she could choose anything she wanted.

"Can the cake be banana-flavored?" she asked.

"Banana?" I asked. "For real?"

"It's the only cake flavor Scott will eat," she said, then turned to the planner. "Can we get that light, whipped icing? I hate the thick, sugary stuff."

"Anything you want," the woman responded.

They settled on a four-tier angel food cake with Italian marshmallow meringue and banana cream filling. Kristin chose rust-orange calla lilies for the bouquets and agreed to have bagpipes playing as she walked down the aisle, a feature the planner seemed proud to be able to offer. The ceremony would be in the Palazzo Waterfall Atrium and Gardens, followed by a reception at Mr. Adelson's private penthouse suite at the Venetian, featuring a buffet-style menu of hors d'oeuvres from the casino's main kitchen. Hair and makeup appointments were made for us in the hotel's salon.

Once all the details were finalized, the wedding planner told us not to get a cab to go dress shopping.

"We'll get you a driver," she said. "Give me a few minutes to set it up." Thirty minutes later, a stretch limo picked us up and drove us to the mall.

The wedding was held on the third day of our trip in front of the three-story indoor waterfall in the Palazzo's atrium. Men dressed in plaid kilts played bagpipes as we walked down the aisle. The guests mainly consisted of wounded guys, their caregivers, and anyone from Scott's family who could fly in at the last minute. Though none of Kristin's family could make it, she understood their reasoning. It was the first Memorial Day weekend since her sister—a military widow—had lost her husband, and they'd already made plans to spend it with her. Kristin's dress was white and strapless with a black bow at her waist that I'd helped her tie just before the ceremony. She wore a pink and orange stargazer lily in her hair. Scott's sister and I—the only bridesmaids— wore black knee-length dresses. Scott wore a black suit and black cowboy hat. The ceremony was quick, but we all lingered near the waterfall afterward, talking to reporters who had somehow found out about the event. We answered their questions and let them take a few pictures before making our way to the reception. The buffet had been set up on the large balcony overlooking the Vegas strip. Not only were Kristin's guests present, but a bunch of people we didn't know attended, too.

"You good?" I asked Cleve. "I'm gonna try to find a bathroom in this maze."

The suite was decorated with modern decor in cool gray tones. A moveable wall had been pushed aside so that the balcony and living room were one large indoor-outdoor space. Inside, servers rushed around, making sure the buffet remained fully stocked. I asked one of them where the nearest bathroom was, and he pointed to a hallway.

"First door on the right," he said.

The bathroom was also gray. Like the rest of the suite, it struck me as sterile, all monochromatic metal and stone.

Sitting on the toilet, I noticed a large pad full of buttons on the wall to my right.

"The fuck," I whispered to myself. It was much more complicated than the bathroom in the suite we had been given. I'd never seen anything like it before. I pushed one of the buttons, and the seat started to feel warmer.

"What? These people can't even shit on a cold toilet seat?"

I was afraid to test any more buttons. I couldn't imagine why a single toilet would need so many, and I was sure I'd push the wrong one and set off an alarm or something.

On my way back outside, I noticed a man who looked familiar on the far side of the balcony. Cleve was talking to Scott, enthusiastically waving his arms as he spoke and laughed, champagne spilling from the glass he was holding. I pinched his butt and he spun around.

"Ooooh! Hey, beautiful," he said with a huge smile. I could tell he was feeling a little tipsy.

"Uh . . . is that Wayne Brady?" I said, pointing toward the familiar man. We'd seen his live show just a couple of nights before.

"Oh shit," Cleve said. "Yes. That is indeed Wayne Brady." He took a sip of his champagne, walked right up to him, and tapped him on the shoulder. "Fancy seeing you here!" Cleve said to Wayne. Cleve's lack of social anxiety always perplexed me.

"You're such a weirdo," I said, hiding behind him.

Wayne turned around and smiled. "Heeey, man! How's it going?" he said with an amused look on his face.

They started chatting as if they were old friends. I listened to them talk a bit before slipping away. I walked around the balcony with a small plate piled high with expensive-looking food. The sun was out, and the sky was cloudless. People in sundresses and shorts and sandals roamed the streets below, the sound of chitchat floating through the air. I took a deep breath, savoring the sense of peace. I knew it was temporary. A distraction. The calm before the storm.

15

PROBLEM CHILD

November 2008

"Baby, wake up. Baby," I said, shaking Cleve by the shoulders. His body quaked back to life, his head still loose on his neck. Pupils the size of pinpricks, his eyes snapped open and scanned the room as he tried to remember where he was. He reached for the towel in his back pocket, bringing it to his forehead and patting it dry. His eyelids sagged as he mumbled some nonsense: *Don't worry, I got you. I got you. Hey! I didn't . . . please, stop.*

Seeing him like this was terrifying, and it was becoming the norm.

To lower the risk of addiction, the doctors had been swapping out his pain pills every few months. But it was always reactionary, when I desperately wanted them to be precautionary.

When I asked Cleve's doctor about the possibility of weaning him off pills, of considering other options—*Acupuncture? Weed? Yoga?*—Cleve looked at me like I was insane.

"I can't live with this if I don't have meds, Doc," he asserted, gingerly rubbing the end of his nub. "I'm in a hell of a lot of pain still."

It was always the same story. And who could argue with it? The doctor certainly couldn't. I couldn't. Cleve was switched from one opioid to another and we were sent on our way.

I didn't know at the time that it was common for people to use prescription drugs to cope with PTSD. I didn't know that the more opioids someone takes, the more sensitive they become to pain, making the opioids less effective. I didn't know that the number of veterans addicted to their prescribed meds had tripled that year. I didn't know there was an epidemic, not just at our hospital, but countrywide, and it was just reaching its peak. The thing is, it wasn't my job to know.

There is no single moment I can point to and say, *That was when! That was when his addiction began!* And that was the problem. Maybe it started with the morphine syrette to the leg on the battlefield. Or the Dilaudid hooked to his body once he was back in the States. Or maybe it was the morphine pills after his amputation. Or the combination of Lortab and Percocet. He was definitely struggling by the time he got OxyContin. Two and a half years of pain meds, every day, multiple times a day. Somehow, it seemed to have both crept up on us and been right in front of us, yelping, the entire time.

It had been six months since our trip to Vegas, and Cleve couldn't even finish a cigarette without passing out. His body would go limp, and somehow his hand always landed near his crotch, the cherry singeing through his pants. I told him I was afraid he would burn the house down. I said it like I was joking, but I really was worried. The other wounded guys would make jokes about the holes in nearly every pair of Cleve's pants.

Nobody loves you enough to buy you a new pair of pants, Kinsey?
Better be glad you're missing a leg, you sloppy motherfucker.
You know that shit doesn't fly in the Corps, devil dog.

His physical therapist at Walter Reed, Sunny, pointed it out once. "What in the world is going on with your shorts, son?" she'd asked, handing him a kettlebell.

Cleve scooted to the end of the treatment table and began lifting the kettlebell with both hands, his legs spread, displaying three perfectly round burn holes on his black basketball shorts. When he told her how the holes got there, he made it sound like he was just exhausted from long days of PT and work. He left out the part about being high on pills. He must have known it was a problem. He'd been pretty good at hiding it, at convincing people they had nothing to worry about, but he was starting to slip. Sunny made a joke, too. We all laughed. Cleve's symptoms had become something people laughed at. But the small voice in the back of my head was insistent: *He is not okay.*

One afternoon, while Cleve and I were watching a movie, I noticed him falling asleep while sitting up, a half-eaten slice of pizza still in his hand. His grip loosened as his eyelids grew heavier, and the slice fell facedown on the floor. Sophie ran to get a bite and almost made it, but Cleve had regained enough awareness to stop her.

"No, ma'am. Get outta here," he said, almost incoherently, reaching his body over the armrest of the oversized chair, so far I thought he might fall out, his amputated leg lifting into the air. He picked up the pizza, casually looked it over with slits for eyes, and settled back into his seat. He took a bite. It must've been covered in dog hair. He stood up and staggered to the kitchen table, picking up a pack of Marlboro Lights before heading toward the back porch. He smacked the top of the pack over and over on the palm of his hand.

I watched him hawkishly. "You good?"

He gave me a thumbs-up. "Need a smoke," he said, clearly irritated. I nodded and gave him five minutes before checking on him.

I found Cleve standing outside with his eyes closed, the bottom half of his body leaning against a porch post, the top half folded completely over with his arms dangling to the ground, a cigarette burning between his index and middle fingers. He'd passed out while standing—a first. When I tapped on his shoulder, he snapped awake and tried to take another drag of his cigarette as if nothing had happened, but only the filter and an inch of ash were left.

"Damn. Was I out?" he mumbled.

"Yeah. I think so." I waited to see what he'd do next. He stared at the middle distance with glazed eyes, as if recalling a memory or trying to find the right words. "Babe, I'm worried about you," I said.

"Aw, stop it. I'm just a little tired. Got a light?"

He pulled the cigarettes from his back pocket, stumbled a little, and steadied himself.

"All right, I guess." I handed him a lighter. I smoked with him to make sure he didn't pass out again.

Later that evening, I found him facedown in a bowl of cereal. My scream startled him awake. For a moment, I thought he was dead. Imagine the headlines: *Local War Hero Drowns in Bowl of Cheerios*. He lifted his head, milk dripping down his stubbly chin. He slurred, "I'm fine. God," before getting up, annoyed, and stumbling to his man cave.

He sat on the floor to clean his guns. When he went silent, I checked on him and found him cross-legged on the floor, folded in half over his AK-47, the back of his military-green shirt reading *I'll Kill You*. The shirt looked just like the military-issued T-shirts service members often wear, only this was a gift from one of the guys in his unit. They thought it was hilarious. I tapped him on the back, but he didn't respond. I shook him and tried to pull him up by his shoulders, but he was too heavy.

"Cleve, I need to get you to the bedroom where I can keep an eye on you," I said. "Do you hear me?"

He mumbled something about sleeping in his cave. It had no furniture, only random belongings of his—guns, military uniforms, car magazines, family photos. It wasn't a comfortable place to sleep. I also knew it wouldn't be safe to leave him there. I persisted until he reluctantly followed me to our bedroom. I laid him down and tucked him in. I crawled into bed next to him and turned out the lights.

First, I dreamed he was snoring. But even in my sleep, I sensed something wrong. A terrified sound, like a wounded animal—a guttural plea in the dark. I fumbled around for the light beside my bed. When it flickered on, I found Cleve sitting up but limp, his back against the headboard. He'd moved at some point from where I put him, which, for a second, made me think he was fine. But then I noticed his skin was tinged purple, his eyes open wide, bloodshot, cloudy, and distant. Vomit dripped down his chin like thin peanut butter, and his chest convulsed as his body fought for air.

"Cleve?" I said, not yet convinced of what I was seeing, but then, "Cleve!"

I'd learned once that if someone was choking on vomit, you should put them on their side. But our bed was so tall. I thought it would be easier to position him on the ground. Panicked and trembling, I tried to lift and lower his 225-pound body. Almost immediately, I dropped him. I grabbed his boxers as he fell, accidentally pulling them to his ankles. He landed on his head. I was horrified. If he wasn't dead already, I was going to kill him. I checked his neck to make sure it didn't look broken. I scrambled to pull up his boxers so he wouldn't be humiliated when the EMTs came. Then I realized I hadn't yet called 911. I ran around my bed to get my phone, hating myself for not thinking to call sooner. The operator coached me through CPR. There was so much vomit. I couldn't figure out how to clear his airway.

The paramedics arrived just as I realized Cleve might be dead. His body was as slack as a doll's, and I was sure he hadn't breathed since before I found him. One man pushed me out of the room as another shoved a needle into Cleve's chest. I screamed at the sight. I don't know what I said, but I imagine it was something like, *Please don't let him die!* or maybe, *God, why do you keep fucking with us?*

A police officer wrapped his arms around me and pulled me through the living room and out the front door. He sat me on the antique trunk on our porch, put his hands on my shoulders, and looked me in the eyes. "I've got you," he said. "I can't promise you anything right now, but I'm here with you, and I'm not going anywhere."

I don't know the man's name, but I will never forget him and the comfort he brought me at that moment. He opened a bottle of water and handed it to me. I closed my eyes and tried to control my breathing. A deep breath in, a long breath out, just like the therapist who came around sometimes when we first arrived at Bethesda had taught me. I took a sip. When I opened my eyes, I noticed the sun had come up between when I found Cleve and when the paramedics arrived. Neighbors were heading to their cars, steaming mugs of coffee in their hands, kids with colorful backpacks trailing behind them. They'd take a moment to look toward our house, probably wondering why there was an ambulance in our driveway, before getting in their cars and driving off. I wondered how many times I'd gone about my day as people were dying on my street. One of the paramedics who had been working on Cleve appeared. They were stabilizing him. He was alive. They would take him to the hospital. I could ride with them or follow behind.

I rode with the cop who'd given me the water. We sped through traffic behind red and white flashing lights and that fucking siren, echoing *Weeooooweeoooweeooo.* I tried to see into the tiny windows of the ambulance's back door. No luck. I sank into my seat, imagined Cleve dying. I closed my eyes. I counted my breaths. *1, 2, 3, 4 . . .*

"You have any family in the area?" the cop asked.

"No. It's just us," I said, and every organ in my body trembled with loneliness and fear.

The cop looked at me and sighed. We rode the rest of the way in silence . . . *7, 8, 9, 10.*

In a single day, I'd seen my husband die and come back to life.

When Cleve woke up, a doctor found me in the waiting room. I was disheveled. I'd flipped through all the magazines. I'd tried and failed to figure out sudoku. I knew I needed to keep busy, but I struggled to focus.

"He's going to live, Ms. Kinsey, but his brain wasn't getting sufficient oxygen for an unknown amount of time, and we don't know how he'll be affected. He's awake now if you'd like to go see him." He said Cleve was disoriented but that it was expected, then he told me to follow him.

When we got to Cleve's room, it was a familiar scene: Cleve in a hospital bed, shirtless, wrapped in a sheet, his heart monitor beeping. Something was off, though. He wouldn't look at me. I walked toward him to give him a kiss. He pushed me away.

"I can't believe you fuckin' called the cops," he said. "What the fuck were you thinking? You know how much trouble I'mma be in now?"

I was stunned. "Cleve, you overdosed. What was I—"

"Get out," he hissed.

"Cleve, listen to—"

"Get the *fuck* out."

I stumbled out of the room in shock. I found a bathroom down the hall and locked myself in one of the stalls, then sat on the toilet to cry. I didn't understand what I'd done to upset him, but that didn't stop me from feeling guilty. Panic and lack of sleep had scrambled my mind— and now this. I felt like I was in a dream. A nightmare. This wasn't real.

None of this was really happening. I remembered getting the call when he was first wounded in Iraq, how I got so little information and then had to wait nearly a day before someone confirmed he would live. How unsure I was that he even wanted me to come to the hospital to be with him, until a couple of days later when he called again, acting as if nothing had happened. He had become unpredictable. Maybe it was the war. Maybe it was something else. I didn't know.

I headed back to the waiting room, curled into a chair, and tried to sleep. A doctor woke me after who knows how long. Cleve had asked for me. When I went back to his room, his face was softer. I stood in the doorway.

"They told me what happened," he said. "I'm sorry I acted like that."

I told him it was okay, but it wasn't. I remembered his face full of hate. I could still feel the venom of his words burning in my veins. After the trauma of seeing him like that, all I wanted was to hold him—to be held by him and hear from his own mouth that it was going to be okay. When he told me to leave, I'd never felt more alone.

"Can I have a kiss?" He reached his arms toward me. As we kissed, the memory of giving him CPR hit like lightning. I quivered and sat on the side of his bed. "What happened, exactly? Your version," he asked. I sighed and then told him the whole story. He shook his head back and forth. He buried his face in his sheet and sobbed.

The doctor later told us that Cleve was clinically dead when they got there, that they revived him with a shot of epinephrine. It only takes three minutes of oxygen deprivation to cause permanent brain damage. I was pretty sure he'd been suffocating for longer.

To buy time until they could place him in a rehab facility, Cleve's higher-ups kept him in the barracks across the street from Bethesda Naval Hospital along with other patients who were considered high risk of suicide, had been making poor decisions, or were there alone without a non-medical attendant. They wanted to keep a closer eye on Cleve to prevent another overdose. There, unlike in your typical barracks, the men had their own rooms and were treated more like patients than employees. Cleve's only job now would be to show up to appointments and check in with his higher-ups each day to take his medications.

I do not remember dropping him off at the barracks. Most of the details are missing. I remember having nightmares that night. In the most vivid, Cleve sat on a crate in the middle of an orange desert. A clothesline ran behind him with a baby's body parts pinned to it. He was in his desert camis, his face smeared with black paint and dirt, his hair overgrown and disheveled. He sat hunched over before reaching behind him and pulling a small leg from the clothesline. He took a bite of the leg. Sandy wind whipped at his body, and hot tears fell down his cheeks.

I was convinced death was still in our bedroom—as if death were a conscious being waiting for me. I couldn't sleep there, opting to sleep on the couch instead. One day, I peeked into the room and saw the vomit stain on the floor. I slammed the door to trap whatever monster was inside. *Demons,* I thought. I couldn't let them out. I had to run outside to catch my breath. Who knows how long I left the stain. Months, maybe. I slept on the couch until Cleve came home.

Cleve's addiction was visible now, and everyone seemed to think he should be more in control of his usage. He, a twenty-something who'd been blown up at war and was receiving next to no mental healthcare, was somehow expected to be more responsible, to know when enough is enough. He was one of the "problem children," as his Master Guns—Cleve's superior, who we called Gunny Marsh—labeled Cleve.

Gunny Marsh called a few of the guys "problem children"—including our neighbor at the Mologne House whose girlfriend had been escorted off base when I'd called the cops. Gunny Marsh chose a tough-love approach, as if the guys were his own sons who had gotten off track and simply needed a little redirecting. When he called them "problem children," he said it almost endearingly. When he looked at Cleve, it was obvious that he saw the good in him; it was obvious he cared. I got the impression Gunny Marsh felt responsible for all the wounded men ranked below him. The weight of that must have been immense. But I didn't like Cleve being called a "problem child," even if it was said with love. It felt like blame, and I didn't blame Cleve or any of the guys who were struggling with addiction, or anything else for that matter.

I blamed the doctors. The doctors were the ones prescribing the pills. They were the ones who refilled them. They were the ones who never explained how to avoid becoming addicted. They never offered anything other than medication—therapy or counseling or support groups (for either Cleve or myself) were never discussed. I was quickly losing trust in them. And as the trust dwindled, I reluctantly took the burden upon myself, even though I knew I wasn't fit for the job. I didn't know much about addiction or PTSD or traumatic brain injury (TBI) beyond what a few internet searches told me. I felt abandoned. Had I known that just a year before, in May 2007, Purdue—the company that created OxyContin—had admitted to misbranding it, claiming it was less addictive than other painkillers when in fact the opposite was true, I'm sure I would have directed my anger toward them. But I wouldn't know about any of that for years.

When anyone mentioned the overdose, I felt like I was suffocating. One evening, I stripped to my underwear and lay on the floor, clawing for something to hold on to, gasping for air. Seemingly out of nowhere, I would become hysterical. *1, 2, 3, 4, 5, 6, 7, 8, 9, 10, repeat.* Kristin, who'd trained as an EMT, told me I was having panic attacks.

I was walking through the main lobby of the hospital one morning when I saw a nurse from the Marine liaison's office jog toward me. I started to speed up a little, hoping to make it to the elevator before she could reach me. I just wanted some lunch and wasn't in the mood to talk to anyone, especially someone new.

"Ms. Kinsey?" she said.

I stopped, closed my eyes for a moment, then forced a smile. "Hi," I said in the most enthusiastic voice I could muster.

"Hi! Sorry to bother you," she said, a little out of breath. She was standing next to me now. Her perfume smelled like cotton candy and her scrubs had colorful cats on them. "My name's Diane. I'm a nurse practitioner that works with families of the wounded sometimes, and I heard about what happened to Jimmy. I can't imagine how devastating that must have been for you, and I wanted to see how you're doing."

She was the first person to ask how the overdose had affected me rather than Cleve. It caught me off guard. I hadn't even noticed until that moment that I'd been treated as a part of Cleve, rather than an individual human being with her own needs. I hadn't realized how much I needed someone to ask me if I was okay.

I could feel tears coming, but I dabbed them away as quickly as they came. I didn't like crying in front of a stranger. "I'm sorry. I . . . it's just . . . it's been a long week."

"Sweetie, don't apologize. I can't imagine how traumatic that must have been. And you two are just so young. Can I hug you?"

I nodded. She wrapped her arms around me, holding me as I sobbed. I ended up telling her about the flashbacks I'd been having, the nightmares. She told me she thought I had secondary PTSD. She said it was probably traumatic stress resulting from hearing about and witnessing the aftermath of the firsthand experiences of someone else's trauma. Apparently, many of the caregivers had been experiencing it. The term sounded made-up to me, so I blew it off. I didn't want people to think I was taking attention away from Cleve. He was the one who had gone to war. Anything I was going through, comparatively, felt silly. I wonder now what about my PTSD was "secondary." Administering CPR on my possibly dead husband is about as traumatizing as anything I can imagine. If I had to guess, it is that military culture prioritizes the wants, needs, and struggles of the veteran above the spouse. Even our trauma isn't our own, only an extension of theirs. I didn't realize it at the time, but my aversion to prioritizing myself had been learned.

We spent Thanksgiving in the barracks. Nobody held at the barracks had permission to leave, even for the holidays. We were served turkey and ham and all the sides you'd expect. It resembled cafeteria food, and we ate off Styrofoam plates. Cleve and I sat alone at a table in a white room with fluorescent lights. A freshwater fish tank, dark with sad-looking fish, stretched across the wall behind us. Other men and women sat around, also alone. Every one of us would've rather been with family, and no one had the energy to pretend otherwise.

"Have they said anything about when you'll be released?" I asked. I was tired of being alone.

"They're sayin' maybe rehab, but not sure when. They haven't told me much yet. They might let me go home with a pill dispenser so I can't abuse 'em. I fuckin' hate it, though. I'm gonna be in pain."

"Really, Cleve? I'm sorry you're in pain, but I'd rather you be in pain and alive than dead," I said. I was so tired of hearing that excuse. I didn't care if it was cruel of me.

"Easy for you to say," he said before taking a bite of mashed potatoes.

"Easy for you to fucking say! You didn't have to see you dying! This isn't a joke!"

He threw his fork down. "I don't wanna talk about it anymore."

We ate the rest of our food in silence.

Later that week, Cleve called to tell me that a friend of his who'd also been staying in the barracks had died. He hadn't come down for breakfast, and at lunchtime, Cleve went to his room and knocked on his door to no response. They had to break in. His body was on the floor, an obvious overdose. Cleve was hysterical, admitting that he and some of the other guys, including the one who had died, had been sharing what pills they had with each other. He didn't know if that was the cause, but it didn't stop Cleve from feeling responsible.

"I fucked up," he said. "It's all so fucked-up."

I was devastated for him. I wanted to scream, *Where are the doctors? Who the fuck is in charge? Why does this keep happening?*

16

GOOD WIFE

Early December 2008

I couldn't stop thinking about fried pickles: their greasy, carb-y texture, crunchy bursts of salty sour on my tongue. I bought a jar of gourmet pickles, cut and breaded them, poured peanut oil into a frying pan, and turned the stove to high heat. As the oil began to bubble and pop, the house filled with the scent of peanuts, and before I could get the pickles into the pan, my stomach turned. I ran to the back porch, flung the screen door open, and puked into the backyard. I got on all fours, my head hung below my shoulders.

"What the fuck?" I whispered, and then I had a thought.

I went through the list in my mind: painful breasts, check; moody, check; missing period, check. I'd been so preoccupied with Cleve's overdose that I hadn't noticed what was happening with my body.

Cleve had been living in the barracks for a couple of weeks, and I was falling apart. I still slept on our couch, only having gone into our bedroom once to get my clothes out of the closet. I quit my job as a vet assistant. I claimed it was because I'd witnessed one of the other assistants throw someone's cat into a cage by the scruff of its neck, causing the poor animal's eyes to fill up with blood. But the truth was, I would have stayed. I liked having the opportunity to be something more than just a caregiver. But after Cleve's overdose, I didn't want to leave the house anymore, so I stopped working. I stopped brushing my teeth. I stopped showering unless I absolutely had to. Sometimes I would burst into tears for what seemed like no reason. I'd sink to the floor, call Sophie to my lap, and rub the small space between her eyes with my thumb until I could breathe again. Existing had become a burden.

After the nausea subsided, I went inside to find Kelsey wrapped in a blanket and watching TV on the couch. She'd flown to Maryland from Alaska after Cleve overdosed. My mom had been the first person in my family I called after it happened.

"I'm so sorry, honey," she'd said. I could tell she wasn't sure what to say anymore.

When I said I needed her, she said she wasn't sure she could get off work.

"Can you just take a few days?" I asked. I hated putting pressure on her, but it was rare that I asked for anything from my parents anymore. I'd learned over the years that asking for things usually resulted in disappointment. If I needed something from them, I had to make it worth it. If they were giving something, they needed something in return. I didn't have much to give. Growing up, I had excused their selfishness as a symptom of the stress of being broke. But now, they owned their own business. They chose their own hours and made more money than I could fathom. I was running out of excuses for them. I wondered what the point was of being the boss—of having money and flexibility—if they still couldn't help, or even show up, during family emergencies. I loved my parents, but they were proving they were not people I could depend on when I needed it.

"I'll see what I can do," my mom said.

To take financial pressure off of them, I contacted the Semper Fi Fund. Ashamed to be asking for another handout, but desperate for support, I asked if they would be willing to pay for my family's plane tickets. They said yes without hesitation. When I told my mom, she insisted she couldn't take off work and suggested I fly Kelsey out. At the time, my relationship with Kelsey boiled down to a couple phone calls a year. We'd both been busy with our adult lives. Kelsey lived with her boyfriend in Anchorage and had just begun cosmetology school. I was worried she wouldn't be able to come either. But her school was understanding and told her to take the time she needed. She arrived several days after Cleve's overdose and stayed for two weeks.

"Whatcha watching?" I asked.

"Real Housewives."

"Wanna make a Target run?"

She looked out the window and back at me with a confused look on her face. "It's kinda late?"

"Well, don't freak out." I paused. "But I need to get a pregnancy test."

She sat up and scooted to the edge of the couch. "Oh my God. Really?"

"I just vom'd all over the backyard from the smell of peanut oil."

"You're not sick, are you?"

"Maybe? I don't know. I can't remember my last period, though."

Kelsey shot me a side-eye. "Okay then," she said. She stood up from the couch and walked to her shoes next to the door, pulling her long blond hair into a ponytail as she went. "Let's go."

Kelsey drove. She pulled up to the front doors of Target, and I hopped out of the car.

"You're sure you don't want me to go in with you?" she asked.

"Yeah, I'm good. I won't be long," I said. I planned to take the test in the store's bathroom, and I wanted to do it alone. I navigated to the pharmacy section and scanned each aisle until I found the one I was looking for. I'd never had to buy a pregnancy test before. Even though I was married, it felt like I was doing something wrong. I had the sensation people were staring at me—like they knew why I was there and were judging me for it.

I chose the most expensive test because I'd heard of false results and wasn't sure which brand I could trust. I pulled the box off the shelf, held it in my hand so my sleeve covered it, and pressed it against my thigh as I walked toward the registers. I chose a lane with a female cashier.

I thought about pulling a candy bar off the shelf so that it looked like I wasn't only there for the test. But then I thought food would make it even more evident because *cravings*. I considered hopping out of the line to find something unrelated to pregnancy, but then it was my turn, and the cashier was looking directly at me.

"How you doin' today?" she said with an exaggerated smile. She wore silver glitter eyeshadow and fake eyelashes. I wished I had the energy to wear makeup. When Cleve and I were first married, I wore makeup regularly, though I never had the patience or money for fake eyelashes. Now, I didn't see the point of it. At the hospital, I'd gotten used to wearing only oversized sweaters, jeans, and Crocs. If I dressed in anything nicer, it was because we were at a special event. Where I once wanted to be considered beautiful, now the idea of being noticed gave me anxiety. I just wanted to be left alone.

"Good," I said in an almost-whisper. I placed the box on the conveyor belt and pretended I'd noticed something interesting on the cover of one of the magazines behind me.

"Exciting!" the cashier squealed. I turned to look at her, and she was holding the pregnancy test in the air, waving it side to side like a tambourine. She seemed *so* happy, and I just thought, *Rude*. If I were ever a cashier, I would pretend I never saw anything I was ringing up— shopping is so personal.

"Sixteen ninety-six," she said. I swiped my card, rejected the receipt, grabbed the bagged test, and went straight to the bathroom.

I pulled out the test, shoved its packaging in the trash, and peed on the stick, then placed it on top of the trash can and held my head in my hands. I tried to imagine how my life would change if I became a mother. I was afraid. I had so little energy, had been feeling so depressed, I wasn't sure I had enough of myself left to give to a baby. I thought about my parents, how I'd felt abandoned by them most of my life. Just that month, they hadn't come to be with me, even for a day, after Cleve overdosed. I loved my sister, but she was not my mother. Would I be like them if I had a baby of my own? Is the tendency to casually neglect your children hereditary? Could I be a good mom at twenty-three? I still felt like a kid myself.

But when I imagined holding a warm, soft baby, my stomach filled with butterflies. Though I feared becoming like my parents, I could only imagine giving that baby everything. I couldn't fathom ever letting a child feel abandoned. Maybe I could be a good mom. Maybe this could be an opportunity to break the cycle of abuse and neglect in my family. Maybe, I thought, this was what Cleve and I needed: a new purpose to keep him motivated and healthy. I smiled when I thought of him holding a baby. I knew he would cry with joy. He would want to be the best version of himself from then on. That child would be the most important person in his life. But would it be enough to change him? To sober him up? If it wasn't, would I be strong enough to take care of Cleve *and* a baby? Or would this kid be abandoned, too?

I took a deep breath and picked up the test. *Pregnant.*

I felt high, suddenly, everything around me melting away, leaving only me and my baby. Placing a hand on my stomach, I smiled. I considered waiting until I could see Cleve in person to tell him, but I couldn't wait. I called him from the toilet. I didn't know when I would see him again, and I've never been good at surprises.

"What?" he exclaimed. Though I couldn't see him, I knew he'd leaped up from sitting. He started rattling off names, most of them girl names, some related to Ford Mustangs.

"We could name her Celine," he said. It was apparently a family name. ". . . but it's also like my car, *Saleen*."

"Oh my God, we are not naming our baby after a car," I said. "Besides, we have plenty of time to choose. I don't think I'm that far along."

"I wish I could hug you," he said.

"Me too."

Cleve told Gunny Marsh that I was pregnant. He was congratulated and given permission to go to my OB-GYN appointments since they were across the street from the barracks. Cleve hadn't been allowed to leave for anything besides his own appointments, and even those were escorted. I was relieved I wouldn't have to go alone. Being in and out of hospitals for so long with Cleve had made me wary.

On the day of my first appointment, two days after I took the pregnancy test, Cleve sat in a chair in the far corner of the exam room. I placed my clothes on a table, put on the backless robe I'd been given, lay on the cold table, and draped a blanket over my hips as instructed. A knock at the door.

"Come in," I said, and the door swung open.

The doctor, a stone-faced young man with black hair and dark eyes, sat on a stool, eye level with my crotch, a small computer screen glowing to the left of him. I remembered a friend of ours saying he once worked in an OB-GYN office as a nurse. He told us how the guys would make fun of women with "funky pussies." They'd mock them in the hallways just outside the exam rooms where the women were lying with their legs still spread, vulnerable and trusting. I'd requested a woman doctor on the phone, but there weren't any available. With military insurance, you took what you could get.

I thought about the shape of my vulva. Was it *funky*? I'd seen my fair share of porn, but I rarely saw a body I could relate to. I wondered if my vagina would be talked about in the hallway, or worse, if it would be a topic of conversation among strangers years later, like it had been when our friend told us about his experience. I started biting the inside of my cheeks as the doctor dimmed the lights.

"How romantic," I said. Cleve laughed and put his hand on my hand, gave it a squeeze.

The doctor pulled a wheeled metal table closer to him. On it: an ultrasound wand, a speculum, and some lube.

"Now, because you're not very far along, this will be a transvaginal ultrasound, meaning we will have to insert this device in order to see anything. There may be some discomfort but let me know if you feel any pain."

I shifted my hips and clenched my fists at my sides, took a deep breath. When I'd imagined the ultrasound, it looked more like what you see in movies—a woman smearing blue gel on my stomach and sliding a stethoscope-type thing across it. My only worry had been whether it would be cold. Now, a strange man was coming at me with what looked like a giant sex toy.

"Should I be jealous?" Cleve said, joking.

I slapped his arm, and he laughed. The doctor ignored us. He put a condom on the wand and covered it in lube. My body tensed. Had I known this party involved penetration, I would've stayed home.

"Ready?" he asked.

"As ready as I'm gonna be, I guess."

"This may be a little cold."

He put the device inside me, pushed it around, shoved it in every corner with a force that seemed unnecessary.

"Sometimes it sits far to the left or the right. They like to hide. You may feel some pressure," he said.

"Yep. Definitely some pressure."

"Oh! There it is," he said, pointing to the screen. "See that little sac? That's your baby."

"Weird," I said. "Babe, we made a thing."

"Well, dang. We sure did," Cleve said, tears welling in his eyes.

Seeing the bean-shaped image on the screen and Cleve's reaction made the pregnancy more real to me. I loved that little bean immediately.

"Hmm," the doctor said, continuing to grind the wand into me. "Looks like you're only about five and a half weeks instead of eight weeks like we thought."

"Is that bad?" I asked.

"Not necessarily. Just let us know if you begin bleeding or cramping in the next few days. I'm sure that won't happen, but just in case. Let's also schedule another ultrasound for next week."

"Are you sure nothing's wrong?" I asked.

"There's no need to worry just yet."

I dropped Cleve off after the appointment and spent the night creating a baby registry, looking at baby names, and watching birth videos. Kelsey had left the day before my ultrasound, so I was alone again, bored and obsessing about how everything had to be perfect. I would have a natural birth, I thought. No meds. A water birth at home. I wanted a girl, and I wanted to name her Madeline. I imagined I would call her Maddie and I would put lavender on her pillow every night. Her crib's bedding would have gold ruffles. I'd read her *Goodnight Moon*.

When I wasn't adding things to our registry, I was obsessing about our life after Cleve's retirement. Carson and the rest of Cleve's 3/8 friends had recently gotten out of the military, which felt strange because Cleve was supposed to get out around then, too. While we remained stuck in time, Carson and Brittany had moved their family back to Birmingham, where they'd grown up. They'd been living in Carson's parents' basement, which his dad had converted into a one-bedroom apartment. Though we didn't have our own retirement date, we knew it would likely come within the year. We wanted to be prepared. We decided that we would move back to Alabama, but not back to Foley. I understood the importance of having his family close, but I also needed some distance from them. Birmingham was our compromise.

We'd visited Carson and Brittany in July, and while we were there we looked at houses together. Our favorite was a new build in a town south of Birmingham called Maylene. Carson's parents had advised us not to do it. They insisted that buying a new house there was a bad investment. But it was only a little outside our price range, and we couldn't resist the opportunity to choose every detail of our very first home.

"It has a Jacuzzi tub!" I gushed to Brittany during our walk-through.

"The stained-glass window is so pretty. I can't believe it even has a TV," she said, pointing to a small flat-screen mounted on the wall above the tub.

I imagined myself taking a bubble bath while watching a movie, lavender candles lit, the jets going. Though the house was small, the neighborhood under construction, and the town less than desirable, the chance to build our own house felt like a dream. We decided to buy. And the best part was that Carson and Brittany would build a house next door. We would be neighbors. Our kids would grow up together. It was a perfect scenario.

Now, four months after that trip, I was pregnant. It felt like our lives were finally beginning. I studied the floor plan of our future home, grateful we'd chosen one with three bedrooms. The room we thought would be a game room would now be a nursery. I imagined pushing the baby in a stroller through the neighborhood. I imagined watching the baby play in our backyard on grass so new it still had lines between the sod. I imagined the child with my eyes and Cleve's nose running in circles around the weeping cherry tree we'd plant to remember our time in D.C. I loved that the child and the tree would grow together, both a reminder of how much time had passed since we began our new life there.

Hope was what I was feeling, something I wasn't expecting so soon after Cleve's overdose. But it seemed that maybe things were starting to come together. Maybe the overdose would prove to be the wake-up call Cleve needed. Now the military had to take his addiction seriously. After rehab, he'd be better. And after retirement, we could move on.

Maybe, somewhere in the future, we would be a happy and healthy family, these days nothing more than a distant memory.

The day after the ultrasound, I woke up in pain. I went to Google and searched *cramping during pregnancy*. I ignored the links that said it could be a miscarriage and focused on those that said cramping was a normal side effect of pregnancy. *I'm fine,* I thought. *This is normal.* Later that evening, I began spotting. Again, Google was divided. It seemed like I could only know for sure if the bleeding was heavy.

When the cramps and bleeding worsened, and the pain was nearly unbearable, I knew it was over. I turned the shower on as hot as I could bear and lay in the tub, writhing. I watched streams of blood snake from my body to the drain. I moaned and wailed and wondered if this was how I would die. I could have taken more ibuprofen. I'd had endometriosis cramps since I'd started menstruating, and I knew that would take the edge off the pain. But I wanted to feel the loss. I wanted to remember the baby that would never be, to prove that I loved it enough to endure the pain rather than masking it with drugs.

I called my mom the next day. I'd told her I was pregnant shortly after I found out. I'd also announced it on Myspace, and I was now frantic to take the post down before anyone else saw it. I'd let myself get too excited too soon. I would have to tell the world that what would have been my baby was now in a sewer somewhere. When I heard my mom's voice, I broke. I wept harder than I ever had, every bone in my body turning soft and folding under the weight of me. I curled into a ball on the floor and repeated over and over again, *Why? Why? Why? I want to die. I want to die. I want to die.*

Christmas came and went, but I have no memory of it. And then Cleve was released at the beginning of January with a bottle of pain pills. Who knows what kind they were at that point—Lortabs? Morphine? Percocet? The military didn't have a treatment plan, or any plan, as far as I could tell. They couldn't find a rehab facility with space for him. They didn't know what to do with him, so they figured they'd give him another chance until they could figure something else out. I should have been angry, but I was struggling to feel much of anything.

Cleve promised he wouldn't abuse his pills this time, and I was told to keep a close eye on him, which terrified me. I'd kept a close eye on him before, and he overdosed. I wasn't sure what they expected me to do and I couldn't fathom going through that again. It felt as though they'd given up and were putting the responsibility on my shoulders.

Not even a month had passed before Cleve started showing signs of abusing his pills again—cigarette holes in his pants from passing out, the inability to eat a whole meal without losing consciousness, slurred speech. Whenever I mentioned it, he became angry, would call me crazy, tell me to get off his back. His anger had been building since he was wounded, but the outbursts used to be spread out. After his overdose, they became more frequent. It seemed like every day there was something new for him to blow up over. I was becoming afraid of him, afraid of what he was capable of. Under normal circumstances, I would have told someone, but I didn't know who to go to. Nobody seemed to hear what I was saying. Or if they did, they didn't know how to help. I wasn't sure anymore if I could keep Cleve alive. But if I couldn't do it, who could?

In mid-January, Cleve went on a milk run that should have taken thirty minutes. After an hour, I started calling his phone, but he wasn't picking up. After two hours, I struggled to shoo away the intrusive thoughts, but the image of his car crushed on the side of the road, his body lifeless in the snowy street, was vivid in my mind. I'd been pacing in the living room, trying to decide whether I should call the cops, when he finally showed up. It had been more than three hours. He stumbled through the door, a whoosh of icy-cold air pushing past him and into the house. He carried a bag of DVDs, candy, who knows what else, and the gallon of milk he went for. I noticed his eyes were glassy, the color in his face washed out, as he walked past me. My jaw dropped when he didn't bother to explain where he'd been, to say sorry, to acknowledge me at all. My worry quickly turned to anger.

"Where the fuck were you?" I asked, almost in tears. "You should have been back hours ago. Why didn't you answer your phone?"

"Whoa, chill out. I passed out in the parking lot," he said, walking past me to put the bag on the dining room table. He seemed annoyed. I was furious. Why was he acting like passing out in a parking lot was normal? I followed him.

"Like, on the ground in the snow? What are you talking about?"

"No, like in my car. It was fuckin' cold, though. I had the window rolled down."

He laughed at himself, tore open a bag of M&M's, and poured a few in his mouth.

"What's so funny? You scared the shit out of me, Cleve! Do you even—"

"I'm fine! Goddamn it!" he said, cutting me off.

"Are you fucked-up again? Where are your pills?"

"No! Fuck, I'm fine! I'm just fuckin' exhausted is all. Calm down!"

I went to the back room, Cleve behind me, still yelling while eating his M&M's. I tore his drawers apart, looking for his pill bottle. He tugged on my arms, demanding I stop. When I found the orange bottle at the bottom of his sock drawer, nearly all the pills were gone. He should've had a couple of weeks' worth left.

"What is wrong with you!?" I yelled, pushing past him and to the bathroom. "I'm flushing them! I'm fucking done with this!"

I hesitated, a little afraid of what he would do if I actually did it. A little uncertain of whether it was the right decision to flush a one-legged man's pain pills.

"Don't you dare flush those, Karie. I'm warnin' you right now. Don't you dare," he said.

But I did it; I couldn't stop myself. I wasn't thinking clearly. I felt I had no choice. The sound of the toilet flushing triggered a rage I'd never seen in Cleve. We called each other names—*piece of shit, bitch, cunt, asshole.* He threw the coffee table and then a curtain rod that hit a glass of cranberry juice. Shards of glass flew through the air and lodged into my hand, streaking my white jacket with blood. I pulled out the glass just before he picked me up by my collar and slammed me into the kitchen cabinets, spitting hot anger into my face.

"You fucking bitch! You stupid fucking whore!" he screamed. He was choking me.

When he let me go, it was sudden—it felt as if he'd snapped out of something. I stood there, trembling.

He went to his room, grabbed his pistol and a cigar, and went to the back porch. He sat in a chair, locked his eyes on me, and cocked the gun.

He put it on a table next to him and lit the cigar, ashes glowing red-orange at intervals as he inhaled.

"Cleve, you need to put the gun away. I'm gonna call 911 if you don't," I said.

I should have just called, but I didn't think he would actually do anything. I'd gotten used to him cleaning his guns when he was angry, cocking and uncocking them. I was certain now that it was meant as a threat, but it never went past that. I thought he was bluffing, and I was trying to call it. I also didn't want to get him in trouble. I thought that if I called 911 and he was arrested for domestic violence, he might end up with the kind of record that would ruin his life.

"No, you're not. Give me your phone," he said as he put his hand on the gun.

"Come on, Cleve. Just put the gun away." Something about him reaching for the gun, about the way he was looking at me, made me wonder if I'd been wrong. Maybe he *was* capable of shooting me.

I began backing away from him and toward the door.

"Give me the fuckin' phone, Karie."

I said no and put my hand on the doorknob. He started to pick up the gun. I opened the door and ran. He ran after me—gun in hand—a hell of a lot faster than I thought he'd be with his prosthetic leg. I dialed 911 the best I could and screamed, *He's trying to kill me! He's trying to kill me!* hoping neighbors would hear. One did: a man built like a linebacker who I'd met in passing a couple of times was outside his house taking out the trash. He ran to where our yards met and opened his arms. I collided into him, and he yelled at Cleve.

"What the fuck are you doing, son?"

It was as if our neighbor had pushed a pause button. Cleve came to a complete stop, dropped the gun, and turned back toward our house. Sirens in the distance got louder, and Cleve sat on a porch chair with a dead stare, waiting for the cops to arrest him, tears streaming down his face. I watched from our neighbor's yard as he willingly got into the back of a police car.

Cleve was held at the police station until sunrise. He wasn't arrested because I refused to file a police report. The cops also seemed sympathetic toward him—a crying vet with one leg. I wondered what the result would have been had it happened off base. I waited in the lobby until he was released. His Master Guns was alerted about the incident, and we were told to report to Bethesda Naval Hospital first thing, so, delirious from lack of sleep, we drove straight there.

The morning was a bright blur. When we got to the hospital, we were quiet. People were talking, but I wasn't registering much of what was said. I just wanted to be in my bed. I had to leave Cleve there, because they didn't trust him to go home. Back to the barracks he went.

As I was leaving, I bumped into a chaplain who knew us. He could tell something was wrong, so I told him what had happened. He looked at me with pity.

"Karie," he said, "eventually, you're going to have to realize that Cleve has been to war and has experienced serious trauma. If you want to prevent things like this from happening, you have to watch what you say and do around him, because he can't control himself."

My heart sank. I barely had the energy to keep back tears. I nodded, thanked him, and made my way to my car. On the drive home, I thought about what he'd said. At first, I was angry. How could he imply that this was my fault? I was the victim here. The gun was pulled on *me*. But I also knew I could have handled things differently. I could have remained calm. But what then? Cleve wasn't going to stop taking the pills. Doctors wouldn't take them away from him. How was enabling him going to fix anything? He was on a path to killing himself, and I was the only one around to keep that from happening. I didn't know what everyone expected me to do.

I thought about leaving. But then I remembered the boy I'd met in eighth grade, the one who loved his mama more than anything, who grew up at the end of a dirt road named after his grandfather, who played football and had dreams bigger than his hometown but not enough money to afford them. Some might argue that that boy had signed up for this and deserved the consequences. Some might say the same about me. But we had so few options. Young, poor, we followed the breadcrumbs we found, and they led us to the Marine Corps. We put our hope and trust in the military to take care of us in exchange for our service. But we had been abandoned, and now we looked to each other to navigate our way out of the mess we'd found ourselves in. I didn't blame Cleve for doing the best he could with what he had. And I couldn't leave my best friend.

That night, I wrote in my journal, *He may kill me, but as long as I am a good wife to him, it's worth it. This is my job. I am serving my country.*

17

MEDICAL RETIREMENT
February 2009

After spending the night at the police station, Cleve was held at the barracks again, something I believed his higher-ups were only doing because they had no clue what else to do with him. There, they could at least keep an eye on him. They checked his room daily and gave him a pill dispenser that only allowed him to get what he was prescribed. But then, after a month of good behavior, it was decided by Gunny Marsh that Cleve would do outpatient addiction rehab. The details of that were murky. Someone would count his pills weekly. He'd go to therapy. *But what else?* I wondered. It wasn't enough for me.

"That's all they're gonna do?" I asked Cleve the day he came home, a bottle of opioids rattling in his pocket.

"They're not sending me to rehab. They're just not. I'm supposed to retire soon. There's no point."

"What do you mean, *no point?*" I snarled. "*They* did this to you. It doesn't just go away after you retire. They need to fucking fix this."

"They didn't *do* anything. What I do is on *me*. I made some mistakes and I learned from 'em. I'm goin' to stop bein' stupid and get my shit together. I don't need rehab."

"Why are you so resistant? What is the worst thing that could happen? If it works, great! If it doesn't, it's just a thing you tried that didn't hurt anything."

"If I go to rehab, that means I'm admitting I'm a junkie. Marines get dishonorably discharged for shit like that. I could get my rank taken away. Even if I didn't, I'd look like a fuckin' loser. Everyone calls me hero now, but if I go there, I'm nothin' more than a damn addict."

"That's not true," I said.

"How do you know?"

I shrugged. "I guess I don't." I turned my head away from him to think. To breathe. I felt like Cleve and I were on a sinking ship. I was begging him to get into a lifeboat and being ignored—and it wasn't just Cleve ignoring my pleas, it was his doctors, his superiors in the military, everyone. They were just killing time until Cleve retired so his addiction wouldn't be their problem anymore. It would be the VA's.

I dropped the subject and locked myself in the bathroom, where I angry-cried as quietly as possible so he couldn't hear me. I was at a loss. Cleve had been my safe space, even if our relationship had never been perfect. But since the overdose and the gun, I no longer felt that way. Our relationship was now more duty than dream, our love the kind bound by codependence, necessity, and obsession. I wasn't worried about his reputation. I was afraid for our lives. That night, without telling Cleve, I sent Gunny Marsh a desperate email.

After near death and arrest for domestic violence what is it going to take to prove he needs more help than he is getting?? These pills are turning him into a monster. There were over thirty of both Oxycontin and over thirty Klonipin [sic] missing in THREE days!!!!!!!!!!!!!!! That's when I dumped all his pills and that's when we got in a fight and he got arrested. You have no idea how much I have suffered as a result of this. I want the hell out of these hospitals and I want out WITH my healthy husband. At this point he is going to end up killing himself. Please take the time to fix him. Please.

Gunny Marsh called me the following day and assured me he'd try to find a place with space for him. Inpatient rehab was in high demand, though, he said. It might take a while. When Cleve found out what I'd done, he was pissed.

"You're makin' me look like an idiot," he spat.

I wanted to say that passing out in parking lots, wearing pants riddled with burn holes, hitting his wife, and almost dying from an overdose made him look like an idiot. But I didn't have the energy to argue and didn't want things to escalate.

"I did it because I love you," I said in a near-whisper.

"They can't make me go."

"If you don't go, I'm going to leave you, Cleve. I don't want to leave you, but I can't play this game anymore. It's on you now."

The next afternoon, I was watching TV in our living room when he sat down beside me.

"I am addicted," he said. He began to cry. "Don't leave me."

I held his head against my chest. "I'm not going anywhere," I said, petting his head. "I'm proud of you. Now we can start to fix this."

"One patch will kill the pain," his pain management doctor told us. "Two will kill you."

Cleve had just admitted to his doctors that he was addicted to his pills. Unsure of how to balance his pain treatment and addiction treatment, the doctor decided to try something different: fentanyl patches. I'd never heard of fentanyl before. They explained that it was typically used for terminally ill patients, like those with cancer, because of its potency and the high risk of overdose. In Cleve's case, because he had a history of abusing pills but not of being suicidal, they thought it might work for him.

I squinted at Cleve. "You wouldn't go and fucking kill yourself, would you? Like, you wouldn't do that to me and your mom . . ."

"Hell no. There's too much to live for." He turned to the doctor. "My whole life's ahead of me. I just want to move to Alabama and start over."

It didn't take long to see a change. He was no longer passing out or slurring his words. He was beginning to get color back in his face, he was less irritable, and he showed up to appointments on time. He seemed happier. We were happier together. We were hopeful, me cautiously so. And then, in late May, Cleve finally got a call that he had been accepted into an inpatient rehab facility in West Virginia. The news was sudden and confusing because we were given little information about what to expect. He would leave in a week.

The memory of him leaving for rehab is blurry, but I know he went reluctantly. He was concerned they would take his pain medicine away entirely. I secretly hoped they would. It wasn't that I wanted him to be in pain. It was that I couldn't tell if he was telling the truth anymore, and my main concern was keeping him alive. My worst fear was burying him. I just wanted to test it, see what would happen. I wanted to be absolutely, positively certain that he couldn't live without the painkillers. I knew, though, that he would get them as long as he said he was suffering. I wasn't sure how rehab could work if the patient left the program with a bottle of drugs in their pocket or, in his case, a box of patches. I wondered if this whole thing was performative. All I could do was wait and hope for the best.

We were expecting to hear back from the Physical Evaluation Board about Cleve's final disability rating, which had to be renegotiated after his leg was amputated. Initially, he was rated 35 percent disabled, but that didn't account for PTSD, TBI, and the latissimus muscle they removed to rebuild his leg. Now, we also needed to add his amputation, his addiction, and the sleep apnea he'd been diagnosed with that required a CPAP machine. All of those things factored into the rating, but only if we could prove none of it was preexisting, which could sometimes be difficult. Something as simple as having attended a special education class as a child could be used against you. Was the Marine suffering from severe TBI inflicted by the war, or was he just dumb? If they found anything that could prove the latter, your disability rating would drop accordingly. Cleve was nervous, because he'd only ever been book-smart enough to get by.

I'd gathered medical records, filled out paperwork, and contacted nonprofits over the last two years, trying to get him the highest rating I could. The rating determined how much money he would get each month after retirement. I was afraid, based on his performance at Walter Reed, that he wouldn't be reliable enough to work and we wouldn't have enough money to survive. The process was stressful, and I knew no matter how hard I worked to put his case together, there was no way to guarantee a good outcome. People joked that the rating you got depended on whose desk the paperwork landed on that day and whether or not they'd had their morning coffee. There were guys with no physical wounds and full-time jobs with the same rating as quadruple amputees. Nobody could make sense of it, so we all had to advocate for ourselves and cross our fingers. This was also the last step before receiving a retirement date, which we assumed would be soon. There was nothing the military could do for Cleve anymore that the VA couldn't take over. By this time next year, we would be on our own.

Cleve started rehab with a rebellious attitude, sneaking his phone in, which was against the rules. I wanted him to do well, to be good, but I was also relieved that I'd be able to hear from him regularly.

"They have a pool," he told me a week after he arrived. "And the people are cool. Everyone here's been through it. Just reminds me I'm not the only one strugglin', ya know?"

"Good, babe," I said. "You think it's helping, then?"

"I do. I just wanna get on with my life."

"Me too."

"I wanted to tell you, too, I put my mom as the emergency contact, so it's not your responsibility this time. I just want you to see I can do this on my own."

I tried not to read anything into it. "You didn't have to do that," I said. "But I'm proud of you for taking this seriously. I can tell you're trying, and that means a lot."

I drove to Alabama the same day Cleve left for rehab. I needed to check on the progress of our home in Birmingham, and then I had to go to Foley to be the maid of honor at my high school friend's wedding. The day after I arrived in Birmingham, Brittany, Carson, and I drove to our new homes. The house smelled like fresh paint. The cabinets in the

kitchen were the color of dark chocolate. Cream-colored granite coun-
tertops with whirls of chestnut and wine sparkled under the pendant
lights that hung over the bar, not a speck of dust. I'd chosen every detail:
the doorknobs, paint color, and crown molding. They had mailed me
samples of carpet, tile, wood, and paint. I had stared at the samples for
hours, laying out different combinations of paint and wood and stone
on the dining room table to see how they made me feel. I wanted something neutral and calming, rich but homey. I would have liked to look
at the samples with Cleve. I wanted it to be his dream home, too. But
he was in the barracks at the time and insisted he trusted me.

"I'm not really into that kind of stuff," he said. I, on the other hand,
was *very* into that kind of stuff, so I didn't argue. Piecing our perfect
home together kept my mind busy and gave me something to look
forward to.

The day after visiting our home, I stood in a garden in a black dress with
freshly curled hair and red roses in my hands. I watched the only friend
I'd kept in touch with from childhood, Fiona, say "I do" to her longtime
boyfriend, Trent, who I'd also gone to school with. Fiona was the girl I'd
met in band class—the girl who'd noticed her discarded shoes on my
feet. We'd remained close after I moved to Florida and through the
years I spent in the hospital with Cleve. Myspace made it easier to keep
in touch. She kept up with my blog updates and checked in on us regularly. I loved that she'd known Cleve for as long as I had—longer,
even—and that she remembered who he had been before he joined the
Marine Corps. She was one of my only connections to that part of my
past—she even kept photos of all of us from high school in a plastic bin
under her bed—and one of the few people in the world I felt comfortable being myself around.

At Fiona and Trent's wedding reception, I sat at a round table under
a tree with candlelit lanterns, eating bacon-wrapped green beans, wondering if I'd ever have a wedding of my own. I'd once assumed Cleve
and I would have a real wedding after he got out of the military. I wasn't
that optimistic anymore. Now, our future was uncertain. If rehab
worked, and I hoped it would, we could start over. I didn't like thinking

about what would happen if it didn't work. The memory of Cleve over-dosing replayed in my mind, so vivid I could taste the vomit, feel his body fall from my arms to the ground. No. Rehab had to work. It had to.

A few days later, I received an email saying Cleve's new disability rating had been raised from 35 percent, which would have equaled $421 a month, to 90 percent, which equaled $1,739. The paperwork that had been scanned and sent to us was difficult to decipher, but it was quickly clear to me that all of his injuries hadn't been included, things like sleep apnea and minor shrapnel injuries on parts of his body. We'd learned from other families who'd struggled to get decent ratings that every tiny wound mattered. Considering Cleve's condition, I thought he deserved 100 percent disability, at least temporarily. That would have given us $2,823 to work with.

I spent the next two days emailing anyone I could think of, trying to find someone willing to help us refile. It would require me requesting his medical records and sifting through them, highlighting every injury they mentioned. I'd then have to redo the paperwork, clearly state what I thought was missing, and include the medical records necessary to prove my case. Then I would have to wait. I was told again and again it would be in our best interest to take the 90 percent rating he received and try filing again after his retirement. Otherwise, retirement would be delayed even longer. Exhausted, I let the issue go.

Cleve eventually gave up his phone. Because I could no longer talk to him, my only contacts were the handful of folks at Bethesda Naval Hospital, including Gunny Marsh, who were coordinating his care. We still hadn't been given a retirement date, so I emailed every contact I had, asking for an update. I needed to be sure the house was finished before we arrived, and I needed to have Cleve's appointments set up at the VA in Birmingham so there wasn't a delay in his care. I also needed to be sure the rehab would be completed before retirement so that we wouldn't get stuck with a bill. An employee at the Wounded Warrior Project whose job was to help make retirement and accessing benefits easier assured me the military wouldn't retire Cleve until he was out of rehab.

"Are they going to pay for our move?" I asked. The Wounded Warrior Project employee said he didn't know. I went back to Gunny Marsh, asking the same question, and he recommended contacting a nonprofit.

"Some would disagree with going that route," he said, "but if you wait for us, it might take too long." I couldn't believe what I was hearing. Nonprofits were constantly making up for the military's shortcomings. It hadn't occurred to me that it was citizens, whose tax dollars were already funding the military, who were really paying for the deficiency. I appreciated the nonprofits. I was endlessly grateful to them for helping us when no one else would. But it just wasn't right. And I was also tired of feeling like a charity case. Of feeling like a burden.

"I guess I'll suck up my pride and ask, then," I said, irritated. "Still no word on a retirement date?"

"Nope. Sorry."

Carson worked at U-Haul now and got me a quote for the move. I contacted the Semper Fi Fund to see if they'd cover it. They were happy to.

Cleve was released from rehab after six and a half weeks. It was July, and because he was so close to retirement, they opted to keep him in the barracks until then. I was busy preparing for the move, so it didn't make much of a difference to us anyway. On August 13, we were told he would officially be retiring on August 30. I would have been upset that we only had two weeks' notice, but I was prepared. Carson would fly to Maryland a week before Cleve's retirement date to help me pack the truck. Carson would drive the truck, and I would drive my car. Everything would be unloaded before Cleve even got to Birmingham.

Since getting out of the military, Carson had done everything he could to help us. I was surprised. He had initially come across to me as selfish, someone who didn't take much seriously. When I first met him, he was only nineteen, and he looked it. He was short and thin, the pitch of his voice somewhere between a boy's and a man's. When he and Cleve hung out, they reminded me of the Looney Tunes characters

Chester and Spike, Cleve moving through the world confidently in his six-foot-three body, Carson bouncing around him, talking a hundred words a minute. Carson had been born in Louisiana to a Creole woman who was too young to raise a baby. He was adopted by a wealthy white family in Birmingham. He described himself as his parents' favorite child, even over his sister, their biological daughter. If he wanted a phone, a car, a house, he got it. He seemed so well-off. I didn't understand why he joined the military, especially the infantry. Most of the guys in their unit had come from lower-income families. It was rare to meet someone who came from wealth. When asked, Carson said it was because he was bored, the military was something to do. But I sensed there was more to it. I just couldn't put my finger on what it was.

Carson was sarcastic, inappropriate, quick to tell me how much I sucked, and kind of a know-it-all. Despite all of this, we formed a bond after Cleve's injury. Carson validated my complicated experience with Cleve in a way nobody else could. He became something like a little brother to me. He was loyal, too, always showing up for us. Carson, Brittany, and Dillon were chosen family.

It took a couple of days after he arrived in Maryland to get the truck loaded. Once the apartment was empty, I sat in the center of the living room and he lay on his back, limbs spread like a starfish, staring at the ceiling.

"Okay, so, what now?" I asked. "Camp on the floor or get a hotel?" It was six in the evening, I was hungry, and the drive was just over twelve hours long.

"Fuck that. If we leave now, we could probably get there by eight A.M., including stops." Carson pushed himself up into a sitting position.

"Tempting," I said. I'd been anticipating the move for so long that I didn't hate the idea, even though I was tired. One big push and I'd be in our new home. I sighed, grabbed my purse, and stood up. "We'll need lots of snacks and Red Bull," I said.

"And dip," Carson said. "That shit'll wake you up."

I grimaced. "I'm not dipping." I'd dipped once in high school, and it ended with me puking beside a campfire in front of the older boy I had a crush on. I woke up the next morning with tobacco stuck in my teeth.

"Yeah. You get back to me when it's late and that Red Bull stops working for you."

I rolled my eyes. "Let's just fuckin' go."

I stepped onto the front porch and turned to lock the door. I stopped and took a final look around, remembering everything that had happened there. I tried to think of something happy, but our memories, even the good ones, were riddled with anxiety and fear.

"I'm sorry," I whispered to the empty home. I hoped that we hadn't ruined it, that the demons would leave, too, and the next family would make happy memories. I closed the door behind me.

We made it to Birmingham a couple of hours after sunrise. We had four days to unpack. My goal was to get the living room, kitchen, a bathroom, and our bedroom set up. The rest of our things could go in the garage, and we could casually unpack when we got around to it. But first: sleep. I was so exhausted I wasn't thinking straight. I didn't care about food or the house. I just needed to lie down. I set up a blow-up mattress in the living room next to the fireplace, curled up under the comforter I'd left unpacked, and slept until that evening.

When I woke up, I stared at the vaulted ceiling, a new fan whirling below it. The paint was perfect. Not a single smudge or drip. Everything in the house was so bright and fresh. I stood up and took a deep breath, giggled. I walked to the bathroom and splashed water on my face. I needed energy. Though the sun was going down, I was determined to at least get a few boxes off the truck. I dried my face with my shirt, then cupped my hands around my mouth.

"ONWARD!" I yelled before moonwalking out of the bathroom and into the hallway. I felt so light. So free. I felt inspired for the first time in years. I hoped that when Cleve arrived and saw this home built just for us, he'd feel the same. I hoped that it would inspire him to start fresh, to continue fighting his addiction, to create a beautiful life with me.

A few days later, Brittany laid a sheet on the floor of her living room. Dillon, now a three-year-old with huge blue eyes and a blond bowl cut, jumped onto it, giggling.

"Mommy, look! Mommy, look!" he said as she urged him to move out of the way.

"This is for Uncle Cleve, monkey. Why don't you come over here and help me? Don't you want to make a sign for Uncle Cleve?"

"Unca Ceve," he said, then ran to his room. I wondered how much he actually understood. Since Cleve had been wounded, Dillon had hardly seen him, save for a few scattered visits.

Brittany opened a bottle of black paint and handed me a brush.

"You get 'Welcome' and I'll get 'Home,'" she said.

Cleve's retirement had finally come. He'd be on his way home from Maryland in the morning, and we wanted to give him the homecoming he didn't get to have after Ramadi. We duct-taped each corner of the sheet to the edges of the new garage door, then sat in the driveway drinking beers.

"Our last homecoming," I said to Brittany, raising my beer.

She raised hers. "Thank God."

IV

I wait for him. Each moment that I wait feels
like a year, an eternity. Each moment is as slow
and transparent as glass. Through each moment
I can see infinite moments lined up, waiting.
Why has he gone where I cannot follow?
—AUDREY NIFFENEGGER, *The Time Traveler's Wife*

18

TWO OF US

August 31, 2009

I heard a car door slam shut. I'd been sitting by the window in the front room for the last forty-five minutes, peeking through the blinds every so often. I jumped to my feet and ran to the front door, swung it open, and squealed, "Welcome home!"

Cleve was bent over, reaching into the back seat for his suitcase. "Let me help!" I said, running over to him.

"I got it," he said as he yanked it out and plopped it onto the driveway. He closed the car door behind him and held his arm out for a side hug. I wrapped my arms around his waist, pressing my face into his chest.

"I'm so happy right now," I said. "You have no idea."

"So am I," he said. "The house is . . . damn. You did a great job."

"You have to see inside!" I said. I grabbed his hand and led him to the front door.

Cleve loved the house. We spent the first couple of weeks unpacking and making plans for the future. He talked about college courses, and I talked about jobs. We decorated the house, took evening walks around the neighborhood, and watched movies, cuddling on the couch. We had a lot of idle time now, something I hadn't really prepared for. We had Carson and Brittany next door, which was great, but they had jobs and family. We often had dinner with them, but we weren't sure what to do with ourselves during the day. We missed having multiple people in one place who intimately understood our experience as an amputee and caregiver and were almost always available to hang out.

The depression, anxiety, and PTSD were worse than we'd realized, too. For both of us. The events that had happened not even a year before—overdose, miscarriage, arrest—made it difficult for us to connect. We trusted each other less. We trusted ourselves less. Time went on, and instead of making progress each day, we isolated ourselves. It was hard to stay motivated without the pressure of the military. Cleve even skipped most of his VA appointments unless they were required to get a prescription refill. It became the root of many of our fights. I was tired of forcing him to do things he didn't want to. I didn't want to be a mother. I wanted to be a partner. A friend. A lover.

Money was also an issue. His disability check was just enough to pay our mortgage and utilities. We still had to cover a car payment, gas, groceries, and everything else we needed to live. We tried to make it work on the leftover TSGLI money we'd saved—we both preferred having me at home so I could clean and cook and help him get around if he needed it—but our savings were rapidly dwindling. Though the thought of leaving Cleve alone for entire days made me nervous, I had to get a job.

I found an ad for a job on Craigslist. *Office Manager,* it said, which sounded straightforward. I wasn't sure if I qualified without a high school diploma, but I applied anyway. That's how I'd approached every job search in the past: apply to everything, and someone would hire me eventually. It usually worked out. When I was called for an interview, I was ecstatic. Ten dollars an hour would make a huge difference for us.

The day of the interview, I sat in front of a desk I was told would be mine if I was hired. The man interviewing me introduced himself as Theo and asked me to talk a little bit about myself and my work history.

"I've never held a position quite like this before," I said, holding my hands in my lap. I could feel beads of sweat growing on my upper lip. "But I'm a fast typer, I have years of experience working with people in both customer service and sales, and I'm comfortable answering phones."

Theo nodded. Though not my type, he was objectively handsome, with gelled brunette hair, piercing blue eyes, and a strong jawline. You could tell through his tight-fitting shirt that he worked out and was proud of it.

"Good, good," he said without looking up from my résumé. He leaned forward on the desk, resting on his elbows and holding up my résumé in front of him so that it blocked the bottom half of his face from my view. "Customer service is good. I was interested in you because of your experience flight attending. I thought it might translate well to this position."

"Oh, yeah! I loved that job. It was one of my favorites. Never a dull moment." I looked at him, confused. "What is it about flight attending, specifically, that relates to this job?" I imagined office managers spent a lot of time alone sending faxes, filing, and fixing broken printers.

He finally looked up. "Well," he said before pausing. "I guess I should mention that the ad is a little misleading. Though you'd certainly be doing office work, a more appropriate job title is Matchmaker."

Every detail I'd noticed since I walked through the doors replayed in my mind: a new office building in the more affluent part of the city, and a sign on the door that said *Two of Us*. Young people led middle-aged folks to private rooms, closing the doors firmly behind them. I was instantly intrigued.

"Like *Millionaire Matchmaker*?" I wondered aloud. I pictured the reality TV show host Patti Stanger with her skintight dresses, perfectly coiffed hair, and brazen confidence. I cringed. Matchmaking was fun to watch on TV, but I wondered what it would be like in real life. Not that it mattered. Two of Us paid more than the other jobs I'd applied to. If they offered me the position, I was going to take it.

"Something like that," he said.

When I got home, I flung open the door to Cleve's game room. "I got a job!" I said, proud of myself.

"Look out! Look out!" he yelled into his headset. He was sitting cross-legged in the center of his game room, directly in front of a massive rear-projection TV he'd picked up from a rent-to-own furniture store. He was attacking the game controller with his thumbs, leaning his body to one side and then the other. I didn't have to look to know he was playing *Call of Duty*.

We'd been in Birmingham for more than three months, and he had a routine: wake up around noon, eat some cereal, start playing *Call of Duty* with breaks for snacks and dinner, then go to bed around two in the morning. Empty soda cans and chip bags surrounded him now in a messy circle. "That's great, baby!" he said without looking away from the screen.

I half-smiled, then left the room, closing the door behind me. I kicked my heels off in the living room, disrobed, and twisted my hair into a bun. I ignored my reflection as I walked past the bathroom mirror. I'd gained so much weight in Maryland that I struggled to look at my body anymore. I drew a bath, turned on the jets, and cried.

It didn't take long before I realized my job would not resemble Patti Stanger's in the least. Two of Us had been successful in L.A. and then decided to branch out into other cities. The branch I worked for was new, which meant there were very few potential matches for anyone. The waiting room filled with beautiful employees was a façade. The cold-calling room was stacked with filing cabinets and paperwork. Most of the employees were just salespeople, carefully selected to be as alluring as possible.

With my ill-fitting slacks, box-dyed hair, and press-on nails, I didn't quite fit the bill. I was stuffed into an office in the back, a space only folks who'd already purchased a dating package were allowed to see. I was relatable. I was comforting. I was someone the clients could trust. And yet, I found myself matching people who had nothing more in common than their age, because we didn't have enough members. When I complained, I was told to make it work. When I struggled, I was told to create a fake dating profile on Match.com. My boss wanted me to pretend to be a young woman looking for love and collect as many phone numbers as I could from unsuspecting men. I'd then turn those numbers over to the phone salespeople, who would call the men and try to convince them that they'd filled out an online form for our service. It would get better eventually, I was told. For now, we just needed to focus on selling more memberships and distracting the members we already had.

Every day I listened to clients talk about their love lives, and every night I returned home to another fight with Cleve. He had become so distant, disconnected, disinterested. I'd hold in how much it bothered me until I got angry, and then I'd attack him with comments about how he never helped around the house, about how he played video games for eight hours a day, about how we never had sex. Though I was hired for forty hours a week, I averaged fifty with no overtime. It was expected. All of us were overworked and reminded of how dispensable we were.

"There's mold on the dishes, Cleve," I'd say, frustrated. "What did you even do today?"

"Get off my balls," he'd say, or "Why are you being such a bitch?" and then I'd call him a dick and then we'd sit in separate rooms until we got over it. He still had multiple guns, and despite being arrested for chasing me with one, he still played with them—cocking and uncocking the biggest one—when he was mad. I didn't care anymore if he killed me. That's what I told myself, anyway. It wasn't that I wanted to die, just that I no longer had the energy to worry about it. Staying was my choice. If I died, I died. That was that.

At work, I felt like a fraud. I had no right to give dating advice. And yet, strangers came to my office every day, trusting me with their stories, trusting me to find them a soulmate who wouldn't hurt them. I was promising these women things I couldn't even promise myself.

"I'm looking for a good man. A kind man," Linda told me. She was in her fifties but looked like she was in her forties. She owned a hair salon and had long, wavy hair. My first impression of her was that she had her shit together. She had just purchased a dating package for a few thousand dollars, hoping I could help her find a new path to a happy relationship. She looked at me and smiled. Crow's feet framed her eyes, but her smile was wide and genuine, and her face glowed without any makeup. She pulled out a piece of paper and held it crumpled in her hands. She told me she'd written the letter because there was something she didn't want to forget to tell me.

"This is kinda weird. I'm sorry." She cleared her throat and began reading. "I divorced my husband two years ago. He hit me for over twenty years. I'm afraid of men, but I don't want to be alone. I am here because I need help." She looked up at me. "That's it."

I wanted to share my experience with Linda, to tell her that I understood. But there was a part of me that still didn't believe the things I'd experienced were actual abuse. The way Cleve was treating me wasn't something I could talk about. Instead, I told Linda I'd do the best I could to help her find a kind man, knowing I probably wouldn't recognize one if he were standing right in front of me.

As the dust in the house grew thicker, I began dreading going home. At first I hoped that Cleve would eventually see how hard I was working and start helping me around the house. I'd park in the driveway, stop at the front door, and imagine what it would feel like to open it and smell food or scented candles. I'd picture an empty sink, folded clothes, and vacuum lines on the carpet. I never expected him to make the house spotless; the tiniest bit of effort would have meant so much to me. But no matter how much I asked for it or how many calendars I marked and schedules I made, that never happened. Every evening, I'd open the door, change into my pajamas, and begin my second job cleaning and cooking while he played video games.

I'd been declining invites to have drinks with my co-workers because Cleve never wanted to join, and I felt bad leaving him. But one night in November, I decided to say yes. I didn't want to go home only to start more work. I just wanted to relax and enjoy the company of other humans. We went out for beer and wings, followed by board games at the home of Holly, one of the women I'd become close to. Cleve called around ten P.M., but I let it go to voicemail. I'd lost track of time and knew he'd be upset. When I checked his message, his voice was roaring. I could tell he was high or drunk or both. His words were slurred as he shouted, "Where the fuck are you this late? You're probably whorin' around or somethin'! I can't believe you left me here!"

I replayed the message for Holly because I needed someone else to witness his outbursts with me. In the past I'd dealt with them alone, and I struggled to know what was normal. The military wives I'd told disapproved of Cleve's behavior but always blamed it on PTSD and brushed it off. They'd shrug like *What can you do?* I'd started to think that way, too.

"I don't know what to do," I said. Holly's jaw had dropped.

"Does he always talk to you like that?" she asked.

"I mean, not always," I said, looking at the ground. I couldn't make eye contact with her. "He has a brain injury. He gets upset and just . . ." I paused. "I don't know. Sometimes I yell back. I'm not perfect, either. He's not a bad person. He's just been through a lot."

"But that's not an excuse to treat you like that," she said. "You didn't do anything wrong. You know this isn't normal, right?"

I started to cry. "I don't know," I said. "I don't know what's normal."

For so long, I thought abuse was a strong, burly man who was evil, with no redeeming qualities. Abuse to me was black eyes and broken bones: something people could see. Cleve, at his core, was kind. And he moved through the world in a wheelchair or on crutches or with a prosthetic leg—his body had become frail. He hadn't hit me with his fists, and I had no broken bones. On paper, he did not fit my image of an abuser. Even hearing the word in my head, *abuse,* made me wince. Was that really what had been happening? Was I sure? I thought that if I said it out loud to someone, they might laugh at me. But what I feared more than anything was making him look bad. I could not reconcile the boy I once knew with the man I was married to now. I didn't want to do anything that would tarnish his reputation. All I wanted was peace for us both.

Holly and I sat on her living room floor, where we'd been playing a board game. She crawled across the floor to where I was sitting and hugged me.

"Stay with me tonight," she said. "I have a spare room. You'll even have your own bathroom."

Holly's eyes were large and full of pity. She was so beautiful to me in a way that required much more time and money than I had. She was tall and curvy with flawless ivory skin. She had brunette extensions to her waist and breast implants and painted her face with MAC makeup. Her nails were always professionally manicured, she carried expensive purses, and she had a closet full of designer clothing she wore as if she were walking down a runway. She was single and had a wild side that intimidated me. On weekends, she went to clubs with friends or went on dates at fancy restaurants with attractive older men. I was also a little jealous. She was so free. She did whatever the fuck she wanted, unapologetically.

"I'm not sure that's a good idea," I said. "He'll be really pissed."

"Karie," she said. She paused until I looked up at her. "Let him be pissed. Take some control back."

She said it so confidently that it was almost annoying. I appreciated that she cared enough to try to help, but she had no idea what we'd been through. Still, she was persistent. At Two of Us, she'd been hired as a salesperson. I assumed it was because men found it difficult to say no to her. I found it difficult to say no to her, too.

"Okay," I said. "Yeah. Thank you for caring so much. You're right. I'll stay one night."

That night, I tucked myself into silver floral bedding and stared at the tray ceiling of Holly's guest room, imagining how upset Cleve was. Holly had suggested I turn my phone off, and I did. He was probably throwing things. He was definitely calling and leaving more angry voicemails. I imagined him polishing his guns and swearing to himself that he would leave me.

The next morning, I pulled into our driveway and found my clothes in a pile in our front yard. They stunk of stale Bud Light. I'd been kicked out. Before picking them up, I looked around to see if any neighbors were watching. I wondered if Cleve was inside. In the past, when he acted like this at night, he'd be in tears by morning. He'd never thrown my belongings in the yard before, though. I thought about the night I found him overdosing, the taste of his vomit in my mouth, the way he'd yelled at me when he woke up in the hospital. My heart began to race. "Fuck him," I said under my breath.

I was starting to feel nauseous. I considered going inside to talk to him, then stopped myself. Nothing had changed. *Would he kill me next time?* I imagined the voices of all of the women who'd confided in me since I'd started working as a matchmaker. They echoed, *Don't do it! Leave! You deserve better!* I closed my eyes and shook my head. "This isn't my battle," I said out loud. It wasn't fair that he'd been left in the wild with an untreated brain injury, PTSD, and addiction. But that was no longer a good enough excuse for me to stay in a situation that made me feel unsafe. "I don't want to die. I don't want to die. I don't want to die," I repeated as I put the damp pile in the trunk of my car. If he wanted to be with me, he was going to have to work harder to get better. He would have to prove to me that he could be my safe place again.

I stayed in Holly's spare room, ignoring phone calls from Cleve and deleting messages before I could listen to them. It was the first time I'd had space from him to think. I realized I'd lost myself in the role of wife and caregiver; my self-worth hinged on how good of a job I was doing. Somewhere along the line, I'd decided that my life was less important than Cleve's. That my life was worth sacrificing to prove I was a good wife. That leaving, or demanding better for myself, was giving up on the only thing that made me worth something. If I could endure his wrath, I was strong. Anything else was weak. I thought about Cleve's friend Nelson calling Cleve a "true Marine" for keeping a cheery disposition even with his leg mangled and lying across his chest. What was it about the military that made us believe it was our duty to not only accept violence against our bodies but find pride in enduring it? I didn't like who I'd become, and I wanted to change. Having Holly remind me I wasn't crazy was key. I would have gone back to Cleve if I hadn't had her.

Days later, I called him with an ultimatum.

"You need to get help. Get your anger under control. I don't know what it will take, but I'm not taking responsibility for it anymore," I said, my heart racing. Saying those words out loud made my stomach hurt. I hoped with everything in me that he would hear me and do whatever it took to get better so that we could move past this and live the rest of our lives together in peace.

"Bitch," he snapped, then hung up.

I gasped as the hope I'd had evaporated. I assumed he was telling me our relationship was over, and I stayed in Holly's spare room until I could afford an apartment.

Holly could sense I was stressed and asked if I wanted to have a few drinks on her at TGI Fridays. It had been two months since I'd left Cleve, and while I used to decline invitations out because I didn't want to leave him at home alone, now I declined because I couldn't afford it. I had my own apartment, and I was struggling to make ends meet. But it had been a long day, and she was offering to pay.

"You're sure?" I asked. "Why are you even friends with my pathetic ass?"

"I sold a 10K package today." Her eyelashes fluttered as she flipped her hair. "Very sure. And I'm friends with you because you're a good person. I know I can trust you and that's hard to come by."

"My queen," I said jokingly. "You are the good one."

It was midafternoon, and the bar was mostly empty except for a few men in white collared shirts and loosened ties. Holly, as usual, made business casual look sexy, while I wore the same slacks I'd worn the day before. I'd pulled my hair into a low ponytail a couple of hours into work. By the end of the day, it was in a bun on the top of my head.

"I need to find another job," I said.

"No! Stay with us!"

"I can't fucking afford it, though. I'm in the cheapest apartment close to work." I took a breath so I wouldn't cry.

"I know," she said. "I'm sorry. Maybe I can teach you to do sales," she suggested, but we both knew I wasn't confident enough to convince millionaires to give me thousands of dollars. She took a sip of her martini. "Well, what's going on with the husband?" She knew some of the story, but I'd mostly kept to myself since getting my own place.

I sighed. Some days Cleve was apologetic and agreed that I was right to be upset. He wanted me to come home, but I'd already told him my terms and I was sticking to them. On other days, he'd get angry and say he didn't need help or me. Then he'd flip again and swear he was looking into inpatient PTSD therapy. On one of his good days, he offered to drive me around to look at cars. I'd given him the Escalade back because I couldn't afford the payments, which left me spending money I didn't have on taxis to get to work. It wasn't sustainable. I'd found a '97 Saturn for four hundred dollars on Craigslist. I didn't have that much money, but I did have one thing of value. I'd stared at the screen, flipping through pictures of the vehicle, and then looked down at my wedding set. Thinking about pawning it made my stomach hurt, but I had to have a car.

The next evening, Holly took me to a pawnshop after work, where I argued with a hairy man about the worth of my rings. To me, they were priceless. To him, their value was six hundred dollars.

"I have the receipt right here. I bought them for three thousand dollars not that long ago." I slid the receipt toward him. "They're in perfect condition."

"Ma'am. I'm sorry, but I have to think of things like resale. If someone wants to pay three thousand dollars for that set, they'll just go buy it new. Get what I'm sayin'?"

I closed my eyes and shook my head. I placed my hands on the glass case full of knives and jewelry and looked down at all of it, wondering about the stories behind each item. *Was any of this precious to someone? Was it worth it?*

Holly put her hand on my shoulder. "You okay?" I nodded.

I stood up straight and looked at the man. "Fifteen hundred," I said, hoping he would say, "One thousand."

He lifted an eyebrow and clicked his tongue. "Eight hundred."

"Come on, man. *My wedding rings.*"

"Eight hundred is my final offer," he said.

I glared at him. "Fine." I slid the rings off of my finger and squeezed them in my hand. Fighting back tears, I placed them on the glass case, and he handed me a wad of cash. I counted it before folding it and putting it in my back pocket. "Thanks a lot," I said as I walked out the door.

Later that night, Cleve drove me in the Escalade to pick up the Saturn. The paint was chipped, the ceiling fabric sank so low it touched my head, and it smelled like mold and cigarettes, but it drove. That's all I'd cared about. I bought it with cash, and after driving it a couple of weeks, the starter began acting up. Some mornings, I couldn't get it to start at all.

"Want another round, ladies?" the TGI Fridays bartender interrupted. I looked at Holly.

"Yep," she said. She looked at me. "You want the same or something else?"

"Same works for me," I said to the bartender, and then looked down at my naked ring finger. "Things aren't great," I said. "The longer I'm gone, the angrier he gets."

Holly put her hand on my knee. Her fingers were long with a French manicure. "You're doing the right thing."

"Well. It feels fucked. On the one hand, he won't answer his phone, but then sometimes I notice his car in the parking lot outside our office. Like, what the fuck?"

"Wait, what?" Holly put down her drink. "Are you safe?"

"I think so," I said, but I wasn't sure. "I don't know, Holly. I haven't heard from him since he helped me with the car. What am I supposed to do? Assume he's planning on going to rehab? Assume he isn't? Do I wait forever?" I took a sip of my bright blue cocktail.

"Have you thought about getting a divorce?" she asked.

I looked at her like she was insane. "No!" I barked, then I sighed. "I mean, I guess sort of. Thinking about it makes me feel sick."

"What if he doesn't go to this therapy thing?"

"I don't . . . I mean, I guess I'd get a divorce." I started to cry.

"You're still so young," Holly tried to assure me. "You're only, like, twenty-four."

I wiped my cheeks. I felt like I was a hundred years old.

That evening I went home feeling buzzed. I filled a pot with salty water, put it on the stove, and lay on the floor. I texted Cleve.

Are you okay? And then, after a few minutes: *Are you giving up on us?*

No response.

Soon after, Cleve was arrested. All his guns, which he'd been keeping in his Escalade for some reason, were stolen. He'd left the doors unlocked. When he reported the incident, he was arrested for unpaid speeding tickets. Carson had to bail him out. The last I'd spoken with Brittany, she'd said she was worried Cleve wasn't paying his mortgage. She said he'd started smoking weed again and had been joking about how he could spend all his money on porn now that I was gone. She said all of this cautiously. She wholeheartedly supported my decision to leave, but she also wanted things to get better. Cleve was her family, too.

Being separated from him left me feeling aimless. I wasn't just heartbroken—my sense of self had been shattered. Even my sense of reality was starting to crack, and I was struggling to keep the pieces together. One minute I loved him more than anything, and the next I loathed him. I felt like I was losing my mind.

Sitting on the floor, I screamed at nothing, "I love you so fucking much!" I punched the carpet with my fists until I couldn't bear the pain in my knuckles. "I hope they fucking break!"

I got off the floor, grabbed my laptop, and went to my room. I shut the door behind me and looked around. I sat on the floor with my legs crossed and typed *Match.com*.

"Fuck!" I slammed the laptop shut and remembered the macaroni and cheese I was going to make. I was hungry, and I still hadn't turned the burner on. I went to the kitchen, turned on the stove, and put my *Yellow Submarine* CD in the boom box. When the macaroni and cheese was done, I sat on my love seat—the only piece of furniture I could afford—eating it out of the pot with a wooden spoon. Mr. Jingles, the Maine Coon mix I had adopted to keep me company, purred in my lap. The apartment was dark except for the bathroom light, which glowed from the hallway. I liked it that way. It was easier to pretend I was somewhere else if I couldn't see what was around me.

"We all live in a yellow submarine, yellow submarine, yellow submarine," I sang. I'd been playing this song repeatedly because it made me feel happy even when I wasn't. Mr. Jingles purred and kneaded my thigh, his claws breaking skin. "Ouch! My dude, you have got to chill," I said, gently pushing him off of me. Though I loved my new cat, I missed how soft and gentle Sophie was. How she always seemed to know when I needed company and had the ability to stare right into my soul. Cleve was keeping her until I could afford a place that would allow me to have a dog.

I stood up and put the pot, still half-full of noodles, on the kitchen bar, turned the music off, and went to my room, Mr. Jingles following. I changed into pajama pants and an oversized T-shirt and sat on the futon mattress I slept on in the center of the floor. I reached for my laptop again. On the screen, Match.com's homepage glared back at me.

19

DON'T LEAVE ME HERE ALONE

February 2010

I followed the man through a maze of bouncing, sweaty bodies. House music blared from four-foot speakers, so we had to scream in each other's ears and use dramatic hand gestures to communicate. As we weaved through the crowd, lights—purple, pink, green, white—flashed across strange faces, glazed eyes, beads of sweat dripping down cheeks, butts grinding, fists pumping, and lips kissing.

We closed the door behind us. The bathroom was small and dingy and covered in graffiti. The man, who wore leather pants, a leather newsboy cap, and a leather vest with chains draped across it, pulled a Ziploc bag out of his pocket, set it on the sink, and began digging through it.

"One or two?" he asked.

"Two, please," I said.

"Fifty bucks, okay?"

"Yep."

I pulled out one of the bills Holly had slipped into my back pocket. I handed it to him.

"Is one enough for the whole night?" I asked.

"More than enough," he assured me. "People don't come to me for nothin'."

I popped one of the pills into my mouth. "Thanks, Cid," I said, and left the bathroom before him.

A drag queen dressed like Rihanna glided across the stage with a sexy femininity I wished I had. The bouncing bodies made it difficult to find Holly, even though she was over six feet tall in heels. After scanning the dance floor, I found her waiting at the bar in the next room, talking to a woman in a white dress.

"Hey. I got the X," I whispered in her ear. It was much quieter in the lounge than it had been on the dance floor. "I just took mine."

"Yes, ma'am!" she squealed. "Where is it?"

I pulled it out of my pocket and handed it to her under the bar. She popped the red pill in her mouth.

"Let's dance," she said with a wink. I didn't love dancing, because I got too in my head, but I figured the drugs would kick in soon. I nodded. She grabbed my hand and pulled me into a sea of light and sound.

The next morning, I woke up on Holly's couch to a text message from a guy I'd met on a dating site. It had been three months since I left, and Cleve still refused to go to rehab. I wasn't handling it well. I was working sixty to eighty hours a week so I could pay my bills. On weekends, I went to the gay club downtown and took every drug I could find, trying to forget the last four years of my life.

I'd become so lonely that I finally made a profile for myself on Match.com. I told myself I'd just put it up and see what happened. Within a day, I had multiple messages. I read them without much interest. Most of them were laughable—dick pics, a man asking if he could pee on me, a shirtless guy who said nothing but "Sup?" But there were a few that seemed nice. I didn't delete those, and after staring at them for a few days, I responded. It seemed innocent enough. As time passed, some of those chats turned to phone calls and then to texts throughout the day. I hated myself for loving the attention, but I craved it. When I was bored, Match gave me someone to talk to. Multiple someones. And all of them took time out of their day to focus on *me*. But I knew they wouldn't want to just talk on the phone forever. Most of them had already asked if I wanted to meet up.

"Go on a date," Holly said. "It's just free food." We were sitting at her table eating breakfast. She took a bite of eggs, and I couldn't help but notice that her cheekbones were starting to look too big for her face. She'd been dating a guy who did meth, and I was starting to get concerned. When I asked about it, she said it was no big deal. But she was rapidly losing weight and had become unreliable at work. Even when we went out, I couldn't depend on her anymore for a place to stay. Sometimes she'd disappear, and I wouldn't see her again until she showed up to work on Monday morning. With time, I saw her less and less.

I called Cleve a few nights later, but he wouldn't pick up. I left a voicemail. "Cleve. Please. I need to know what we're doing. I love you no matter what, but things can't be like this forever. Remember who we are." The last time I'd talked to him, he'd called me crying, begging me to come home. I was tempted, but I'd made my decision, and I wasn't going to budge. When I reminded him he had to go to therapy first, he screamed, "Fuck you!" and hung up.

I gave up hope after a few weeks. I started accepting dates from the Match.com guys. One of them was sweet and would show up to my work with gifts, including a basket full of random small items from World Market. It included an *Amélie* DVD, a bonsai-growing kit, a small gnome figurine, Gouda cheese, and a bottle of Malbec. I imagined him shopping, carefully deciding what to include, and it gave me the good kind of butterflies. It was cute, funny, out of the ordinary. I'd never gotten such a thoughtful present from someone I hardly knew. He wrote me letters and took me camping at his favorite spot by a river. He introduced me to Thai food and sweet tea vodka and portable hammocks you could string up anywhere as long as there were two trees close enough. I liked him a lot, but I wasn't sure why he was interested in me. He was also understandably wary of the fact that I was still married. He had reason to be. As great as this guy was, if Cleve started therapy, I would have chosen him in a heartbeat.

Then there was a cop who was ten years older than me, who would pick me up from the club when I was too fucked-up to get home. He would lecture me in his cop car about how I should care more about myself. He'd say I deserved better than an abusive relationship; he'd tell me how much potential I had. Then he'd insist I stay at his house for the night so I could sober up. He'd urge me to shower to get the grime from the club off of me, and then I'd hear a tap on the shower's glass door and turn around to find him naked and getting in with me. He'd fuck me before the lights and the sounds had a chance to stop spinning around in my head. I knew whatever this was was toxic. It felt like the punishment I deserved to have this man do what he wanted with me. It was humiliating; hooking up with him was my way of expressing to the universe that I just didn't fucking care anymore.

My greatest fear was being alone. Alone, I was drowning in endless space around me. Alone made my skin hurt, made me want to peel it off and maybe, for once, breathe without the weight of a thousand regrets on my chest. I'd never been alone. I didn't know what to do with the silence. My thoughts were enemies, reminders of everything scary in the world. Alone, I kicked and screamed and flailed until someone bigger than me caught me and held me. I hoped eventually someone would catch me and protect me from myself, but I learned quickly that most people are more interested in taking advantage of the weak than they are in protecting them. *I will do anything,* I thought. *Just don't leave me here alone.*

One night in late March, Cleve called as I was getting ready for bed. I spat toothpaste into the sink and answered.

"Hey," I said cautiously. "I didn't think you'd call."

"Baby, I'm sorry," he said. He hadn't called me *baby* in months. "I know I've been a piece of shit and don't deserve you, but I don't want a divorce." His words felt like déjà vu.

"Okay," I said. I was holding back tears. "But I've told you—"

"I know," he interrupted. "I talked to the Wounded Warrior Project. They're gettin' me into this inpatient PTSD program in Texas. It's called Victory somethin'."

"Wait. Really?" I said. I rinsed the toothbrush off and put it on the counter. "You're actually going?"

"Yes. I promise I'll go. I don't want to lose you like this."

I started crying. "Why the fuck did you take so long, Cleve? Why did you do that to me? To us?"

"Please don't cry."

"No, you don't understand. We can't get that time back. Don't you see that? So much damage ha . . ."

He started to cry, too. "Baby, I'm sorry. I'm so sorry."

"It sounds so fucking weird to hear you call me that," I said, pacing from the sink to the bathtub. "What if it's too late, Cleve?"

I was overwhelmed with guilt over how I'd acted over the last three months. *I should have waited,* I thought. I considered confessing—to the partying, to the dates—but I was too afraid of how he'd react. I wasn't even sure I trusted that he would go to the program in Texas. I decided if rehab went well, I'd tell him while he was there so he'd have the support to work through it and decide what he wanted to do. I'd also be safer if he were states away.

I wiped my eyes with the collar of my T-shirt and took a deep breath. "When do you leave?"

"A week, maybe. I told them I was ready ASAP."

"Oh wow. Okay. Okay, good. This is really good. Do you feel good?"

"I don't know how I feel. What if it doesn't work?"

I shook my head. "It has to work. Let's just try to stay positive. Just take it seriously, ya know? Put everything into it," I said. I stopped at the sink and, holding the phone between my ear and shoulder, leaned toward the mirror, examining my face. I had circles under my eyes and the tiniest crow's feet were starting to form. My chin was breaking out. My eyes were bloodshot. I took a deep breath, willing the tears away. The truth was, I was also afraid it wouldn't work. But I had to keep my shit together if Cleve stood a chance. My mood directly affected his, and I knew that. If I wanted him to be positive, I would have to be positive, too.

"Can you come over?" he asked.

I considered the pros and cons for a moment. "I don't think that's a good idea," I decided. I was afraid he would want to kiss me or even have sex, and I didn't want that. I was still afraid of him. What if we fought? I didn't want to ruin the hope we'd found. If inpatient therapy did work, maybe he would come back changed. Softened. It felt safer to wait until then. We could start over with a fresh slate.

On the way to the airport, Cleve drove, Carson sat in the passenger seat, and I sat in the back. Alison Krauss's "Baby, Now That I've Found You" played on the radio, one of our favorites. Otherwise, the car was silent. The two weeks since he'd told me he was going had flown by. I couldn't believe it was already happening.

"Her voice is so damn beautiful," Cleve said, his head swaying from side to side. "Like angels fuckin'."

Carson and I laughed and then went back to silence. When we got to the airport, we decided to park so Carson and I could go into the airport with Cleve. I dragged his suitcase for him out of habit. Carson joked about how he wasn't sure he'd like Cleve without PTSD, said it made him relatable, but that he'd deal. I slapped him on the arm with the back of my hand.

We stood in line with Cleve at the ticketing counter. We walked him to TSA. Carson and Cleve hugged.

"Proud of you, man," Carson said.

Cleve put his hand on Carson's shoulder. "Means a lot, brother." He turned to look at me and put his hands in the air in a half shrug. "Can I have a hug?" he asked.

"Of course," I said, and we hugged for the first time in months. "I love you," I said.

"I love you, too. I'm gonna fix this." He kissed me on the cheek before pulling away.

Carson and I watched as Cleve made his way through TSA. He grabbed his belongings from the belt, put his shoes and backpack on, then turned to wave before disappearing around the corner.

Unlike at the inpatient rehab facility he'd gone to for addiction, Cleve was allowed to keep his phone. He called me after he arrived and told me he was staying at a hotel across the street from the hospital. I expressed my concern—I was under the impression that this was a true inpatient facility where he would be monitored around the clock—but he assured me he'd be fine. I wish I could say I called the program right then and asked questions, but I didn't. And that decision would be one of the greatest regrets of my life.

"Remember that time when we were sixteen, maybe fifteen, and you snuck out to meet me by the church?" Cleve said. He'd been in rehab now for weeks and called every evening. I could tell by the tone of his voice that he was lying down.

I smiled. "Which time?"

"It rained right before I got there. I brought a joint, but you wouldn't smoke it. You had that job at Lambert's and just got off work. You were still wearin' those damn red suspenders."

"Yeah," I said, laughing. "I remember." It was humid that night. The still-wet road had glistened under the light of streetlamps. Moths and mayflies and crane flies spun in mesmerized clouds around the lights. I was afraid I smelled like fried food from work, but Cleve had shown up unannounced and I didn't want to leave him waiting while I washed up and changed.

"Do you know why I wanted to come see you?" he asked.

"No." I remembered wondering why Cleve had come by that night. We didn't hang out much, and when we did it was usually at a house party or school event.

"I heard you were datin' that asshole, Jonathon," he said, referring to the twenty-year-old guy I'd lost my virginity to. "I was worried and wanted to check in. But also . . ." He paused. I waited. "Also, I was jealous. I never got over you after you broke up with me. I kept thinkin' maybe you'd come back around, but then you never did. That night, I was goin' to tell you how I felt. But, I just . . ."

"You never told me anything like that."

"I know. I chickened out. I remember you walkin' up to me. I was waiting for a little while—not too long, though—and then you came around the corner, and you were just so beautiful, and I knew I was goin' to chicken out right then."

"So beautiful in my suspenders? I'm sure," I joked.

"Yes, ma'am. Suspenders and all."

I remembered how seeing him had made me feel: warm, relieved somehow, like finally taking a breath after being held underwater. I loved him as much as I could love anyone back then, but I hadn't been confident enough to tell him that.

"You should've said something," I said. I turned and put my forehead on the cabinets. "I had feelings for you, too."

"Really?"

"Yes. I never stopped. I was just . . . scared."

"Scared of what?"

"I don't know. I hardly ever know what I'm afraid of. I just wander around waiting—knowing something bad is gonna happen. I've lived long enough to know something bad is always coming. You just have to wait long enough. I mean, look at us now. Proof is right here in front of us."

"I don't know if I believe all that. Look at us? We're working through it."

I walked to the living room and curled up in the corner of the love seat. "But is this it? Or will we be working through *it* forever? Does the hard stuff ever end? Will we ever just be happy? Just boring ole happy?" I paused. "Sorry. I'm being negative."

"I'm tryin' to get us there. I'm tryin'," he said. "Things have been goin' real well, I promise. I just feel like I've had some breakthroughs in therapy. I'm figurin' some stuff out. I'm not perfect, and I have a long road ahead of me, but I'm hopeful."

I exhaled. "No, that's good. That's *great*. I'm proud of you. I really am."

"I've had a lot of time to think here. I'm goin' to fight to be good enough for you."

I wanted to believe him, but I'd heard him say that before. "I know. God . . . life hasn't been fair to you. Hell . . . to *us*. What a mess."

"I believe in us."

"Can I be honest without upsetting you?"

"Yeah."

"I want to believe in us, but I have a lot of doubts," I said. Cleve was silent, and I could feel my throat closing up. "Just . . . I just hope you know, no matter how rehab ends and no matter what happens to us, I will never forget who you are at the core. And I will always love that person."

"Please don't give up on me," Cleve pleaded.

"I'm not giving up on you."

20

AMERICAN NIGHTMARE
April 2010

Emily was a flight attendant. She had wavy auburn hair past her shoulder blades and large hazel eyes. She loved her job because it allowed her to travel, but her real passion was writing. She'd started taking an online creative writing course where she was working on a novel based on her life, but she wasn't ready to talk about the details of that with anyone yet. Emily lived alone in an apartment with her cat, Freddie. She had a friend group she adored, including her best friend, Sasha, who she'd grown up with. Her hobbies included camping, traveling, and baking when time permitted. She'd been single for a couple of years. She was so busy with work that she hadn't had much time to date. She wanted to change that, though. At twenty-seven, she was ready to settle down and maybe even start a family. That's why she'd made herself a Match.com profile.

Slumped in my office chair, I sipped my third cup of coffee. Emily looked at me from the computer screen. Her profile picture was pretty and sexy but not overwhelmingly so. It was a selfie taken on a sunny day somewhere with trees. She had a girl-next-door vibe, and that's exactly what I was going for. The other pictures—there were five total—showed her with friends, traveling, at home with her cat. I'd stolen them from someone else's real profile because I needed to be sure they were convincing. I opened my desk drawer, pulled out a tube of mint-flavored ChapStick, smeared it on my mouth, and smacked my lips a few times. I cracked my knuckles. I stared at the ceiling, trying to think of something creative to say to the man who'd just asked Emily about her family. Guys like this annoyed me. Why ask about something so personal over the internet? I sighed. All I needed was a number, and then I could block the dude and add it to my cold-call list. We'd had an influx of twenty-something straight women join our service that month and I needed men to match them with. I sat up in my chair and began typing.

Sounds like a good question for a first date, I responded. I thought about what he might say back. I'd been talking to this guy for days and was ready to get on with it. "Fuck it," I said out loud to myself. To speed up the process, I sent another message. *Can I get your number? We can text about it.*

I hated being the one to ask for a guy's phone number. I preferred they offer it up so that when I blocked them immediately after, they might assume they'd been too presumptuous and scared Emily off. In that case, our salespeople could cold-call them within two weeks, and it was unlikely they'd put two and two together. When I had to ask for it first, the number ended up on my special list titled *Call in Three Months.* Three months, I thought, was plenty of time for the guy to have forgotten about Emily before one of our salespeople called him with their pitch about why he should come in to learn about our matchmaking services.

I stared at the screen, waiting for a response. When my cellphone rang, I looked to see that it was Trent, Fiona's husband, calling. They still lived in Foley and we'd see each other every couple of months. It was odd for him to call me, but I let it go to voicemail. It was eight at night, and I wanted to get my work done so I could go home—no time for distractions. I figured if it was important, Trent would send me a text. Otherwise, I'd call him back in an hour. The cellphone rang again. I sighed and clicked the minimize button on my computer screen to hide the shameful thing I'd been doing. Though everyone in my office knew how we got new folks into our system, I didn't like them knowing anything about the profiles I made. My profiles felt personal. They were alternate identities, pictures of what I wished my life was, who I wanted to be. In a way, I was jealous of Emily. She'd made a successful career out of flight attending, she was independent and content and knew exactly what she wanted. I kept her locked away like a diary.

"Eyo," I said to Trent before wedging the phone between my ear and shoulder. "I was going to call you back aft—"

"Hey, Tang," he interrupted. It was short for Kurtango, a nickname he'd given me years before. "Where are you?"

"Work, as always," I said. I'd stopped partying so hard after Cleve left for Texas, and instead spent most of my time working. It was Tuesday, and I'd already clocked thirty hours that week. "What's up?"

"Are you sitting down?" he said. His voice was shaky. Something was off.

My skin tightened. I leaned back and spun myself in the chair to face my office door. It was cracked open, but I decided it wasn't worth getting up to close. There was no one left at the office anyway. "Yeah. Tell me what's going on. You're freaking me out."

"You haven't seen Facebook or anything?" he said.

"No. Dude, you're scaring me. What the fuck is going on?"

"Goddamn it. I don't know how to tell you . . . I . . . uh . . . fuck . . . My dad wrote on Facebook that Cleve died," he said. The walls began closing around me until everything disappeared except for the phone in my hand. I forgot how to breathe. To speak. Trent went on. "I called him to see why he'd say that, and he said he heard from a cousin. I hadn't heard from you, so I wondered if . . ."

"Stop talking," I said. Tears turned the room into a kaleidoscope. This was a dream. I was dreaming. "Trent. I need you to hang up and call his family right now and make sure this is real before you say another word. Please."

"Anything you need," he said. I gave him the number to Cleve's parents' house—the same one I'd called when I was thirteen. "You're calling now?" I asked.

"Yes. I'll call you back when I know what's going on."

I sat on the floor of my office, waiting. I couldn't think straight—my head was ringing, my skin felt hot and tight, the overhead light grew brighter and brighter, my vision narrowing to a pinpoint. Part

of me knew this couldn't be real, and another part was already grieving. I thought about our phone call the night before. Cleve had
sounded so hopeful. Had I said something wrong? Was I too negative? Could he have killed himself? I pushed the thought out of my
head.

My history with him played in my mind out of order. I thought of
the baby I lost, how I could have had a piece of Cleve forever if she'd
lived. I thought about how he cheated on me before he deployed, and
about how he surprised me with Sophie, and about how he told me
over and over that he'd never loved anyone the way he loved me and
then how he threw my clothes on the lawn and let me leave him. He
just let me fucking leave. And now maybe he was gone forever, and I
thought about the drugs I'd done, the cop I'd slept with. I thought about
all the nights I'd cried myself to sleep, begging God to make me stop
loving him so fucking much. I thought about how both of us had put so
much hope into our future. That was where I knew we'd find our re-
demption. We had time, we thought. We were young, and there was still
time to repair all the damage we'd done.

This can't be it, I said to myself. I started rocking, my knees tucked
into my chest. *This can't be it. This can't be it. This can't be it. They would
have called me,* I thought. But then I remembered Cleve probably put
his mom as his emergency contact again.

What do you call the emotion that is all of the emotions combined?
That was what I was feeling. I rocked and rocked until my mind went
dark.

The phone rang, and I stopped rocking. I pulled my knees tighter
into my chest and stared at it, afraid to move. *He's fine,* I thought. *Trent's
dad is old and misinformed and Cleve is fine.* I picked up the phone.

"Hello," I said. Trent was sobbing. He didn't have to say a word.
"No!" I wailed. I threw the phone out the door. I couldn't stand the feeling of it in my hands. I lay my cheek on the carpet and wept. The rest of
the night is darkness.

A nurse from Project Victory called around noon the next day. After
apologizing for taking so long to get in touch with me, she told me

she'd seen Cleve's body. Her voice quivered. "How detailed would you like me to be, Ms. Kinsey?" she asked.

I wondered if she'd volunteered to call me, or if she'd been made to. I imagined having to make this sort of call, how difficult it must have been for her. "Tell me everything," I said.

What she told me was more baffling than clarifying. He was found on the ground in his hotel room in a pool of blood next to what looked to be a homemade aluminum-foil pipe. There was a tarlike substance in it. He didn't have his prosthetic leg on. It looked like he had hit his head "pretty hard" on a coffee table, but they couldn't be sure if that's what killed him. He was found just after eleven A.M. on April 20, and they estimated his time of death to be around one A.M. She was sorry she didn't have any more details. She wanted to know where she could send flowers.

Cleve's mom and I sat beside each other at the Wolfe-Bayview Funeral Home located less than a mile away from Foley High. I could've left right then. Taken a right out of the funeral home's parking lot, then a left at the Krystal where I ate chicken sandwiches and sipped sweet tea the first time I ever skipped class. I'd pass Walmart on my right, the one where I spent so many nights swinging my legs off the backs of tailgates, smoking cigarettes, and flirting with crushes. Just beyond that, I'd come to a stop sign before crossing the street into the parking lot of a long, rectangular building with a bright blue roof and a *Foley High School* sign out front. I thought of the cafeteria and the time that one kid stood on a table and chugged a gallon of milk before puking it all over the floor, and the hallways lined with blue lockers where I'd found Cleve that one time, crying after he found out his cousin died. The ghosts of our teenage selves were still hugging in that hallway, I just knew it. I wished I could go back in time and warn them. *Don't join the military! Do anything else!*

I had passed that funeral home countless times throughout my life. I had witnessed many processions leaving that gray building's parking lot. I remembered the heaviness of those strangers' grief, the sinking chest feeling that lasted no longer than it took for the light to turn green. Never once did I imagine that one day I'd be inside that building, sitting next to my mother-in-law, planning my husband's funeral only days after his death.

My relationship with Cleve's mom had never fully healed. She was still upset that Cleve and I had eloped, still thought I did not fit well into her family, still wished he'd married Lisa. The table we sat at looked like something meant for a boardroom. The ceiling was adorned with shiny gold light fixtures, and the windows were dressed in gaudy curtains with ruffles at the edges. We both wore short sleeves, and our shoulders were touching, skin against uncomfortable skin. I wanted to move, but my body was frozen. I hoped she would move first. She didn't.

Cleve's dad sat across from us, wearing a houndstooth Alabama hat that matched the one Cleve often wore. His head hung, his thin arms pulled into his body. His dad always looked as if he'd worked hard his entire life—skin like tanned leather, underweight enough that his head looked a bit too big for his body, creases in his face that made him look perpetually stressed. Like Cleve's, his eyes were warm and optimistic. Even after everything he'd been through, he still believed that hard work paid off. But that day, the sparkle in his eyes had dulled. Jimmy Sr. had worked his entire life for the American Dream, and there he sat, defeated, waiting to plan his eldest son's funeral.

On the other side of me, Fiona sat with perfect posture. She wore a black top I'd given her a few years before because it no longer fit me. She'd straightened her black hair, slicked it into a ponytail, and painted her lips red. Bold lipstick for Fiona was confidence in a tube—her secret weapon. She didn't need a reason to wear it other than to add a little color to her day.

Everyone was so quiet. When no one else was watching, I shot Fiona a quick look I knew she'd recognize meant *Get me out of here.* She forced a fake smile, wiped tears from her eyes, and squeezed my hand twice. Fiona had hardly had a chance to grieve because she was too busy making sure I was okay. The day before, she'd brought me a cup of Earl Grey tea with honey and insisted on going to the funeral home with me. My parents weren't sure they would make it to Alabama before the funeral, and I was anxious about planning it with Cleve's family. "I'm not letting you do this shit alone," Fiona had said. I was relieved not to have to do the "Are you sure?" dance with her. When I thanked her, she said, "Girl, I got you."

The door behind Jimmy opened, and a man in an ill-fitting gray suit with a manila folder tucked under his arm walked through. He moved too quickly for a room thick with grief. Fiona squeezed my hand again and looked at me from the corner of her eye.

"Good afternoon," the man said. He sat at the end of the table, the king of the funeral home. "I'm very sorry for your loss." His eyes darted to each of ours before looking down at his folder. Cleve's dad was the only one to respond verbally. The rest of us just nodded.

"Thank you, sir. I think we're all still in shock," Jimmy said.

"I know it's so hard to bury a loved one," the man said.

Cleve's mom looked up. "Our son," she said. "He was our oldest son."

The man cleared his throat. "Yes, ma'am," he said. "My sincere condolences."

There was an awkward pause, and then the man began pulling paperwork out of the folder. He looked at Fiona and then at me.

"Who is Jimmy's wife?" he asked.

"Cleve," I responded. "He has the same name as his dad, so we call him . . . called him . . . Cleve."

"So sorry," he said as he scribbled something onto the paperwork in front of him.

"This is his wife," Cleve's mom said, putting her arm around my shoulders in a half hug. "Karie."

I wondered if the hug meant something. Was she finally going to call a truce? The man turned his attention to me.

"Ms. Kinsey, have you thought about the kind of funeral you'd like to have for . . ." He looked down at his notes and then back up. "Cleve?"

"Uh, I mean"—I could feel my face turning red, could feel the tears forcing their way out—"not really? I . . . he said he wanted a wood casket once and said he wanted to be buried in his hometown."

"We bought the plot already," his dad interrupted.

"You did?" I said, shocked. "When?"

"We called them yesterday," his mom said. "He has to be with the family."

"Right," I said. I agreed he needed to be in the same graveyard as his family, but I didn't understand why nobody had talked to me about it. I didn't know where I wanted his plot to be, but I knew I wanted a say in it. I wondered if I could be buried next to him when my time came, if that's what I wanted. I was afraid to ask. I assumed his parents wouldn't want me buried next to their family, but I didn't want to hear them say it out loud. Their rejection of me over the years was salt in wounds I'd carried since childhood. Now, I was a twenty-four-year-old widow. I needed mothering, but the only mother around merely tolerated my presence. Rather than cry about it, I told myself lies: *I don't care about them. I don't need their approval. I don't fucking like them, anyway.*

The funeral director stood up. "How about we look at some caskets?" he said. He led us to a much smaller room attached to the boardroom. The walls were beige, which was hardly noticeable, because they were lined floor to ceiling with caskets. There were metal caskets, wooden caskets, blue caskets, white caskets, brown ones, all packed so tightly into the room that the only space left was a short maze just wide enough for an average-sized person to navigate their way comfortably through them. Not one casket had a price tag.

"Take a look around and see if there's anything you like," he said.

"Okay." My voice cracked.

Jimmy stopped in front of a baby-blue metal one with a soft ivory interior. At the back was an ivory insert with bluebirds holding a blue ribbon embroidered on it. "I like this one," he said. "I like it a lot."

"Oh God, no," I blurted out. The words had pushed their way to my mouth like vomit. I instantly regretted it. It looked like something built for a child, and I couldn't imagine a grown man's body lying in it.

"Sorry. That one's really nice," I lied. "I just . . . Cleve said he wanted a wood one once, and I can't get that out of my head." It was a weird fact that I'd held on to since he'd first overdosed. Shortly after, we discussed our wishes after death, just in case. He didn't want much, but what he did want was specific. "I was thinking we could add this insert, too," I said, picking up one with an eagle, globe, and anchor embroidered on it from a pile on the floor. I held it up to the back of a chestnut-colored casket. "I just think this looks so good. This one looks really soft, too," I said as I rubbed the cream-colored interior. "I think he'd like it. I think it would look sharp with his dress blues."

His dad gazed at the blue casket for a moment, almost longingly, before making his way to the one I liked. He ran his hand across the length of it, then stopped to look it over, stroking his mustache with his thumb and forefinger. He pressed down on the interior to test its softness. "Yeah," he said. "I think you're right. This is a good one. Whatcha think, Penny?"

Cleve's mom walked over to us and stared at the empty box, her arms stiffly folded. "Guess it doesn't matter what we choose now, does it?" she said.

I wanted to respond with something comforting, but there was nothing there.

"Sir," I called to the funeral director, who was in the next room. I'd forgotten his name.

"Yes, ma'am," he said, rushing toward me.

"How much is this one?"

"Let me see," he said, flipping through stapled paperwork. "That one is just under three thousand dollars."

Penny gasped. "How are we supposed to pay for this?" she said.

"The military is supposed to," I said, even though I wasn't sure what the military would do for someone who'd medically retired and then died. The casket price made me feel ill, but I didn't want to spend all day budgeting for a funeral. I just wanted to get what felt right and get the fuck out of there. I also didn't want his parents to worry about finances.

"I think that's how it works, anyway. Either way, this is my responsibility, and I'll handle it." I turned to the funeral director. "We'll just take this one with this Marine Corps insert."

We followed the man back to the boardroom and spent an hour writing an obituary we could all agree on. The final product came to 209 words at $1.20 a word. By the time we were ready to leave, the cost of the funeral was more than twelve grand. It seemed outrageous. I wasn't even sure what I was paying for. But I was too heartbroken and exhausted to fight it.

"It's fine," I assured his parents, even though I only had a few hundred dollars in my bank account. "I'll figure it out."

The next day, I went to Target with Fiona to find something to wear to the funeral. I told her my size, and we pulled anything black for me to try on.

"I feel like Miranda looking for a shitty black dress," I said, referring to the *Sex and the City* episode where Miranda's mom dies. "I don't want to fucking be here."

Fiona rubbed my arm. "Let's just get this shit over with," she said. "Here." She handed me a pile of black clothing. "Something in here will fit."

The first thing I tried on was a black short-sleeved cowl-neck sweater and some ill-fitting black slacks that hit above my ankles. I pulled my Wayfarer sunglasses from my purse, put them on, and stared at myself in the mirror. *Wow,* I thought. *I look like shit.*

"Just gonna go with this," I said to Fiona, who was sitting on a bench in the waiting area of the dressing room.

"Do you want my opinion?"

"Nah," I said as I checked out my ass, which looked flat and uncomfortable. "It's like . . . if Kate Gosselin and Johnny Cash had a baby, then one of them died, and the baby had to go to their funeral. I think this is what the baby would wear."

Fiona laughed. "What the fuck, Karie. That is so specific."

"It looks like shit," I said with a shrug. "But I feel like shit, so it's perfect."

At the checkout counter, I stared at the cashier's hands as she rang up the clothing. Everything else seemed to disappear. It was just me and her hands and the voice in my head asking unanswerable questions. *Why is this happening? Is this real? Where am I? What if I run away? What if I burn this store down? What if I die?*

"Ma'am?" a woman's voice echoed. "Ma'am?"

I looked up. It was the cashier. She wanted money. My card. I pulled my bank card from my purse.

"Sorry," I said and then swiped it. She handed me the receipt, and as I walked toward the door, I began to sob. I'd been holding it in for two days and my body couldn't take it anymore.

"Hey, girl. You okay?" Fiona asked. I nodded. I couldn't make words.

In the car, I beat the steering wheel with the palm of my hand.

"No. No, I'm not okay. Fuck!" Fiona nodded but didn't say anything. Sometimes no words are the right words, and I could tell she knew this was one of those times. "Do you have time to go to Gulf Shores?"

"Today is your day."

"Thank you," I said. I wiped my eyes and started the car.

I stopped at the first tattoo shop that didn't look sketchy. Inside was a small waiting area where a man with jet-black hair and tattoo sleeves sat behind a partition. A large sign behind him read *Gulf Shores First and Finest*.

"Can I help you?" the man asked. Tattoo machines buzzed in the back room. Someone was playing "One" by Metallica.

"I want a small tattoo. Is anyone available now? It's super small," I said. I didn't want to wait. I needed to feel something other than grief and anger, and I needed it right then. If I couldn't get a tattoo, then I would go somewhere and pound a few shots or find some drugs or, fuck, anything. I would take anything.

"I have an hour or so. Whatcha need?"

I held up my left hand. "A red heart on my ring finger." I wanted something permanent that nobody and nothing could take away from me.

"Oh, that's nothin'. Fifty bucks work for you?"

"That's fine," I said.

"Well then, my ladies. Follow me. My name's Magic Mike."

Magic fucking Mike, I thought. I bit my lip to keep from laughing. I looked at Fiona from the corner of my eye and could tell she was holding in a laugh, too. His chair creaked as he got up. I followed him down a short hallway and into a room that smelled vaguely of cigarettes. "Have a seat," he said, patting the top of a black chair in the center of the room.

It didn't take long for him to do whatever he was doing, and then he was sitting next to me on a black leather stool with wheels. Fiona sat on another stool on the opposite side of him.

"What's this for?" he asked.

I debated whether I should tell him the truth or make something up.

"It's for my husband," I said, hoping he wouldn't ask any more questions. Fiona squeezed my hand.

"Okay, okay. You must really love the guy. Does he know you're getting it, or is it a surprise?"

I sighed. "He died last week."

"Shit. Oh shit. I'm so sorry for your loss."

"It's fine," I said because I didn't know what else to say.

Magic Mike said "Damn" under his breath, and then the machine started buzzing. I closed my eyes, exhaled, and lost myself in the burn.

21

EVERY GOOD AND TERRIBLE THING

April 24, 2010

I sat on the floor of Cleve's childhood home, looking through photos. His mom wanted to hang posters on either side of his casket, and she'd asked if I wanted to help. I pulled a photo of Cleve as a baby from a tin box. In it, he wore nothing but a diaper and stood on all fours as if he were in mid-crawl across the same green shag carpet I was sitting on. In twenty-five years, the trailer hadn't changed except for serious aging—same wood paneling, same layout, family photos lovingly hung on the walls. But now, there were holes in the floor covered by rugs, the front door looked like it had been shredded, the deck was falling apart, and it smelled of cheap cigarettes from the many years Cleve's dad had smoked inside.

"I like this one," I said, handing the photo to Penny. She nodded and placed it on the white poster board she'd picked up from Dollar General, moving it around the other pictures until she found the perfect spot.

"What's goin' to happen to all his stuff?" I heard Cleve's youngest brother, Daniel, say behind me. I turned around to look at him.

"What stuff?" I asked.

"All them DVDs and games and stuff he has in Birmingham." Daniel was sixteen years old and six foot two, almost as tall as Cleve. He sat at the top of the couch, his feet on the cushions. "Who's gettin' the Mustang?"

My chest burned. It had been days since Cleve died, and I wasn't ready to talk about divvying up his belongings. Too uncomfortable in their home to respond, I looked at Cleve's mom, hoping she would tell him that Cleve's things were my things, too. They were our things, things we'd collected together throughout our marriage.

"We can discuss it after the funeral," she said, and my heart sank.

Later, a man in a strange black suit with a white square at the neck met with Cleve's parents and me in their front yard. We sat around a weather-worn picnic table under the shade of oak and pine trees. I sat across from the man in the suit with my hands in my lap, picking my cuticles. As he talked, I looked past him to dozens of kittens scurrying over a pile of cat food Cleve's mom had dumped into the yard earlier that morning. Stray cats had overrun their property for as long as I could remember. They kept showing up pregnant at their doorstep, and Penny didn't know what to do with them besides feed them. A small tabby with fur so fine it reminded me of a baby bird's feathers sat in a patch of dirt near my feet. It looked up at me with one eye sealed shut. One of its ears looked like the tip had been chewed off, and patches of fur were missing. It meowed, and I ignored it, and then it meowed again, so I reached down to pet its head. Its skin felt gritty. I wondered if it was fleas.

The man continued to talk about God and the Bible and how Cleve was in heaven now. I thought of my childhood. I'd been taught that if there were a heaven, which I wasn't so sure of anymore, Cleve would have had to work much harder than he had to get there. People who went to heaven didn't cheat, didn't do drugs, didn't abuse people, didn't spend all their money on porn. Hell, I was taught drinking, sex before marriage, and even masturbation were tickets to hell. Cleve and I had never gone to church together. We'd never owned a Bible besides the one he'd been given as a teen that we'd kept in storage our entire marriage. We weren't even sure if Cleve had committed suicide or if he'd died of an overdose. If his death had been a suicide, I was pretty sure that guaranteed hell, too.

I was too raw, too stunned, to be angry with Cleve about any of it. I'd sinned, too. If he was going to hell, I was going with him. Everyone at that table was, I was certain. What I was mad about was that everyone was pretending he had been perfect. Since his death, his family had been working overtime to scrub him clean of all the unpleasant things he'd done before they would have to bury him.

"He carried his Bible with him always," his dad said.

I guffawed. The "ha!" just sort of fell out of me. I looked at his dad, visibly confused, waiting for him to take back what he'd said, but everyone just sat there looking at me like the asshole I was, as the preacher or pastor or priest—whatever he was—wrote down the lie. I wanted to say that Cleve believed there was a God and loved Him, but he was so preoccupied with all the bullshit he'd been dealt in life that he had difficulty finding time for Him. I wanted to say that God had betrayed him. I wanted to say fuck God, grab a fucking kitten, and leave. The funeral was starting to feel like more than just burying Cleve's body. It felt like burying the truth of who he was. I wanted to remember every good and terrible thing about him. I wanted to laugh and cry and scream over the loss of him—every single bit of him—with everyone else who'd loved him exactly as he was. I wanted to stand on the table and scream, *What the fuck are we doing?* Instead, I went back to picking my cuticles and tuned out. I watched cats on a hill of cheap cat food, and I dug the tip of my shoe into the cold dirt beneath the rotting picnic table, and I pretended I was in a glass case, separated from the rest of the world, protected from it, too. Every detail of this funeral made me uncomfortable—all of it felt entirely out of my control and wrong—but I let it go because Cleve was dead, and none of this shit mattered anymore.

On April 26, 2010, I sat in the back room of the funeral home, waiting for the service to begin. Someone, I wasn't sure who, had gotten me a Frisco Burger meal from Hardee's, and I was eating it as quickly as I could. We'd gotten there just after noon to prepare for the service. Folks were supposed to arrive at two, but it was one-thirty and people were already showing up.

Lopez, the Marine who'd befriended us at Walter Reed and helped coordinate our trip to Vegas, had medically retired since I'd last seen him. He wore his dress blues and stood next to me, nearly at attention, staring into the distance as if that was his duty. The day before, after he'd arrived from California, his home state, he asked if there was anything he could do to make the day easier for me. I asked for two things: that he look over Cleve's body to make sure his uniform was correct and that he keep strangers from touching me. He'd already gone to check Cleve and he assured me the medals were correct and that his makeup wasn't terrible.

"I won't lie," he said. "Our man's looked better. But they did a good job. His uniform is sharp."

"Thank you," I said. "I just couldn't do it."

I'd never been more afraid than I was of Cleve's dead body. It had been six days since his death, and I'd managed to mostly keep myself composed. But I knew that once I saw him lying there lifeless, there would be no way to convince myself ever again that everything was fine; there would be no coming back from the truth of his death. I couldn't imagine surviving it. I knew there was no reality in which I would walk away from him as the same person. The only thing scarier than seeing my dead husband was meeting the monster I was sure I would become after witnessing it.

"I know," Lopez said. "That's what I'm here for."

At two p.m., I emerged from the back room surrounded by some of Cleve's and my closest friends. I wished my parents could have been there, but they couldn't make it. My dad said he couldn't cancel appointments. Mom planned to fly to Birmingham when I was ready to begin organizing and packing our things. I was upset that they weren't trying harder to be there. I suspected it was because they didn't like Cleve and they had never taken our relationship very seriously. Or maybe it was work; I couldn't know for sure. What I did know was that it hurt.

The lobby was full of chatter turned white noise. Strange faces. Looks of pity directed at me. The funeral director announced that everyone should get in a line in front of the door to the viewing room. He offered to let me and my friends go in first, but I said no. I wasn't sure I was going to go in at all. As people filed in, the sound of women wailing echoed through the building. I watched as people entered dry-faced and composed and exited with mascara running down their cheeks, their bodies curled into themselves.

"I'm sorry," they'd say as they passed me and then made their way to the chapel. "He will be so missed," they'd say. "I can't believe he's gone," they'd cry. "Why him? Why him? He was too young. He was a hero. A real hero."

The line grew shorter and shorter, and I sat on the floor in the lobby with my legs crossed, questioning whether I was making the right decision. I tugged on Lopez's pant leg, and he knelt next to me.

"I think I have to go in there," I said.

"Do you want me to come with you?"

"Yes, please. You and Brittany and Fiona."

"I'll go tell the director," he said, and as he walked away, I felt a little less safe and wished someone else had gone instead.

"Hey, Brittany," I said, still sitting on the ground. She was very pregnant with her second son, her stomach swollen. I was with her the day she took the pregnancy test. She'd collapsed on her kitchen floor in tears. It was unexpected, and she was scared. She and Carson hadn't been doing well. It was bad enough that she'd been considering divorce. But she couldn't imagine being the single mom of two kids.

"Hey," she said in a careful tone. "What's up?"

"Will you go in there with me?" I asked. She'd already gone with Carson, and I felt bad asking her to go again.

"Of course," she said. "You sure this is what you want to do?"

"Yeah. I'll always wonder," I said. "Can you find Fiona and ask her if she'll go, too?" I assumed she was in the line somewhere or maybe looking at Cleve as we spoke.

"Yeah, I'll go find her." She put her hand on her hip and made her way through the crowd.

Cleve's nose was the first thing I saw when I walked into the viewing room. The familiar curve of it extended above the sides of the casket. My legs went limp, and I fell to the ground. Lopez knelt and wrapped his arms around me as I cried. Fiona and Brittany held each other be-hind me.

"I'm sorry," he said. "I'm so sorry."

I willed myself to get up and, gripping Lopez's arm, inched toward Cleve's body. I stopped a foot away. The sight of him—makeup-caked skin, chin pressed unnaturally to his chest, his hands purple-tinged marble folded at his waist—turned my insides from searing lava to cold, hard stone. All at once, I wanted to puke and run away and crawl into the casket with him and take a sledgehammer to the walls of the funeral home and scream and cry and bury myself in the deepest, dankest hole. My brain felt like it was glitching, unable to compute. What was in front of me couldn't possibly be real. What was this monstrous, lifeless thing? *Who are you? Who am I? What have we done?* I couldn't touch him. I could only turn and walk away one last time.

Hours later, I sat in a metal foldout chair in front of a hole in the ground. Lopez and a volunteer from Pensacola Air Station lifted the flag from the top of Cleve's casket, which hovered over the hole. Care-fully, they folded it like origami into a perfect triangle. Lopez walked over to me and said with tears in his eyes, "On behalf of the president of the United States, the United States Marine Corps, and a grateful nation, please accept this flag as a symbol of our appreciation for your loved one's honorable and faithful service." He leaned over to hand me the flag and whispered in my ear, "He died a hero, and he will be missed."

That night, I went with our friends to a bar on the beach because we didn't know what else to do but get drunk. I was sipping a margarita, watching my friends laugh and cry and dance, when I overheard some-one next to me talking to the bartender about an oil spill.

"Excuse me?" I said, waving her down. "Hey. There was an oil spill?"

"Yeah, you haven't heard about it?" She dried a wineglass with a towel and hung it above the bar. "It was horrible. Oil's still just, like, gushing into the water. A buncha people died."

"What the fuck? When?" I asked.

"The twentieth, I think. I can't believe you haven't heard about it. Everyone's talking about it. Are you from here?"

"Yeah." I paused. I didn't know how to tell her why I hadn't been paying attention to the news. "Um . . . my husband died that day, so I . . ."

"Oh my God, I am so sorry."

"No, don't be. It's fine."

"No, it's not," she said, shaking her head. "What was his favorite liquor?"

"Crown Royal."

She poured Crown into a shot glass and then pushed it across the bar toward me. "Here. On me," she said. "May he rest in peace."

V

Forests may be gorgeous
but there is nothing more alive
than a tree that learns
how to grow in a cemetery.

—ANDREA GIBSON, Twitter

22

FOREVER CHANGED LANDSCAPE

End of April 2010

The folks at Project Victory sent a box filled with Cleve's belongings. It arrived a few days after the funeral. I had it sent to my office because, once again, I wasn't sure where home was anymore. I sat on my office floor looking through it. A bottle of Yves Saint Laurent L'Homme, the cologne we discovered at the Navy Exchange on Bethesda Naval Base. Cleve's prosthetic leg, his favorite Converse shoe attached to the foot; its match was missing. A houndstooth Alabama hat. Some clothes. His wallet. His cellphone. I turned it on to look for clues. Maybe he called someone after we talked. Maybe he sent someone a suicide note. I checked recent calls. *Karie,* it said. He'd called just before seven P.M. the night he died and we talked for almost an hour. I looked at his messages. *Karie* and then *Mama* just under it. The remaining texts were from earlier in the week. I knew what we had texted. I'd analyzed every word since he died. So I skipped our messages and checked what he'd sent to his mom. There was nothing of note. Casual chitchat. Him checking in. I expected as much. Had she gotten anything that could explain what happened that night, I would've known about it.

My boss peeked into my office. I was despondent, and he'd been tiptoeing around me, probably wondering why I didn't wait until I got home to open the box. But I needed to know what was left of Cleve—what had been in the same room with him when he took his last breath—and I needed to know right then. To wait for anything was to risk losing everything. I knew that now. When Cleve died, there was a shift. The concept of waiting, of being patient, had seemed so simple before. Not any longer. Where once I thought we had time to figure things out, now I knew there would never be enough of it. I'd been told my whole life that time was on my side, and I'd been lied to. I saw it now for what it was: time was amorphous, fluid, a thing without beginning or end, a thing that had the power to speed up or stop, a thing I could neither grasp nor control. Time had betrayed me, and I no longer trusted it would be there. Everything was urgent. Everything had to be done immediately. I put Cleve's belongings back into the box, stood up, and told my boss that I quit. I didn't care about money or what would happen to me. I just knew there was no way in hell I could continue working at a place like that after experiencing something as life-altering as this.

I didn't want to be alone, so I stayed with Fiona and Trent, where I slept most of the day except to eat and practice guitar. I had Sophie, who'd been with Cleve's mom, back with me, and she'd stay up letting me pet her soft ears. In the evenings, Trent taught me chords. Fiona, Trent, and I would sit cross-legged in a circle on the floor with cheap beers next to us and nag champa burning. Trent would show me where to put my fingers, and I'd strum. I found the practice soothing. I found their apartment soothing. Unlike me, who'd moved so many times and had whittled my belongings down to a few boxes, Fiona kept anything that held a happy memory. On every surface of their home was a knick-knack or a photo that meant something to her. The couch was draped with cozy blankets crocheted by family members, her laptop rested on a pillow tray Trent had made her for her birthday, and in the corner of the kitchen, a goldfish they'd won at the state fair stared at us with bulging eyes. This was my safe space. They accepted me as I was. They didn't ask questions or expect me to do anything in return for my spot on the couch. They simply gave me a place to be and grieve. I loved them for this. Food, music, and a comfortable place to rest, I learned, are the best things that you can gift someone grieving.

By the first week of May, I knew I had to go back to Birmingham. I went to the house first. It smelled musty, like cleaner hadn't been used in ages. The wood floors at the entrance had footprints leading to the living room, where they ended at the carpet. The living room had clothes on the floor and draped across the back of the couch. The coffee table was covered in gun and car magazines, a glass half-full of syrupy liquid, a pipe with a bowl of half-smoked weed, and various random junk. The table was filmy with dust. I sat on the couch and picked up the pipe, poking the contents of the bowl with my pinkie, searching for mold or drugs other than weed. I decided it was safe and used the lighter lying beside it to take a hit. I'd never liked marijuana much. I'd always preferred uppers. But I knew being high would be more pleasant than the hollowed-out feeling I carried as I navigated our war-torn home. So much hope had gone into it, and now it was nothing but a giant reminder of my failure. I wished I could burn it to the ground.

I couldn't afford to keep the house on my own. I needed to go through our belongings, decide what to do with them, and figure out where I would store what I kept. Cleve's family had asked again about his things. Unable to hide my disgust, I'd reminded them that his things were my things and that I would be the one to decide what to do with them. His mom wasn't pleased, and our relationship slid back to where it had been when we first met in Bethesda. I had hoped his death would show her we had more in common than not. That it would show her we were, in fact, family. I had hoped we could continue to mend our relationship and maybe even lean on each other for support. I had been very naïve, and my heart broke just a little more every time we interacted. To make things even more complicated, his mom was the executor of the estate.

Cleve and I had updated his will while at Bethesda. All of the families at Bethesda were instructed, one day, to sit in an auditorium-style room and wait for someone with a clipboard to help us update any information that needed it. Cleve transferred his life insurance and other after-life benefits to me and made a new will that included me, making me executor of his estate. Naïve twenty-somethings that we were, we never made a copy of it. After he retired, the military destroyed any documents they didn't need, including the will. I knew this, because I called about it after being told his mom had an age-yellowed copy of the will he'd made when he first enlisted, well before we reunited on Myspace. That old version of the will listed her as executor of the estate. Bank accounts, car titles, and possessions were legally mine, but it was her job to make sure they got to me. When she asked me if their family could come to our home to shop our things and I said no, she refused to release a couple of bank accounts that equaled just over three thousand dollars. I didn't get the sense that she wanted the money for herself. I'm sure she knew it wasn't legally hers. But she never handed it over. She was grieving. She needed someone to take it out on. What mother wouldn't? I just happened to be standing in the way.

Exhaustion trumped anger. In the end, I let the bank accounts go and decided to give his Mustangs to his family. They'd been keeping one of them since his second deployment and the other since he left for PTSD therapy. Though at first I considered fighting to get one of them back—they were the only cars we had paid off besides my Saturn, which was starting to smoke—I ultimately decided it wasn't worth it. I would have to get a lawyer. I would have to take them to court. I didn't have the money for it. I didn't have the stomach for it. I had no interest in fighting. Instead, I filled a box with Cleve's personal items. Despite everything, I couldn't imagine what it must be like to bury your own child. My plan was to fill the box, leave it on their porch the next time I was in Foley, and never see them again.

The day after I came home, my mom flew in from Alaska to help me get organized. When I picked her up from the airport Arrivals line, she waved enthusiastically, her arm clear over her head, and smiled in an almost childlike way. I noticed how much she'd aged and was hit with a moment of grief over all the lost time between us. Her eyes and the corners of her mouth were creased, her cheeks had given in to gravity. She'd finally let her hair go gray but had cut it so short it was nearly buzzed. I imagined she'd had a panic attack before the trip, and to regain control, she found the kitchen scissors and started cutting her hair, something she'd done my whole life. Unable to get it perfect, she cut more and more and more until it was too short to continue unless she wanted to be bald. The short gray hair looked good on her. Combined with the oversized artisan-made earrings, bohemian dress, and brightly colored glasses she wore, she looked artistic, or "artsy-fartsy," as she would say. Her hair looked purposeful. But I knew her well enough to know she was probably ashamed of it. I, however, thought that she had always been beautiful, and this was no different. Even with age, that beauty shined through. I wondered if I'd age as gracefully as her.

I popped the trunk of the Escalade and got out to help her with her luggage.

"Hey, Mom," I said.

"Hey, baby." I could tell she was holding back tears. We hugged, and I nearly wept at the scent of her perfume.

"Here," I said, picking up her bags. "I'll get these."

When we arrived at the house, I warned her before going in that it was dirty. I hadn't cleaned anything yet. Whatever I moved could never go back to how he left it. So, I slept among Cleve's clutter—his clothes at the foot of the bed, a chip bag on the nightstand, a porn magazine on the floor—and waited for my mother to help me. Though I did hide the magazine before she arrived.

Mom always joked that she might not be good at much, but she was good at organizing. And when she puts her mind to getting anything done, she does it quickly and efficiently. The morning after she arrived, I woke up to the scent of cleaning supplies and a sparkling kitchen. She'd pulled out large black trash bags and laid them on the living room floor.

"One of those is for keep, and one is for toss," she said as she wiped down the refrigerator. When she cleaned, she did it frantically. When I was younger, she would even clean while on the toilet. She didn't like wasting time. "We can go through the keep bag later. For now, let's just get it out of the way."

"Okay," I said. I felt a little sick, wondering what she'd already moved. It wasn't even eight A.M. and tiny pieces of Cleve's existence had already been scrubbed away. I knew I was supposed to be grateful. I knew this was the point of her being here, and it needed to be done. So I took a deep breath. "Can we eat first?"

"Sure, honey," she said. She put the rag down. "What can I make you?"

The next day, a gray-haired volunteer from Montgomery sat with me on the floor of my living room, helping me fill out paperwork for survivor benefits. I didn't know who sent him; he just called one day and asked when a good time would be for him to visit. He told me I'd get two thousand dollars for the funeral. I'd already gotten a bill for over twelve thousand dollars in the mail. It was in a landfill now, and that's where I planned to file away every bill I got from them for the rest of eternity. The man said I might get monthly annuities, depending on how Cleve died. It had to be considered service-connected by the military. Because Cleve died stateside, and I wasn't sure yet of the cause, there was no way of knowing. I would just have to wait. First, for the autopsy report to get a death certificate. Then, after filing the death certificate with the military, I would have to wait for their judgment. The volunteer said if it did end up being deemed service-connected, I'd also get life insurance money. But only if Cleve had opted to extend coverage when he retired. I wouldn't know if he had until all of the paperwork was submitted and processed. The man gave me an address to send it all to. I thanked him, but I wasn't feeling hopeful. I assumed I wouldn't get any of it. Nothing had worked in my favor so far; there was no reason to assume it ever would.

I felt conflicted about receiving benefits, anyway. Our relationship wasn't exactly healthy when Cleve died. I wasn't the kind of military widow Americans liked to imagine. Though, one could argue, he wasn't the kind of hero they liked to imagine, either. When I expressed my concern to the man, he reminded me that most people have time to repair their relationships. We were young, he said, and marriage is hard, but that didn't change the fact that we were, in fact, married.

"Take what you can get," Mom advised from the kitchen bar, where she was eating a sandwich and eavesdropping.

"Mother, please," I said.

"Honey, you two were put through hell. You were part of that. Those assholes owe you." She hardly ever cussed and you could tell she wasn't totally comfortable doing it. But it was her way of letting me know that she felt strongly, that she was on my side.

"Mom! Can you just . . ." I mimed zipping my mouth shut.

"Well . . ." She raised her eyebrows, shrugged, and took a bite of her sandwich.

The word *benefits* didn't sit right with me, either. It sounded as if the check I'd get in the mail each month was something worth trading Cleve's life for. I imagined an infomercial with a fast-talking man and a big head saying, *All you have to do is bury your husband, and the benefits are huge! Thirteen hundred dollars a month! A school scholarship! On-base privileges! Call 1-800-Ded-Hubs and get all this delivered straight to you today!* It felt fucking gross. It felt like blood money.

Mom was only in town for a few more days, but that's all it took for her to get the house back to living condition. It seemed like that was her main concern, which was helpful, but I was surprised by how alone it made me feel.

"I can't let my daughter live in filth," she said repeatedly.

She was so concerned with cleaning the house that it was difficult to know if she understood that I was grieving. She had hardly mentioned Cleve's death at all. It was as if that fact was only a small detail of the visit. I waited for her to ask about the funeral or say she was sorry she'd missed it, but the apology never came.

When I would break down, unable to decide what to keep and what to toss, she would hug me and tell me it was okay, then say something that was meant to be comforting but wasn't.

"You're young, sweetie. You have your whole life ahead of you," she'd say. I'd tell her I didn't care and remind her I just buried my husband.

"Well, I'm just glad he didn't kill you first," she'd say, shaking her head, her cheeks pink with anxiety. I'd known she didn't like him. And though I understood why, it bothered me that she couldn't let it go—he was very much not a threat anymore. I just needed her to be my mother, to tell me she saw my pain, and to hold me as long as it took for that pain to go away. I endured the passive-aggressive comments about Cleve in a quiet rage, stuffing things into bags and wishing I could have the house to myself again.

That weekend, Mom flew back to Alaska and Carson met me in my garage with a bottle of cheap tequila, ready to help me go through the rest of Cleve's and my things. When he arrived, he stood in the driveway and held the bottle in the air with a huge grin.

"You ready for this shit?" he said.

For him, the cheap liquor added levity to an otherwise depressing situation. He could have afforded something nicer, but what's the fun in that? We passed the bottle back and forth, wincing with each sip, then split up and started ripping open boxes to see what they contained. Carson laughed to himself as he rifled through a large box in the corner.

"You keeping this?" he asked with a shit-eating grin. I walked over to see what it was and found the sex swing Cleve had purchased and surprised me with when we first moved to the house. It was typical for Cleve to surprise me with gifts that were actually for him. The sex swing was very optimistic of him, considering how our last year had gone. He had lots of plans for it. I promised him that once all the boxes from the move were unpacked and our belongings put away, we would maybe install it, and maybe, if I was really very drunk and feeling generous, we could possibly use it. We never got to all the boxes. We never really had sex, anyway.

"Oh my God, stop," I said to Carson. I threw a combat boot at him. "Burn it!"

By the time the sun had set, Carson and I were drunk and sitting on the garage floor, digging through a box of Cleve's pictures and letters. Somehow, I'd never seen most of the photos before. Some were of him as a kid or of his family, but many were of ex-girlfriends.

Most of the letters were from young women he'd been dating just before he went to Fallujah on his first deployment. I recognized their names as girls we'd gone to high school with. I took a swig of the tequila, inhaled, and reminded myself that none of this mattered anymore.

"You gonna read them?" Carson asked, gesturing toward the pile of folded notebook paper.

"I dunno," I said. "I feel bad, but I'm curious. What if some of these are important and should go to his mom or something?"

"I can scan them if you want. I'll give you the ones I think are important."

"Sure. Thanks."

Carson, too drunk to have a filter, still shared juicy highlights from the letters.

"Wow. He was leading on at least three girls at the same time. Impressive."

"I don't want to know, Carson."

"Fine, fine," he said, and then, in a high-pitched voice, started reading from one of them anyway. "'I'll never forget the night you held me . . .'"

"Stop it!" I said. "It's not funny!"

"Oh, come on," he said. "You know it's kinda funny."

"Literally not funny," I said, and then laughed. Carson's sense of humor had gotten darker since his last two deployments. He took very little seriously anymore. It could be annoying and was probably one of the reasons his marriage was failing, but usually I found it comforting. It helped me to stop taking myself so seriously, too. "You are so fucked," I said.

We spent the next few days going through the boxes. That weekend, I went back to the apartment I'd been living in. I'd called to cancel my lease before leaving Foley but hadn't had time to deal with it. Being there felt like a lingering bad dream. Hardly anything in that space mattered to me. I dragged the futon, the love seat, and everything else I had to the dumpster. I tried to set it all up in a way that would make someone want to take it and use it. I would have sold it, but I didn't have time. I couldn't afford movers. I was planning on skipping that month's rent and ignoring the fee to cancel the rental agreement. I needed to get out of there fast and didn't know what else to do. I'd already rehomed Mr. Jingles. I'd had to do it quickly the week Cleve died, so I listed him on Craigslist as *Free to a Good Home*. A young woman and her son whisked him away in a black sedan. I was so overwhelmed, I didn't even say goodbye.

Days somehow turned into weeks. My bank account was so low I had to sell things on Craigslist to buy groceries. I sold our TVs, some of my furniture, my purses. I still wasn't motivated to work. Just the thought of it—of leaving the house at all—made me want to dig a hole in the backyard and bury myself in it. I'd let myself die of starvation first. Instead, I sat in bed all day with a bottle of wine, watching back-to-back episodes of *Lost* and pretending everything was fine.

A month after the funeral, another mortgage payment was due. I'd scraped enough together to keep the utilities on, but that was all I could afford. Cleve hadn't been paying the mortgage for months before he died, so the amount it would take to keep it from foreclosing was huge. I knew I couldn't pay it and that the home would eventually foreclose. I just didn't know when. The lease on the Escalade hadn't been paid in months, either. I hadn't realized that until I woke up one afternoon to a knock on the door. I peeked out of the window to see who it was. A man with a ponytail, jean shorts, and a neon-green tank top was standing there, waiting. He knocked on the door again, only this time it was more of a *bang bang bang*. He placed a notice on the door and then left. When it seemed safe to check, I cracked the door open and grabbed the piece of paper. He was there to repossess the Escalade. I ran to the garage to make sure the door was locked. The Saturn was on its last legs. I needed time to figure out where I would live and how I would make money before I could give up my only reliable transportation.

By the end of May, I was running out of things to sell. The only things of value I hoped to keep were a TV, Cleve's banjo, his Xbox, a pistol he'd bought me, and my laptop. Everything else was up for grabs. I'd saved up a small nest egg, just over a thousand dollars, in preparation for my move. I knew it wouldn't last long, but it was something. Fiona and Trent offered to let me live with them in Foley until I figured out what I would do next. I hated relying on others, but they insisted, and I trusted they meant it.

Meanwhile, I was obsessing over the oil spill. Eleven crew members aboard the rig had died in the explosion. Animals were found dead all over the Gulf. I searched the internet, reading articles about the spill, looking for meaning. I was convinced something bigger was happening. It wasn't just Cleve's death or the largest oil spill in history, it was the universe trying to tell me something. But what? When the news said blobs of oil ranging from the size of BBs to small pancakes were expected to hit the coast of Alabama by June 11, I knew I had to be there. I had to see it. I had just over two weeks to get out of that house and get to the beach.

The same repossession agent came back several times after his first visit. I never opened the door for him. One time he yelled through the door that he knew I was in there, that he was sorry, but he had to do his job. I sat on the floor next to the door, out of sight of any window, listening. Another time, he said through the door that he knew my husband was a veteran. He thanked me for his service and said he was so sorry he was the one who had to do this. Finally, the day I parked the SUV on the street to be picked up, he gently knocked one last time.

"I know it doesn't make up for it," he said. "But I made you something."

When he and the Escalade were gone, I opened the door to see what he'd left me. Carefully propped against the doorstep was a customized license plate. The background had been airbrushed green camo, it had an eagle, globe, and anchor on it, and it said *In Memory of Jimmy Cleveland Kinsey II*. I couldn't decide if I loved it or hated it. Either way, I appreciated that the guy wasn't just an asshole. I walked out to the Saturn, opened the door, and threw the gift onto a box of Cleve's things in the back seat. The car was almost completely packed, containing the items I'd decided I couldn't live without, mainly consisting of my clothes and Cleve's belongings. I would leave for Foley the next day. I wasn't sure when the house would foreclose. If it didn't in the next month, I would come back for more things. If it did, I would try to forget everything I'd left behind.

Brittany came over to say goodbye. Carson was working.

"Visit me?" I asked.

She looked at the tiny newborn in her arms and said she'd try.

"I love you."

"I love you, too."

I made it to the sands of Gulf Shores two days later. I chose a popular spot that Cleve and I had frequented as kids, but with so many new restaurants and bars, it was almost unrecognizable from the beach we'd grown up on.

I sat in the sand and stared at the endless water that went from shades of green to dark blue to sky. I closed my eyes and took a deep breath. In that moment, I felt deeply connected to that place: the pristine white-sand beach I knew so well, quietly and helplessly awaiting its oily fate. I walked to the shore until my feet were submerged and savored the cool water lapping against my ankles. And then I saw it in a wave reaching toward crest: a large, nebulous shadow. A cluster of black globules. In the distance, a seagull plummeted into it. I tried to imagine the moment Cleve gave in to his addiction, to the promise of escape from his broken body for the last time. My childhood friend, my first middle-school crush, sitting on the bed of his hotel room, sucking a tarlike substance from the aluminum-foil pipe that had been found next to his body. April, I thought, was so fucking cruel.

Six months after Cleve's death, the news reported thousands of animals dead from the oil spill, and I received a check from the military meant to make up for killing my husband. After finally receiving the death certificate, the military ruled his death service-connected. He'd died of an accidental overdose of the fentanyl that had been prescribed to him by military doctors for the leg he'd lost at war. They also confirmed that he'd extended his life insurance policy just before retiring. My bank account went from under one hundred dollars to three hundred thousand dollars in an instant. I'd seen that number on the paperwork I'd filled out on my living room floor. It was one thing to see a number like that on a form. It was a whole other thing to see it in my bank account, ready to be spent in whatever way I chose. I'd given years of my life to caring for Cleve, to loving him. And for what? Now he was dead, and I had no idea what to do next. Three hundred thousand dollars didn't make me feel better. I wished it did, but it didn't.

The house foreclosed and everything inside was put into a storage unit. I had a month to get everything out, but I couldn't get to it in time. I lost everything. Deep in grief, I couldn't fathom the life ahead of me, where this money would give me the freedom to do and be whatever I wanted. I could finally go to college without going into debt, buy a reliable car, buy a house anywhere in the world I wanted to live. I'd never had such an open road ahead of me. And neither had Cleve. I struggled to reconcile the sacrifices I'd had to make to be in this position. At once, the money's presence disturbed me and made me feel freer than I ever had before.

23

THE WIDOWS
February 2011

I dreamed I was inside a run-down house, everything in shades of gray except for brightly colored plants creeping through windows and doors. I walked into a room covered in peeling paint and ripped wallpaper and found Sophie in the middle of it, standing on a closed casket. I wanted to pet her, but I couldn't move. My feet were rooted to the ground. Suddenly, she was gone and the casket opened. Cleve was inside. I could see his entire body vividly, exactly as he was at his funeral—caked makeup, eyes and lips sealed shut, his chin pressed uncomfortably against his chest, his hands folded at his belly.

When I woke up, my pillow was wet. I'd been crying in my sleep again. Cleve's prosthetic leg, which I'd been sleeping with at night, was tucked under the covers beside me. It made me feel less alone. I reached toward it, gripped its cool metal center, and took a deep breath. The room was pitch-black, silent. I guessed it was three in the morning. I'd been waking up every night around then. I sat up and waited for my eyes to adjust to the darkness. I needed to pee. When I was ready, I whispered, "Don't fuck with me," then ran across the room to the bathroom, flicking on the light as soon as I was through the door. Ten months had passed since Cleve's death, and things were getting weird.

I was convinced that Cleve's ghost was living in my apartment. Sometimes I would look for signs he was there—a flickering light, a bird at my window, my car's radio changing stations on its own. I'd ask Cleve questions or make requests like a prayer, then wait for a sign.

"Am I on the right track?" I'd ask and then wait. Clouds could part, letting sunshine through, and that was enough for me to know the answer was *yes*. If a cloud covered the sun, I knew it was a *no*. I'd had enough time to consider God's role in my life since Cleve's death and had decided, once and for all, that there was no God. If there was, I didn't like him much anyway. He was judgy and demanding and let people suffer for his own benefit. No thanks. But I couldn't shake the need to pray. So, I prayed to Cleve.

I also couldn't stop thinking about dying. I was too aware now that it could happen at any moment. That week, I'd passed a semi on the freeway and seen so vividly the truck losing control and crashing into my lane. I could feel my body thrown from side to side as my car spun, could hear the glass shatter as the truck landed on top of me. Danger was everywhere. And anyone could die. That was the part I feared most— losing someone I loved and feeling that pain all over again. *Never let anyone get too close again,* I thought. *That's how you get hurt.* But I didn't want to be alone, and there were already people in my life that I loved. So, I drank. You can't hurt if you're numb. On weekends, I frequented a bar called Flora-Bama, where bras hung in the rafters and local bands sang songs like "Poontang on the Pontoon." I ordered their strongest drink, the bushwacker, chased one after another after another until all the terrifying things in the world melted away, leaving only a stage and country music and sweaty bodies bouncing and shimmying around me.

During the week, I obsessed over losing weight. I traded bush-wackers for vodka sodas. I cut sugar. I cut carbs. I cut calories. I went to the gym on Pensacola Navy Base each morning. My workout started with a cycling class run by an older man with thick skin and a white high and tight.

"Stand up! Sit down! Stand up! Sit down!" he yelled gruffly. "Hustle, hustle, hustle, you're stronger than you think!" I pushed myself until the muscles in my legs felt like they might snap. After an hour on the bike, I ran a mile or two on the treadmill before lifting weights, alternating between arms and legs, depending on the day. I shed as much of myself as I could. If I couldn't control anything else in the world, I could at least control my body.

"Girl, you're lookin' good!" a friend told me at the beach once. Nobody had complimented me like that in a long time, and it felt good. All it took to be beautiful was a punishing workout, a prescription for phentermine, and a diet of steamed vegetables and water.

I'd gotten good at hiding my grief, disguising it as self-care and living my best life. I lived in a one-bedroom apartment near the beach, and it had furniture in it—a couch and a bed and a bistro table, some generic art from Ross, and a Yankee candle that smelled like pine trees. I bought a Subaru Forester and a kayak I could strap on top without anyone's help if I angled it just right and pushed with all my strength. I didn't know what I wanted to be yet, so I took classes to get a real estate license, a worthy goal that would buy me more time. Nobody knew how self-destructive I'd become. From the outside, it looked like I was really getting my shit together. But behind closed doors, I felt alone and stuck, my complicated marriage playing on a loop in my mind. I was leading a double life.

As the first anniversary of Cleve's death approached, I visited his grave often. It comforted me despite my knowing what was beneath the ground. There, I had nothing to hide. I'd bring flowers and Crown Royal and sit in the grass next to the patch of red dirt, sipping the whiskey. I'd update Cleve about my week, remind him I missed him, and cry. I couldn't bear how easy it had been for the world to continue without him. People talked about his death less and less, but it felt to me like it had just happened. His grave didn't even have a headstone yet.

That night, after waking up from the nightmare, I looked in the mirror and wondered how many others like me were out there. I went back to bed, leaving the bathroom light on so it wouldn't be so dark, and googled "military widow." The website of a nonprofit called the American Widow Project (AWP) appeared in the search results. I clicked on it and found pictures of women my age hugging, laughing, and going on adventures together. A woman named Taryn had founded it. The purpose was to bring military widows together through free retreats. I got goosebumps as I read. They had a few retreats listed. The one I was most interested in was in New Orleans that April, just over a week after the anniversary of Cleve's death. They called it a Give Back Retreat because the widows would spend the trip helping to rebuild a home Hurricane Katrina had destroyed. I nervously filled out their form and then tried to go back to sleep.

A month later, in early March, I received an email saying I'd been selected for the trip. We were given the contact information of the other widows attending. Two of them, Kelly and Tiffany, lived within a couple of hours from me and would also have to take I-10 if they were driving. I added them on Facebook and messaged them to see if they wanted to caravan. They said *yes*, even offering to ride together. I considered it, but ultimately opted to drive my own car. I preferred having a way to leave if I needed to.

I left for New Orleans in the early evening and met the other widows at a Shell station about thirty minutes down the route. I parked in front of the store while Kelly and Tiffany, who had opted to ride together, pumped gas. I was too nervous to get out of the car, so I rolled my windows down and waited for one of them to come to me. Kelly, all green eyes and perfect curls, popped her head in the window.

"Hi!" she said cheerily. "I'm Kelly Green. Just like the color!"

Well, that's adorable, I thought. I laughed and told her my name.

"You're still welcome to ride with us if you want," she offered. "Plenty of room!"

"Oh, thank you! I really don't mind driving," I said. "I appreciate you meeting up with me so I can follow, though."

"No problem!" she said. Her voice reminded me of a bird's. "As soon as we're done pumping gas, we'll head out."

I looked behind me and waved at Tiffany. She waved back and then pulled the nozzle from her SUV before they both got back in it.

It was dark out by the time we arrived. The GPS led us to a brick building with multiple apartments. After parking, we helped each other with our bags. As we approached the door, we gave quick introductions. Tiffany was a twenty-two-year-old mom who lived in Navarre, about two hours away from me in Alabama. She was tall and thin with straight chestnut hair, hazel eyes, and freckles sprinkled across her nose. She had a half-sleeve tattoo of a skeleton woman with a black veil on her upper right arm, which added a little mystery to her otherwise clean-cut but casual mom aesthetic. Kelly was a twenty-three-year-old biology major living in Pensacola, only an hour from my place. She had brown curly hair to her shoulders and large green eyes that reminded me of Mila Kunis's. She wore a sundress, a cardigan, and ballet flats, and spoke with a sugary sweetness. She was a big fan of cheesy, G-rated one-liners and recited them anytime she had the chance. There was a warmth to her that reminded me of an elementary school teacher or librarian.

"I can't believe you two lived so close and I didn't know it until I found AWP. It would've been cool to connect sooner," I said.

"Right?" Kelly said. "Where have you been *hiding*?"

Tiffany stopped and yelled, "MY HUSBAND IS DEAD!"

"Yeah, he is." Kelly laughed.

"Is that the secret code to get into the building?" I asked.

"Perfect," she said. "Neither of you gave me that fucking sad face everyone else does every time I have to say that. This weekend is gonna be great."

We knocked on the door, and nobody answered.

"Should we just go in?" I asked, and Tiffany pushed the door open.

A hallway of redbrick and warm lamplight greeted us. I could hear giggling but couldn't see where it was coming from.

"Welp. I hope this is the right place," I said.

"I'll go first," Tiffany said, pushing past us and through the door. I could tell she was a no-nonsense kind of person, and I loved it.

"Following you, ma'am," I said.

We made our way down the hallway in a line. When we turned the corner, we found a living room with a group of women sitting in a circle on the floor. Taryn, whom I recognized as AWP's founder, stood up.

"My duuuudes," she said with open arms. Her large almond eyes were inviting. "Welcome to the widow circle. We were just sharing our stories with each other." She stopped and scanned the group, then pointed to an area where a few women were sitting with plenty of space between them. "Can you guys scooch closer to each other so these guys can squeeze in?" They obliged.

I sat on the floor next to a woman with long bleached-blond hair in a ponytail. I looked around at all the faces in the group. Everyone was so young. Not one of them looked to be older than twenty-five. A wave of anxiety washed over me. I wondered if their husbands had all died overseas at war. If so, would they accept me even though Cleve had died stateside? One at a time, the women shared their stories of how they were widowed. It quickly became clear to me that I had nothing to worry about. Each of their stories was unique. One woman's husband had died eight years before, while another widow's husband had died four months before. Some were already engaged, while others swore they'd never date again. Some women told love stories that sounded like fairy tales, while others were on the verge of divorce when their husbands died. Many of their husbands did die overseas, but it wasn't always due to enemy fire. A few of them had even died of suicide.

Kelly and her husband, Gatlin, had eloped before he deployed. While he was gone, she kept herself busy planning their dream wedding, which was scheduled for after his return. She was stuffing envelopes with wedding invitations when a man in uniform showed up at her door with the news that Gatlin had died. It was a work accident. She could hardly talk about it without breaking down. Her husband was her soulmate, she said. The way she described their relationship sounded like a dream. I wondered what it was like to grieve for a perfect relationship. In that way, my experience was so different from hers. So much of my grieving was wishing I'd had more time to make things right with Cleve. So much of it was feeling remorse for all the ways I'd failed him. But for her, it seemed she was mostly angry that her perfect love story had been cut short.

Tiffany, a soldier herself, had just given birth to a baby girl when she found out about the death of her husband, Brad. He'd met their daughter briefly after she was born, before having to fly back to Afghanistan to finish his deployment. He died before their daughter's first birthday. Brad had been her best friend. He had wanted to leave Afghanistan and come home to be a father. Tiffany was pissed that she'd been left a single mother, that her daughter would never get to know her dad. But she was also grateful: she'd fallen in love again. Her new boyfriend had been in the same unit as her husband and was there for Tiffany after Brad's death. He supported her, but also accepted that she was a grieving widow; he gave her as much space as she needed to work through it.

After everyone in the circle had shared their stories, Taryn showed us where we'd be sleeping. There were fourteen of us, not including her, and we were each assigned a bedmate. I was led to a queen-sized pull-out bed with gift bags on each pillow. A woman with brunette hair, dark almond-shaped eyes, and colorful tattoo sleeves was already sitting on the edge of the bed.

"I figured it would be rude to pick a side of the bed before meeting the person I'm sharing it with," she said in a jokey tone. She stood up and held out her hand. "I'm Lulu, and I'll be sleeping with you this weekend."

I laughed and shook her hand. "Nice to meet you, Lulu. I'm Karie, I don't care what side of the bed I sleep on, and I'm pretty sure I don't snore, but I can't guarantee that?"

"Oh, God. I might snore. If I do, you have my permission to smother me with your pillow."

"Fortunately for both of us, I brought earplugs!" I said as I dropped my bag on the bed. "I guess we can save the violence for another time."

"Oh, good," she said. She pulled the blanket back, crawled into the bed, and bounced a little. "Hmm. Springy."

I knew from the widow circle that Lulu was from Salem, Massachusetts, and her husband had died in Afghanistan only seven months after Cleve. They were one year apart in age. Her husband's twenty-sixth birthday was that day, and Cleve's twenty-seventh was coming up that June. Taryn matched us as bedmates because she thought we might have some things in common. She wasn't wrong. I was drawn to Lulu's dry humor and quirky, witchy, nerdy-but-in-a-cool-kid-way persona. And though our lives were so different on paper, it was enough that we were in a similar place with our grief. Our husbands even had similar names, Jimmy and James.

I got into the bed next to her. "Now what?" I said. "Pillow fight?"

"I mean, I'm down," she said. "This might sound weird, but . . ." She looked around the room. "I'd like to think all the guys are here, too. I'm just, like, imagining them all hanging out and making fun of us for sitting around crying together."

"God, I hope so. Sometimes I wonder if Cleve's a ghost just following me around, lonely. I selfishly feel comforted by the idea of him being with me, but I like imagining him with friends."

"I'm sure they'd like seeing all of us together, too," she said. "This is cool."

"Definitely."

The next morning, we loaded into a van and were taken to a large white home in the St. Bernard Parish that Hurricane Katrina had ravaged. A nonprofit called the St. Bernard Parish Project, which we would be working with that weekend, was rehabbing the home. They'd already gutted the house, the interior stripped to its studs. They split us into work groups. Some of us helped put up drywall, some of us were tasked with sanding, and others painted. I was handed a sander and led to a room upstairs with two other widows. I found a spot that nobody had worked on yet, put on my gloves, and got to work.

I'd never done construction work before. I was shocked by how difficult even sanding was. Dust from the drywall filled the room. My arms began to burn. After forty-five minutes, I stopped, got water from a community cooler, and sat down in the room I'd been working in.

"I suck," I said out loud to the other women working.

"Nah, I think you have the right idea," one of them said. We'd been working side by side silently. She pulled her gloves off, wiped sweat from her forehead—the heavy southern humidity wasn't making the work any easier—and grabbed a water before sitting down next to me. "This shit's hard, right?" she said.

"Very," I said.

"I'm Natalie."

"I'm Karie."

Natalie and I kept the same schedule for the rest of the day. We'd work for thirty minutes to an hour, then take a break together, chatting about our lives since our husbands had died. She'd been widowed for a few years now and had four kids, all boys. She was still single, mostly because she didn't have time to be in a relationship.

"It's a lot being a single mom," she said. "I barely have time to get laid."

I laughed. "At least you're getting that," I said. "Any hotties recently?"

"A few." She paused. "Can I tell you a secret?"

"Yeah, of course," I said.

"It's embarrassing, but . . . you know people post ads for sex on Craigslist?"

"Oh shit."

"Yeah. I just do that, get mine and done."

"Kinda genius. But aren't they creepy?"

"Sometimes. We meet up somewhere public first. If I get creepy vibes, I tell them there's an emergency with the kids and leave."

I admired Natalie's ability to put herself out there like that. Though I'd had casual sex before, it wasn't something I sought out or openly admitted to. I kept my sex life private, mostly out of shame.

"Do you think you'll ever want anything serious again?" I asked.

"I don't know," she said. "He was my soulmate, ya know? My kids' father. It's hard to imagine something different."

I nodded.

We spent the next two days at the home, sanding, painting, and learning to use nail guns. There was lots of laughter and chatter, and by the end, our progress was obvious. The house felt more like a home. Instead of bare studs, it had insulation and painted walls. I was amazed by how much we could accomplish together, even though we'd never done anything like that before.

That evening we went out for dinner, followed by barhopping on Bourbon Street. As a group of fifteen young women, we received a lot of attention.

"What brings you to New Orleans?" someone would ask, and then one of us would inevitably blurt out, "Our husbands died," and we'd stare at the person as they squirmed in discomfort, waiting for a reaction. Our collective sense of humor was dark.

I was relieved to see how the veteran widows handled their widowhood in public. It was something I'd struggled with. When someone new would ask me questions about my life, there was always a point where I would have to tell them about Cleve's death. I anticipated an uncomfortable silence as they took in what I was telling them. Though people knew there was a war going on overseas, it was rare that they had to face the consequences. I knew that I was a living, breathing symbol of the suffering our country and the countries we'd invaded had endured. My presence forced people to consider the sins our country had committed. Hearing a widow talk about her loss is never a fun time, but talking to one who was a teenager only five years ago is downright depressing. It was a heavy thing to drop on someone at a bar, and I felt guilty every time I did it. But these women were unapologetic. They owned who they were, and it made me feel more confident.

Bourbon Street was wet with beer, humidity, and sweat, the scent of gumbo and sewage in the air. People of all ages wandered up and down, drunk on oversized drinks, some stopping to dance in front of a club playing "Cha Cha Slide." Colorful beads hung from necks and trees and littered the gutters. As our group strolled along, we joked that Taryn was a mother hen. When she moved, we followed as if we were her newly hatched chicks. When she stopped, we stopped too. I was holding a hurricane the size of my forearm, taking sips from a neon-green curly straw.

"I guess we're gonna be BFFs now," I said to Kelly. She, Tiffany, and I had plans to meet up after the trip.

"Yeah! We're the beach widows!" she said, holding her drink in the air. I assumed she was referring to our proximity to the Gulf.

I met her drink with mine. "Beach widows! I love it!"

One of the women in our group shushed us and pulled us to a window. They were all looking at a TV on a wall over the bar.

"What's going on?" Kelly asked.

I shrugged. "Not sure."

I couldn't hear the TV, but I recognized bin Laden's face on the screen.

We moved closer. Under his face, I read the words *Osama bin Laden Dead*. Cheering echoed through the streets, strangers high-fived strangers, and the widows in our group jumped up and down in glee. I had stopped paying attention to what was going on overseas after Cleve got home and I didn't know what bin Laden's death meant for our future, but I jumped and cheered, too. In that moment it felt simple: bin Laden was the bad guy, and this was justice.

———

A week after the trip, I met Kelly and Tiffany at a divey pizza place in Pensacola for a belated celebration of Cleve's and Gatlin's lives. Taryn had called the anniversary of a loved one's death an "angelversary." As cheesy as it was, we couldn't think of anything better, so we called it that, too. Gatlin, Kelly's husband, had died on April 24, just four days shy of a year before Cleve did. Because their angelversaries were so close, we decided in New Orleans we'd try to get together annually to honor them.

When the waiter asked what we wanted to drink, I ordered a Sweetwater 420.

I looked at the girls with a cheesy grin. "Because that's the day Cleve died."

"Ayyyy," Kelly whooped. "Bring us a pitcher of 420!"

A couple of months later, Kelly and I sat on her porch in rocking chairs, sipping wine. It was past midnight, but the air was warm and humid, the sky speckled with stars.

"I still don't know what to do with my life," I said. I looked down at the rocking chair's armrest and picked at a piece of chipped paint. "I feel stuck. Like, now what? Who even am I?"

"Well, what do you want?" Kelly asked. It sounded so simple.

"A billion dollars."

She smacked me on the shoulder. "Shut up. I'm being serious. You're more than a wife, caregiver, or widow. Figure out what makes you happy, and I think you'll start to see that, too." She stood up. "I want to show you something." She wrapped the throw blanket that had been in her lap around her shoulders.

I followed her to her living room, where she sat on the floor and reached for a journal on her coffee table. She opened it and pulled out a piece of paper that looked like it had been folded and unfolded a thousand times.

"I made this list after Gatlin died," she said, handing it to me. "Some of them are things he wanted to do, some things we wanted to do together. A lot of them are goals I have for myself."

I read through the list: *learn to scuba dive, dive with great white sharks, participate in an archeological dig, visit Belize, skydive.* The list went on for a full page.

"You really wanna swim with great whites?"

Kelly smiled. "Oh, they're much more docile than you'd think. Very misunderstood creatures," she said. "Plus, I'd be in a cage. You should come with me!"

"Nope. Not happening," I said. "I've always wanted to learn to scuba dive, though." Diving was one of my dad's hobbies when he was younger. I had hazy memories of him leaving on weekends and returning with treasures he'd found in the sea. After one of those trips, he returned with a diamond ring he had found. It had a few diamonds missing, but I still couldn't believe there was real treasure down there. My mind ran wild imagining all the other things hiding in the depths that hadn't been found yet. I wanted to be the one to find them.

"We should go!" she said. "I already researched it. I can send you the info if you want."

"Yeah. I'd love that."

Kelly folded the list and put it back in her journal. "Anyway. I wanted to show you this because I wrote it when I was struggling with a lot of the same questions you are now. I wasn't sure who I was without Gatlin," she said. "But I wanted to take advantage of the time I have. We know it's precious now, right? Don't get me wrong, I cried in my parents' basement a lot at first. But when I was ready, making a list helped me figure out what to do next."

I grabbed a throw pillow sitting next to me and hugged it. "Maybe I should try making a list."

"My totally unbiased opinion is that I think that's a great idea."

Kelly's list inspired me to set my fear of failure aside and dream a little. And when I allowed myself to really consider what I wanted, the top three things that came to mind were: school, move to the Pacific Northwest, and write Cleve's and my story. I wanted a degree, I wanted to be surrounded by mountains, and I wanted to find my voice, to take back some of what had been stripped from me. A week after my night at Kelly's, I applied to the University of South Alabama in Mobile.

24

IT TOOK ALL THREE OF US
October 2011

When I was a kid, someone told me it was disrespectful to play music when driving past a graveyard. The advice stuck, and when I turned sixteen and was handed a set of keys, I did my best to turn my radio down whenever I saw a group of headstones in the distance. Sometimes I'd even hold my breath, enacting a rule that might've had to do with driving through tunnels. I wasn't sure. There were so many superstitions. But with the music down, even my breath seemed too loud, so I'd suck it in and hold it deep in my lungs until the graveyard disappeared into my rearview mirror. For me, this wasn't about respect for the dead—it was that I didn't want to risk waking them up and bringing them back to life. I didn't *really* believe in ghosts or zombies, but I believed that the universe was just chaotic enough that either was possible, and it wasn't something I wanted to test.

Whenever I pulled into the graveyard where Cleve was buried, I always turned my music's volume down. This day was no different. What was different, however, was a gray rectangle at the head of his grave. My chest tightened when I saw it. I'd been waiting for his head-stone for almost a year and a half. I couldn't wait to get a closer look. I parked parallel to the dirt road that weaved through the graveyard, just below Cleve's plot. I jumped out of the car before even turning it off. With the car door still open, I walked hurriedly to the foot of his grave, took a deep breath, and allowed relief to wash away the anxiety I'd been holding on to for so long. *Finally,* I thought, *his burial is complete.*

I put my hand on the headstone and read the words etched in the granite. His first name, his middle name, his last, a sigh of relief. And then, *Persian Gulf,* the headstone read, instead of *Operation Iraqi Freedom.* And although I'd included it in the paperwork, his Purple Heart wasn't listed either. I was devastated. Neglect is what killed Cleve, I thought, and it was continuing even after his death.

"How do you get an entire headstone incorrect?" I scoffed.

I thought about how difficult it had been for me to get the headstone in the first place. I'd spent months after Cleve's funeral overthinking it. I didn't want to look at the paperwork. I didn't want to be in the same room with it. I had to print it out. Read the questions. Answer them. Drive to the VA. Wait. It all made me feel panicky. Eventually, I shamed myself into getting it done. I read the first question on the form—NAME OF DECEASED TO BE INSCRIBED ON HEADSTONE OR MARKER—and fell into a sobbing mess. Cleve was deceased and his name—twenty-two symbols that formed three words—was all that was left of him. I wrote that name on the line, filled in all the blank spaces with the details of his birth and death, and then brought it to the VA and handed it to a woman who took the paperwork out of my hands, put the information into a computer, then told me it should arrive in a month to six months.

It was all so official. Cleve was dead. Cleve was dead. Cleve was dead.

After turning in the paperwork, I let a month pass before revisiting the grave. I found it still unmarked, but that was fine. A month wasn't that long. Week after week, I continued to visit with fingers crossed, but nothing changed. It looked so unloved. I hated myself for not filling out the paperwork sooner. Now, a year and a half later, I was sitting next to a headstone with incorrect information. I was furious.

I called the VA from the graveyard. The person on the phone apologized flatly and said to resubmit his paperwork. I hung up on them.

"Fuck!" I screamed to the sky.

This time, I didn't hesitate. The next day, I printed out the paperwork again, filled it out, and brought it to the nearest VA, where I handed it to the same lady I had seen before. She began to type.

"The headstone needs to say *Operation Iraqi Freedom*," I said.

She looked at me from the corner of her eye. "Right," she said and continued to type.

"And it needs to include that he's a Purple Heart recipient," I said. I pointed to the paperwork where I had that underlined. "You can do that, right?"

"Yeah," she said. "That's fine."

"Can I look at the form when you're done to make sure it's correct?" I said. "Sorry if that's annoying. I just don't want to have to do this again."

She sighed. "Sure." When she was done, she turned the screen toward me. All the information was correct.

I decided I would wait awhile before visiting Cleve's grave again. I knew now how long it would take for the new headstone to arrive and didn't want to obsess over it. I'd received an acceptance letter to the University of South Alabama, only an hour and a half from where I lived. I would start classes in the spring semester, just a couple of months away.

It was early January 2012 when I took a selfie and posted it to Facebook with the caption *First day of school pic!* I was terrified and excited and proud and everything in between. In my English 101 class, I chose a seat at the front, something I would never have done before. I was sure I didn't know as much as the kids who'd just graduated from high school, but I was determined to catch up. I wanted to make straight A's, even if it meant studying twice as hard as everyone else. As we went over the syllabus, the professor explained that we could have physical dictionaries and thesauruses for essays written in class. I raised my hand.

"Do these need to be in cursive?" I asked. Chuckles filled the room.

"Oh, no. No, we don't do that anymore," the teacher said. I shrank in my chair, my face hot with embarrassment.

After class, I waited until the rest of the students were gone and I walked up to the teacher.

"Ms. Emily," I said.

She put the eraser down and turned to look at me. "Hi! What's up?" she said with a warm smile. I noted how young she looked and wondered how she was already teaching at a university.

"I have a possibly dumb question." I paused. "Uh . . . can you explain what an essay is? It's been a long time since I was in school. Is it just, like, five paragraphs or . . . ?"

"Oh! Yes! Sort of! It doesn't have to be, necessarily, but that's a good model to start with. There are different kinds of essays, but we'll go over all of that in class. As long as you show up and pay attention, I think you'll be just fine. If you ever have questions, though, please come to office hours," she said. "I'm more than happy to help."

"Okay. I really appreciate that," I said, though I couldn't imagine bothering someone in their office. "Can I ask another question?"

"Shoot!"

"Are you a professor or a doctor or . . ."

"Ha! No, no, no. I'm a grad student. I'm getting my master's in English. We teach the 101 classes."

"Oh! Well, that's cool," I said. "Thank you."

I walked away, trying to imagine what it would be like to be in a graduate program where I could teach actual college courses. I had butterflies in my stomach thinking about it. I added grad school to my list.

As the weather began to warm up, Kelly and I signed up for scuba diving lessons. We met at Dive Pros for our PADI certification class. Our first test was to see if we could swim from one end of the pool to the other ten times and then tread water for five minutes. Having grown up at the beach, I thought it would be easy. I'd had swim lessons in the third grade and never looked back. But by the sixth lap, I was swapping between a doggy paddle and sloppy backstroke—anything I could do to finish. Kelly and I finished around the same time and then faced each other as we began treading water.

"It's just . . . five . . . minutes," she said, her head bobbing out of the water to suck in air before she dipped back in up to her nose.

I felt confident at first. I was just relieved not to be doing laps anymore. But my legs became weak a few minutes in, and I, too, was hardly keeping my head above water.

"Oh," I said as my mouth emerged from the water and then dipped back down again, ". . . my God." I tried to pace myself, kicking my legs back and forth methodically. *Strong and slow,* I thought. *Strong and slow.* I just had to keep moving. It would be over soon.

When the timer went off, we swam to the side of the pool and high-fived.

"Piece a cake," Kelly said between heavy breaths.

"Piece of fucking cake." I coughed.

The course was two weeks long. Most of it was spent at an indoor pool, familiarizing ourselves with the gear and practicing diving skills. We also had to complete an academic course online. The last two days were our open-water dives. The first would be a more leisurely dive in the crystal-clear water of Vortex Spring. The second would be a more difficult ocean dive.

When we arrived at Vortex Spring, we unloaded our gear from the van and began suiting up. All around us were families in swimsuits, sunbathing. A country song played in the distance, and a little boy with red, white, and blue swim trunks ran by screaming, "Jamie's tryna eat my hot dog," nearly knocking my oxygen tank over.

Once we were all geared up, we weaved our way between the beachgoers toward the water. I thought we must look like aliens in our wet suits and masks and flippers. Everyone turned to watch us as we reached the water's edge and then submerged up to our necks. Treading water, which is much easier with flippers, I adjusted the mask over my eyes and put the mouthpiece in my mouth before dipping into another world. The water was as clear as freshly Windexed glass. There weren't as many fish as I imagined, only a few silvery-beige ones here and there. To the bottom left was a cave we were instructed not to go near and a log that ran in front of it as if to say, *Stop here.*

One of the instructors gestured for us to follow him, pointing toward a cement platform around twenty feet below us. It was just big enough for us all to fit. On our knees, we watched the two instructors pull their mouthpieces from their mouths and then swap them so that they could breathe from each other's oxygen tanks. It was a skill we'd learned back at the pool that could save someone's life if something happened to their tank. The problem was, if you put the other person's mouthpiece in your mouth upside down, you suck in water rather than air, and it's difficult to tell underwater which way is up and which way is down. This terrified me. Kelly and I stood across from each other. With my fingers, I counted: *1, 2, 3*. On three, we took out our mouthpieces and let go of the only thing keeping us from drowning. They floated freely in the water for a moment, and my heart raced. I reached out to grab hers, but the closer I got to it, the farther away it floated. I scrambled to grab the hose, with no luck. It began wrapping around Kelly's back, out of my reach, and I could feel the pressure in my chest, my body demanding air. Kelly, who'd already managed to get my mouthpiece into her mouth, reached around her back to grab hers. She didn't bother handing it to me. Instead, she put it directly into my mouth. When I breathed in, I was relieved that it was right side up. A breath had never felt so good. While it would have made sense to be scared, I wasn't. The entire experience was exhilarating. I was trying new things, exploring new corners of our beautiful planet, and learning to trust again—others but also myself. Kelly probably didn't realize it, but she was showing me how to live in a way I hadn't known was possible. For the first time in my life, I wasn't afraid of my future. Instead, I was excited by all the possibilities the world had to offer and eager to experience as many of them as I could. The list of things I wanted to do grew and grew. I wanted to see and taste and smell and touch everything. And the more I wanted for reasons rooted in curiosity rather than survival, the more I discovered about who I was at my center. And the more I was able to see my own potential and worth. The next day, we did our final test and passed.

Cleve's second angelversary was approaching, and I was obsessed with the idea of having the correct headstone by then. Once a week, I visited him to see if it had arrived. Week after week, I was disappointed until, finally, a week before the anniversary of his death, I could see the new headstone from the road. The error was obvious: it had been placed at the foot of his grave, and the original remained at the head of it. I checked to make sure the information was at least correct. It was. That's *something*, I thought, exhaling. I crossed my arms and stared at his grave, trying to process what I was seeing. The sight of the headstone thrown at the bottom was absolutely absurd. Infuriating. And so predictable it was almost funny. After years of this kind of negligence from the military, all I had the energy to do was laugh.

"Thank you for your service?" I scoffed. "*Right.*" I got on my knees and, as if there were a crowd of people around me, said to no one, "Don't worry, guys. I'll fix this, too."

I got on all fours and dug around the edges of the incorrect headstone with my fingers to see if I could easily move it myself, but it was partially buried. I didn't want to waste my time digging it out if it was still too heavy to lift, so I tried lifting the new one. It was too heavy.

That night, I called Kelly.

"I need your help," I said. When I explained the problem with the double headstones, she met my sadness and rage with her own.

"Fuck this! We can move it ourselves."

I laughed. "Don't you think we might get arrested?"

"That's *your* husband in the ground. You can do whatever you want. If you're worried about it, though, we can go after dark."

"Right. Okay." I thought about it for a second. "Let's fucking dig up some headstones. I'll call Tiffany."

When I called Tiffany, there was no need to convince her. She just needed to know when.

We decided to do it on the day of the anniversary. I arrived at the cemetery while there was still plenty of sun left. I wanted to spend some time alone with Cleve before the ladies arrived. We took shots of Crown Royal: one for me, then one poured over his grave. A woman with a cane hobbled by and nodded with a stiff smile. I watched her and wondered if she was there to see her husband, too, but instead of stopping at a grave, she strolled along each row, reading about the people buried there. By the time the beach widows arrived, the woman was gone.

Tiffany swung open her car door. "I have wine!" she said.

We sat around Cleve's grave, sipping cabernet from red Solo cups, waiting for night to fall. As the sun set behind the pines, the trees transformed into black silhouettes, then into ghosts. When only a glow remained on the horizon, and we were confident it was dark enough that people driving by couldn't see us from the road, we got on all fours and felt around the gritty dirt for the bottom edges of the original headstone. It was deeper than it looked, and the dry clay proved difficult to penetrate with bare fingers.

"I should've brought a shovel," I said. I couldn't believe I'd forgotten something so obvious.

Tiffany, without flinching, pulled the corkscrew out of her back pocket as if this was precisely why she had brought it.

"Screw this," she said, plunging the metal into the clay, removing one tiny shovelful at a time—pieces of hair sticking to the sweat on her forehead. Finally, we were able to fit our fingers underneath the stone.

"On three," I said. We all nodded, then: "One, two, lift!"

It took all three of us to carry the headstone to my car, though I left them with it for a moment. I had to get a picture. As usual, my car was a mess, especially my trunk. I'd had to push aside shoes, bills, purses, and beach gear to make room. When we dropped it, the whole car bounced under the weight. We stared at it, our hands on our hips, Kid Cudi's "Day 'n' Nite" playing so loud my car vibrated. The whole scene was ridiculous and somehow felt wrong, as if we'd just thrown Cleve's body back there. But it also felt powerful. For the first time since my husband's death, I felt like I had gained some control over my grief.

We stood in front of the trunk and stared at the headstone in the middle of all my clutter.

With my hands on my hips, I asked, "Do y'all think it's okay to play music in graveyards?"

"Sure. Why not?" Tiffany said. "Not like they can hear you."

"Right," I said, closing my trunk. "Well, I guess I'm the proud owner of a headstone now. Let's move the other one and get the fuck out of here before someone sees us."

25

FIND HIM NEAR WATER

November 2012

I had been in school for almost a year and I was killing it. I had recently changed my major from journalism to creative writing after Dr. Walker, the instructor of a poetry class I'd taken as an elective, convinced me I had natural talent. I was skeptical, but I preferred the freedom creative writing offered, and I remembered Kelly's advice to do what I love. And I did love it. I spent most of my free time studying and reading and was getting good grades. I had a friend group of poets, writers, and artists who taught me about things like social justice and climate change. I'd taken up running long distances, had trained my body to run more than ten miles without needing to stop for a break. I spent weekends on my kayak, exploring Gulf Shores' waterways, a side of Alabama I'd never seen before and was falling in love with. I had a purpose, a schedule, a routine that was mine and no one else's. But beneath the surface of my wonderful new life, guilt festered. Guilt for being alive when Cleve wasn't. Guilt for feeling happy without him. I was desperate for relief from it.

I texted Lulu. *Tell me more about mediums. How do they work?*

Lulu worked at a small but popular witchcraft shop in downtown Salem. She'd once told me she'd spoken to a medium a couple of times to get in touch with her husband, James.

I'd responded with an uncomfortable laugh. It reminded me of when my mom found Kelsey and me playing with a Ouija board on our bedroom floor. With flushed cheeks and eyes wide with horror, she snatched the game off the floor.

"This is a sin!" she yelled. "The devil's game!"

Speaking to a medium felt risky in the same way. But Lulu had only positive things to say, and I trusted her. She claimed that the medium had helped her to find some peace.

Cleve's third angelversary was approaching. When I texted her asking for details, she answered almost immediately. *Can I call you?* she wrote. I said *yes,* and the phone rang.

"Oh my God, you have to come!" Lulu said. "Bring the other beach widows, too! Come to me, my pretties," she said in a witchy voice.

"I might, but I have questions. What would we be doing? Do you know who would do it? Do you really trust this person?"

"Her name's Leanne Marrama. I work with her. She's fucking fabulous. I trust her with everything."

"How does it feel hearing from him?"

"Healing."

"I want healing," I said.

"I want you to have healing."

Later that night, I put on pajama pants and one of Cleve's T-shirts—a bright-green one with a piece of anthropomorphic broccoli on the front and the words *Keep It Green!* In the kitchen, I pulled a bag of tortillas and a bag of shredded cheese from the fridge and placed them on the counter, and then called Kelly. I couldn't get the idea of seeing a medium out of my mind. I held the phone between my cheek and shoulder as I sprinkled cheese onto a tortilla.

"Hello, hello!" Kelly said cheerily. When I told her what Lulu and I had discussed, she responded, "You know I'll never say no to a date with my man."

We talked about possible dates in January, which was only two months away.

"Bradley's angelversary is around then," Kelly said. "I wonder if Tiffany would be able to go."

Tiffany had just given birth to her second baby. David, the guy she'd been dating who served in the same unit as her husband, was the father. Tiffany couldn't remarry without losing the widow benefits she received from the military, but she and David had decided to start a family together anyway. Earlier that year, Kelly and I had thrown her a baby shower. We'd made clouds out of tissue paper, set up a crepe bar, and laid out white onesies for guests to decorate. It had been nice to celebrate a birth when so much of our friendship revolved around death.

"We should still ask," I said. "I could see her making it work."

"If anyone could, it's her," Kelly said.

Tiffany, the only one of us who'd been a mom when she was widowed, was the kind of person who would tell women never to have kids. She was mostly joking, of course. She adored her children. But she didn't sugarcoat the sacrifices that came with being a mother.

"If you do it, just be ready to kiss your freedom goodbye," she'd say. "The cute little shits show up and make you fall in love with them, and then they take over everything."

There was no way I could understand what it was like to be a newly widowed mom, but I assumed it sucked, even if part of me was envious of her for having a piece of her husband living, breathing, growing in front of her eyes. Olivia, her first child, had been born only months before Brad was killed, and she looked just like her dad. Kelly and I fell in love with her instantly. Before long, she called us "Aunt Kewwy and Aunt Kawwy." In my eyes, Tiffany handled being a mother exceptionally—bitterness, sarcasm, and all. She was a badass. One of the strongest people I'd ever met. I had so much admiration for her.

"Let's call her tomorrow," I said. "I don't want to wake up the kids."

"I'm supposed to meet her for lunch. I could do it then?"

"Yes! Perfect. Let me know."

"Will do!"

Kelly called a day later to let me know Tiffany was in. We booked the flights.

Even before considering seeing the medium, I'd realized I could speak to Cleve whenever I wanted. It didn't matter if he was really there or not: our one-way conversations made me feel better. I began talking to him out loud daily. It was always in the bath or shower. I'd close my eyes, imagine him, and tell him or ask him anything I wanted. Sometimes I would imagine him responding. I knew it wasn't really Cleve answering, but I still accepted the responses as coming from him. It was comforting. And even if the answers were coming from my subconscious, it made decision-making easier. It helped me to stop overthinking everything and go with my gut. After each conversation with Cleve, I felt like a weight had been lifted.

The night before our flight to Salem, I sat under the shower with my eyes closed, imagining that Cleve was in front of me. We were both on our knees, facing each other. He was silent, waiting for me to speak. "Cleve," I said out loud. "Tell her we talk in the shower." It was the only thing I could think of that I hadn't mentioned to anyone, even the widows, and that couldn't be googled. Though I was open to the experience of speaking to a medium and was ready to trust the process, I couldn't resist the urge to test it. I waited for a response, but he said nothing. I switched my focus to the steady sound of water hitting the tub, letting it put me in a trance. *Cleve? If the medium tells me we talk in the shower, I'll know for sure you're here with me.*

Salem was a forty-five-minute cab ride from Boston. Lulu's neighborhood had narrow roads lined with colorful, old houses. Everything was blanketed in at least six inches of snow. Her home, a large blue-gray two-story, sat on a corner lot. When the cabbie parked, I handed him ten ones and wished him a happy New Year. At the door, Lulu met us with a smile and led us to our rooms.

Leanne, the medium, was scheduled to arrive Saturday, the second day of our trip. On Friday night, David called in tears, Tiffany's baby screaming in the background. The baby was sick. David was overwhelmed.

Tiffany sighed. "I need to come home, don't I?"

"I'm so sorry," David said. "I need you."

Tiffany flew out the next morning. Her one request was that we try to get a message from Brad.

Because she was a friend, Leanne had offered to do the reading at Lulu's house. When she arrived, Kelly, Lulu, and I were already on our second bottle of wine.

"Come in!" Lulu shouted, and a curvy woman with curly black hair and dark eyes walked through the door. She introduced herself and went straight for the wine.

"Can I just say something?" she said in a strong Boston accent. Her voice boomed. "You girls married a buncha nerds!!"

Lulu, Kelly, and I laughed.

"Well, yeah," Lulu said.

"They all like each other! They think it's funny to talk to me at the same time. They think it's hilarious that it's confusing me!"

"So they're, like, hanging out right now?" I asked.

"Oh yeah. When you ladies are together, those boys are together too."

"I love that!" Kelly said. "I'm just sad I can't be a part of their shenanigans."

"Right?" I said. "I want to meet James and Gatlin."

"Let's bring this party to the living room," Lulu said.

I grabbed the bottle of wine and followed her. I sat on the floor next to a coffee table and draped a blanket over my legs. Leanne sat on the floor across from me. At her instruction, we all introduced ourselves by our first names only. She said she didn't want any other identifying information. I appreciated that.

Lulu insisted that Kelly and I go first.

"You should go first," I said to Kelly.

"No, you! Ladies first . . ."

"You just want me to be the guinea pig," I said.

Kelly shrugged and took a sip of her wine.

"Fine," I said. I looked at Leanne. "Don't tell me things I don't want to hear."

She explained that she only shares what is beneficial unless the person specifically asks. "The goal is for you to leave here feeling better, not worse."

She told me to say my first name one more time. After I did, she closed her eyes for a moment, then said calmly, "He's here."

"Really?"

"Oh yeah. And he's a jokester."

I laughed. "Yes. That's accurate."

"He's a loud spirit." She paused. "What I mean is that he wants to communicate. Have you ever noticed anything strange like lights flickering or items around the house moving?"

"Yes," I said without hesitation. Since his death, I'd noticed a few things that were strange. I'd wanted to believe it was Cleve, but my better sense wrote it off as coincidence. "My car stereo changes channels sometimes," I said. "And the bathroom light turns off sometimes when I take my shirt off before taking a shower."

"Well, it's him," she said. "That's him trying to get in touch with you."

"Huh," I said. I was still skeptical. Ghosts manipulating things in the physical world was a cliché concept, an obvious way for the medium to open the session. But I was still listening.

"He's okay with how he died," she said. "He wants you to know that. He knows you worry about it."

I pulled the blanket up to my chest. I tried not to cry because I didn't want to give anything away, but I couldn't stop it. I'd struggled with the fact that he died of an overdose, alone in a hotel room. I worried he would have preferred to die in Iraq, rather than come home to suffer for four years, only to die anyway. Memorials would not include his name among those lost to war. Instead, his memory would disappear with time, and that made me angry. He deserved the same recognition as everyone else who'd lost their lives to the war. I looked down at my hands and started picking my cuticles.

Leanne's eyes were still closed. She went on. "How do I say this?" She paused. "So, after his death, your souls became bonded. If you're happy, he's happy. If you're sad, he's sad. When you're in pain, he feels that pain, too. You could think of him as part of you now."

"Great," I said. "He's sad a lot, then."

"Well," she said. "When you get really sad, he sort of checks out. It hurts him so badly he can't handle it. But! There is a but . . ."

"Give me the but."

"When you're happy and laughing—it's like a drug to him. That's when he's the closest to you. I'm seeing something about water, too. He's drawn to it. He says that if you want to be closer to him, go to the ocean," she said.

"Like, just bodies of water or any water?" I asked. "Like a shower?"

"Showers work, too!" she said. "But the more water, the better."

"Wow," I said. I told her what I had asked of Cleve before I left. She smiled. "See?"

By then, I was all in. The session went on for an hour. She guessed the first letter of Cleve's first name. She said he, too, was upset about where he was buried; he said his body was mine, and I should have had a say in the matter. He said I needed to stop feeling guilty about my fraught relationship with his family. He knew I tried to love them and that they never loved me back. He wanted me to move on. He also wanted me to forgive anyone in my family that I'd pushed away over the years. She said he wanted me to forgive God. At that, I winced.

"Not sure about all that," I said.

Leanne shrugged. "Just relaying what I'm hearing," she reminded me. "I think more than anything he just wants you to find peace."

"Yeah. Yeah, all that has been kind of holding me back a bit, I guess."

She guffawed. "Oh, man. This guy," she said. "I'm sorry. I didn't mean to interrupt. He's just so loud. I don't even know how to say this." She closed her eyes. "You're bad!" She shook her finger at the air. She was obviously talking to him and not me. She looked at me. "So . . ." She paused. "This might sound crazy, but he says he would have rather been cremated and turned into a dildo."

"What?" Kelly and I said in unison. I laughed and shook my head. "I'm ashamed to admit that he would actually fucking say something like that," I said.

After settling down, the medium said someone else was trying to contact me. A child. They didn't say much, but she was pretty sure it was a child I would give birth to sometime in the future.

"Maybe five years?" Leanne guessed. I asked her if it could be the child I'd miscarried. "No, I don't think so. It's pretty clear that this child will come later." She tried to channel the baby I'd lost but got nothing.

"I think we can wrap it up unless you have anything specific to ask him," she said. I shook my head. I was more than satisfied. "One more thing before we finish," she said.

"Oh no," I said, anticipating another dildo story or similar.

"No, nothing bad. Just that he says your marriage was never given a chance. Lots of passion. Lots of love. But also, lots of fighting. Things were hard from day one. But he wants you to know he's made peace with it. He wants you to make peace with it too. None of it matters anymore."

I nodded. "Thank you."

"He wants you to know you'll see him again."

"Well, that's the dumbest shit I've ever heard," Carson said a week later. He'd called to see how the trip went. He was one of the first people I told about it, even though I knew he'd make fun of me for it. He'd been calling a lot over the last year because he and Brittany were getting a divorce. He was devastated, and I was one of the only people around as their marriage fell apart. I was also the only person willing to listen to him work through it.

"Fuck off. It was cooler than expected. And weird. But whatever."

"You know she probably googled your name before you showed up."

"She didn't know my name," I assured him. "Some of what she said couldn't be googled, anyway."

Carson laughed. "Like what?"

I told him about how she mentioned my relationship with his family, how she guessed his first initial, and how I talked to him in the shower and asked him to tell her to reassure me.

"The wording wasn't the same, but don't you think that's weird? That she specifically said I was closer to him when I was near water?"

"I guess," he said. "I still don't think dead Cleve is talking to you."

"Fair enough. Oh, and get this. She said he wanted to be cremated and turned into a dildo." I laughed, but Carson was silent. "Isn't that funny? So fucking random."

"Karie," he said. "He did."

"He did what?"

"I can't believe I'm even saying this, but when we were filling out paperwork before our first deployment to Fallujah, he wrote that he wanted to be turned into a dildo if he died. They made him trash it and redo the paperwork."

"Fuck off."

"Do you think I want you to believe in ghosts so bad that I'd lie to you? You know I'd much rather make fun of you for doing this."

I shook my head. "No. You're definitely supposed to be making fun of me right now."

"Exactly. This is very disappointing for me."

"Does that mean you think this could have been real?"

"This is weird enough that I will admit maybe there are ways for spirits to exist."

When the call ended, I sank to my kitchen floor and attempted to process the conversation. I really hadn't anticipated that sort of validation, especially in the form of a dildo, especially from Carson. This was the sort of evidence people hope for after talking to the dead. Even still, I wasn't ready to say I believed in ghosts. Maybe I was talking to Cleve, or maybe it was a lucky coincidence. It didn't matter. Whatever happened in Salem, I found the answers I needed to move on, and that was good enough for me.

"Cleve?" I said. I looked around for a sign he was there, but there was nothing. I sighed. "Thank you."

26

HOME
Spring 2015

Dr. Walker sat behind a messy wooden desk that looked like it had been in her office since the school was founded in the mid-1960s. The room was full of books. Books on shelves. Books in piles on the floor. None of them alphabetized. Organized chaos. Dr. Walker had once been Alabama's poet laureate, but she was now the director of the small creative writing department at the University of South Alabama. Her passion was to cultivate the next generation of writers, and she was good at it. She saw potential in most of us and had a way of convincing us of that potential, even if we'd never seen it in ourselves before. Her special power was turning prose writers into poets. She believed learning to write poetry would improve prose, and she encouraged all the students in the English department to take one of her classes. She often held them in her home a couple of miles away from campus. There, we would sit in a circle in her living room, eating a from-scratch custard her husband had made, drinking red wine, and discussing craft. At the end of the semester, she'd tell the students to give themselves the grade they thought they deserved. I'd given myself a B+, but when the transcripts were posted, I had an A.

After I found my bearings at school, everything in my life seemed to click into place. I was dating again. I had more friends than I'd ever had—smart, funny, talented, kind humans who loved and appreciated me in a way that made me feel worthy and like, maybe, I'd finally found home. And like a toddler who is securely attached to their mother, knowing I had a place I belonged and could always come back to made me feel safe to explore the rest of the world. I spent a month backpacking across Europe with a couple of girlfriends from my writing program. Traveling did something to my brain. I wandered through foreign cities, listening to people I would never see again speaking languages I didn't understand, and a pressure in my chest released. I was in absolute awe of our planet—of its beauty and vastness and diversity. I mused about the miracle of being a living thing in this infinite universe full of so much nothingness and, suddenly, felt grateful to have had the privilege to grieve at all. Because if I was grieving, that meant I'd loved someone enough and lived long enough to be able to. And then I would think about all the people I'd grown to love: Brittany, Carson, Scott, Kristin, Lopez, Fiona, Trent, Holly, the widows, my family, my new friends from school. Social media had made it possible for us to keep in touch forever if we wanted, even as our lives moved in different directions. Knowing I would always have them in my corner made me feel at ease. *This* was joy. Finally, I had found some peace.

Dr. Walker rifled through piles of paperwork on her desk before pulling out an essay I'd titled "American April," which I'd submitted for one of the school's writing awards. She adjusted her glasses and flipped through the pages.

"You wrote this in Jesmyn's class, right?"

"Yes. Her memoir class."

"Have you thought about MFA programs?"

"Not really," I said. "I haven't written much other than blogging until now." I could feel my cheeks flush. I thought of my friend Rachel, a talented poet I'd met in class who had dreamed of being a writer most of her life. Though I'd worked harder toward my degree than I'd ever worked for anything before, I felt like I was only just getting started. There was so much I didn't know. "I know MFA programs are hard to get into," I said.

"They are," Dr. Walker agreed. She opened a drawer and pulled out a magazine called *Creative Nonfiction.* "Have you read this before?" she asked.

I hated that question. Since I'd started college, people asked me all the time if I'd read one thing or another, and my answer was almost always *no.* Though I loved reading, for most of my life it was a luxury I didn't have time or energy for. I hadn't read most of the books people considered classics, and I spent a lot of energy hiding that about myself. But this time, I nodded. "I have! It's one of the first publications you introduced me to when I said I wanted to write a memoir."

"Well, take this one," she said, sliding the shiny magazine across her desk. "You'll find ads at the back for MFA programs. It's a good place to start."

"Okay," I said, picking up the magazine and flipping to the back.

"You're a talented writer, Karie. Your past doesn't matter," she said. "I can help you with the applications. We can get you any recommendation letters you need." I continued to flip through the magazine so she couldn't see the tears in my eyes. My sense of self had always been formed through the eyes of others, and no one had ever shown me the version of myself that Dr. Walker envisioned. She saw me as a writer, someone who had talent, someone who could get a *master's.* Maybe for the first time, I was starting to like who I was. And I was excited about what might come next in my life. When I didn't respond, Dr. Walker said, "But you're the one who has to take that leap. Believe me, any of these programs would be lucky to have you."

I looked up and clasped my hands in my lap. "Well. There is this one program in Oregon . . ."

The semester before, I'd read the memoir *Son of a Gun* by Justin St. Germain. After the class finished reading and discussing it, I'd looked Justin up. He'd been teaching at the University of New Mexico but had recently taken a job teaching nonfiction in Oregon State University's creative writing program. *Oregon,* I thought. Over the course of my undergraduate career, I had tried to imagine a life outside of the South. In my mind, Washington, D.C., and Maryland had hardly counted. I hadn't chosen those for myself and what we were doing there didn't feel like living so much as surviving. Now, I could go anywhere I wanted. I could do whatever I wanted. Oregon, with its rocky coast and mossy trees and quirky cities, had been at the top of my list. To be able to live in Oregon *and* get an MFA? It seemed like an impossible dream. But I couldn't stop thinking about it.

It didn't take much for Dr. Walker to convince me to apply. I spent the rest of that fall piecing together an application. Then, one day in March, I pulled into the parking lot of my favorite coffee shop right as my phone started ringing. I took the phone from my purse but didn't recognize the number. I never answered random phone calls, so I pulled up Google on my phone and searched the number's area code. *New Mexico.* My cellphone dinged with a new voicemail.

"Oh my God," I said to myself. I brought the phone to my ear. Justin St. Germain's voice was deeper than I expected. My heart raced as he talked about how much he loved my application and then invited me to be a part of Oregon State's nonfiction writing program.

"Holy shit," I said to myself, shaking. I was going to move out west. I was going to be a *master*. And maybe, one day, I'd be able to tell my story.

The only thing left was the leg. Everything else was already in the Subaru, every inch of the car thoughtfully packed so that as much of my past could make it to Oregon as possible. I'd whittled my belongings down to a pile that barely fit, leaving a space just big enough for Sophie. She looked at me from the back seat, panting, with a stupid smile on her face, her bubblegum tongue hanging from her mouth. She would be eight soon, and her rapidly aging body was a reminder of how much time had passed since Cleve's death. For six years, I'd been a widow. Now, at the age of thirty, I was ready to see what else I could be.

"This goofy girl is gonna be your road-trip buddy," I said to the prosthetic leg in my hand, placing it carefully on the floorboard beneath Sophie. I scratched the fluffy spot behind her ear and kissed her wet nose. "Let's get out of here."

I checked the straps on the top of the car to be sure they were tight enough around my kayak. I checked my bike rack. Checked the tires, just in case. I took a deep breath and pulled the driver's door open, then sank into the seat. I closed the door behind me and started the engine.

I was surprised by how unsure I was. Running from places I didn't want to be with nowhere I wanted to go was my norm. But I was going to miss Mobile. It felt strange, wanting to stay, while also wanting to be somewhere else. I had choices, suddenly. And good ones. But it was bittersweet. So much had been sacrificed to get here. People had called me a hero for rebuilding my life after Cleve's death. But if this was what it took to earn that label, I didn't want it. I'd give it back in exchange for his life in an instant. The idea of the war hero, to me, was nothing more than a fantasy designed to assuage America's guilt. *Hero* is much more palatable than *casualty*. Cleve and I weren't heroes. He was just a boy who loved his mama and hoped to afford her a better life one day. And I was just a girl searching for home. I was the lucky one. I'd found what I'd been looking for. But not before Cleve ran out of time. My joy had been birthed from grief, and I was sure I would spend the rest of my life trying and failing to reconcile that.

As I drove across the country, I was overwhelmed by the weight of Cleve's absence. I thought about that night in a hospital room ten years before. "Happy Alive Day, man," Addair had said. Cleve had been given a second chance at life. We couldn't have known that meant only four more years. He would never get to grow up. He'd never get to explore his potential or experience this kind of freedom—an open road toward a future with endless possibilities. I knew how precious the future ahead of me was. Time would eventually run out for me, too, and I couldn't predict when. I had to take advantage of my own "Alive Day." This was *my* second chance. I gripped the steering wheel and swore, to myself and to Cleve, that I would make the most of it.

AUTHOR'S NOTE

I fell in love with Oregon's landscape and with being in a master's program, continuing to learn about writing and beginning to find ways to tell my story. But I found myself unexpectedly longing for Alabama. In undergrad, I had made new friends—people who introduced me to books and music and art and travel. I learned what it was to forge relationships that were based on an excitement about life, about the world, and weren't rooted in grief or trauma. I'd found community there—a chosen family that I'd grown to love and trust. Being away from them felt wrong. The South, I realized, had a grip on my heart. Alabama is part of who I am, whether I like it or not. It is in my blood.

I'd started dating someone in Alabama a few months before I moved to Oregon. Brent—born and raised in Alabama—was a yoga instructor with large blue eyes who lived in a camper on his grandmother's property. He was different from anyone I'd ever dated before—a reserved jack-of-all-trades who was just as interested in meditation as he was in Dungeons & Dragons, who had an affinity for obscure documentaries and cared about things like where our food comes from and where our recycling actually goes after it's picked up. Our connection was instant. Soon after I moved, he followed me to Oregon—we wanted to see if our relationship could work. We became best friends and built a life together. Then, in the spring of 2020, at the height of the Covid pandemic, I found out I was pregnant.

For years after my miscarriage, I told myself I didn't want kids. But I know now that I was just trying to avoid heartbreak. Brent softened me to the idea of a family. He cared about things so deeply—politics, human rights, our planet's health—and had an idealistic view of the world that I respected, even if I didn't think it was realistic. Like all of us, Brent has his own scar tissue. He'd been hurt in the past, and he carries the thick skin to prove it, but not so thick it stops him from trying to make the world a better place. He was all in on us from day one. And he wanted a family more than anything in the world.

In February 2021, I gave birth to my daughter in a blow-up pool in my living room. After hours of pushing, she shot out of me so fast she created waves in the water, her arms stretched out above her like she was some kind of superhero. The midwife placed her on my chest, and everything changed. In an instant, I knew what mattered more than anything else in the world: my baby. I'd known love, but I'd never been so sure of it. Her dimpled knuckles, the way she rooted around on my chest looking to reconnect after being so suddenly severed from my body. She put a mirror in front of me and forced me to look at every imperfect and still-beautiful piece of who I am and then said, "I love you. All of you."

Being in Oregon without my community was even more difficult with a baby. Brent and I needed our friends and our family. So, we moved back to Brent's hometown in Alabama. There, our daughter would be near her grandparents and I would be closer to my friends. For the first time in my life, I knew exactly where I belonged.

I think about Cleve every day. I carry the memories of our marriage like tattoos etched onto my skin. Though they might fade with time, they will always be a part of me. That part of my life changed the chemistry of who I am. In the years after Cleve's death, I began to embrace the rage I'd long ignored in order to do what I believed was my duty: to care for him, to keep my head up, to carry on his legacy, and to remember him as a hero who sacrificed his life for our country. Through my rage, I was finally able to see the truth of what happened to us.

So many of my peers and I have memories of sitting at desks in classrooms with American flags hung above the doors. Of pledging allegiance with our hands at our hearts and then, only hours later, watching our teachers turn on the CRT TVs at the front of our classrooms just as the Twin Towers fell. I dropped out of school around the time President Bush declared war with Iraq. We were told that the military was protecting our country, that there was honor in service, that if we fought, we would be heroes. For eighteen years, my generation was embroiled in that war.

I have come to see that Cleve and I were mere parts of the machine that is the military-industrial complex. Nothing is as simple as we once believed it to be: Cleve wasn't just a young man choosing to fight for his country, and I wasn't just a young woman choosing to marry and support him. We grew up with so few choices, as so many Americans do, and facing war head-on seemed like the best of our options. I know now that Cleve's death, and every casualty of any war, is anticipated. Everything from widow stipends to prosthetic legs is part of a very large budget. And people like me and my husband—poor, uneducated, young—are chosen by recruiters who seek out the economically disadvantaged, knowing that those kids are more likely to enlist and stand on the front lines during wartime. Cleve and I were chosen, and we played our parts.

What happened to Cleve wasn't fair. War is never fair. Our story isn't even special. It's just one of many. As I write this, 7,085 American service members have died in conflict since 2003, and 60,620 have been wounded.[1] As Cleve's and my story shows, these are not the only war casualties: 130,000 veterans have died by suicide since 2001;[2] more than one in ten veterans struggle with a substance use disorder,[3] tens of thousands have overdosed and lived; hundreds have overdosed and died.[4] Thirty-five thousand veterans are homeless.[5] One in three veterans end up arrested and jailed at some point in their lives.[6] More than 180,000 are incarcerated.[7] Twenty-three percent of veterans who use the VA have had PTSD at some point in their lives.[8]

And every service member counted in those numbers has a family who is also affected—moms, dads, wives, girlfriends, children. Wives are caring for wounds, mothers are looking at pictures of the babies they had to bury, and kids are growing up in one-parent households. Around fifteen thousand cases of military domestic violence are reported each year.[9] And an unknown number of women have been murdered by the veterans they love. Many, many family members live with untreated PTSD, too.

And then, we cannot forget the hundreds of thousands of innocent civilian lives lost in these wars, their blood forever on my generation's hands, the weight of their families' tears on our backs.

The wars might be over for now, but my generation is still carrying the weight of so much loss. My hope is that, by writing this book, I've conveyed that the cost of these wars is paid for not only by those who fight, but also by innocent civilians and family members, like me, who love the ones doing the fighting. Many of us are so very young. And the truth is that our country depends on its least powerful citizens to carry the burden of protecting us all—and in return, those citizens are neglected. Forgotten.

When Cleve died, I thought I'd die, too. I couldn't imagine living in a world without him. I wondered if the lucky ones die before they know grief. I thought nothing could hurt more than seeing the lifeless body of someone who loved you, who used to make you laugh and cry, who you promised to protect. But eventually, with time, I came to see that wasting the life I was given when so many didn't have that option was selfish. So, I chose to live. I started to ask myself big questions: What would I do with this new understanding of mortality? What would I prioritize now that I know nothing lasts forever? How will I face the inevitable pain of being human? What will I do with the gift of breath, a beating heart, and time? Who will I choose to be?

Everyone deserves to find that thing that cracks them open and softens them enough to see the beauty in the world. While that kind of happiness comes in many forms, mine is in the form of a little girl with giant blue eyes. Every day, my daughter heals me a little more. When I hug her, I hug myself. When I love her, I love myself. I will never forget where I come from and where I've been. But she reminds me that I'm right where I'm supposed to be, finally.

ACKNOWLEDGMENTS

Some might say this book exists because I pulled myself up by the bootstraps. But that's not true. While the path from high school dropout to grad school to published author did take a hell of a lot of hard work, determination, and sacrifice, I couldn't have gotten here without help along the way.

Cleve, thank you for choosing me, for learning how to love with me, and for growing up with me. When you were still alive, and I was writing our story in a little blog called *Wife of a Wounded Marine,* you believed in my voice and supported me 100 percent. I wasn't quite ready to tell our whole story yet, but it helped knowing that I had your blessing when I finally was ready. I love you. I will always love you. My biggest regret in life is that I wasn't there to save you a second time. You deserved a chance to grow up.

Thank you to my agent, Chris Clemans, for seeing the potential in this story and helping me get this thing published. You've always been in my corner as both an agent and a friend. I got really lucky. And part of the reason I got so lucky was because of you, Matt Young, for seeing potential in my work and sneaking one of my essays to Chris without me knowing. That move was a life-changer, and I'll never forget it.

Thank you to everyone at The Dial Press for believing in and making space for my voice and story. Whitney Frick, my dream editor, you've shown me so much grace over the years—especially during the pandemic, when I was very pregnant and very much not able to write. You continued to stand behind me and this book, even when I thought I wasn't going to be able to finish it. From the bottom of my heart, thank you for not giving up on me.

Thank you to my sisters for continuing to love and support me through a lot of hard shit. Thank you to all the military widows, caregivers, and wives I befriended over the years. Each of you helped carry me through some of the hardest times in my life.

To all the war-wounded men and women I met and befriended at Bethesda Naval Hospital and Walter Reed, you inspired me then and inspire me now. Thank you to the Marine who pulled Cleve to safety after he was wounded, and to the physical therapist and doctors and nurses and everyone who gave him four more years of life. Thank you also to all the 3/8 Marines who served with and loved my husband.

Thank you to my hometown friends (you know who you are) for being my safe space no matter what phase of life I'm in. And for always being honest with me and showing up for me. I swear, y'all saved my life more than once.

Stephanie Land, thank you for not only responding to my awkward Facebook message asking for an early blurb but for being one of my closest friends. Erin Khar, Simone Gorrinodo, Tiffanie Drayton, Natalka Burian, Lauren Hough, Lauren Depino, Shannon Luders-Manuel, Melissa Petro, Debbie Weingarten, and all the other talented writers who were part of my writing group at some point—you are the life raft I needed to get to the end of this book when pregnancy and the pandemic had me convinced I wasn't capable. Thank you.

Dr. Sue Walker, Jesmyn Ward, Justin St. Germain, George Estreich, Elena Passarello, Dorothy Allison, and all my writing teachers and mentors over the years—thank you for seeing potential in me, for helping me find the story I needed to tell and the words I needed to tell it.

Thank you to all the friends I made at Oregon State. I came to that MFA program feeling like an undereducated outsider from Alabama, but you welcomed me as one of your own. Jenna, Jessie, Emily, Paisley,

Robin, Sarah, Taylor, Holly, Chessie, Addy, I know I'm forgetting people.

I miss all of you so much. Like, so so much. I'm especially grateful for my cohort: Natalie, Andrew, Kay, Zoe Bossiere, Joe, Victoria, Pete, Eric, Bridgid, and Adeline, for reading so many shitty first drafts in addition to being great friends. Every one of you influenced this book.

Thank you to all of my beta readers for your time and honesty. You helped me see the book more clearly. And to the women and gender nonconforming writers I met over the years in online writing groups, but especially to Tamara Gane for always being so willing to answer my questions about freelancing. You've always been such a generous friend.

Jenn, Rachel, Rachael, Tay, Corey, Mo, Brandon, Aryn, Daniel, Nick, Leah, Natalie, and all the friends I made in Mobile, you helped me find myself when I'd been lost for so long. You've always accepted me for exactly who I am. You helped me find the confidence I needed to keep reaching for this wild dream. You never once told me that I was silly for wanting to be a published author. Instead, you met my dreams and passions with your own and inspired me to grow and become a better version of myself. I love you like family.

Thank you to the universe for throwing me a bone here and there. I am so grateful for the life insurance money, even though I have such a complicated relationship with it. And for the school scholarship I was given for being a military widow. Between those two things, I was able to afford a reliable home, a reliable car, health insurance, healthy food, and time to pursue my dreams for the first time ever. I was given a once-in-a-lifetime gift I didn't want or ask for, but I never once took it for granted.

Thank you to all the nonprofits who helped Cleve and me over the years: the American Widow Project (AWP), Tragedy Assistance Program for Survivors (TAPS), the Semper Fi Fund, Fisher House Foundation, Yellow Ribbon Fund, Operation Homefront, Wounded Warrior Project, USO, the Bob Woodruff Foundation, Hope for the Warriors, and all the others I'm sure I'm forgetting. You save lives. Economic Hardship Reporting Project, thank you for seeing potential in my story and helping me place my first big byline. Your support boosted my confidence and my résumé, which helped me sell this book.

K and D, thank you for making me a part of your family, no questions asked. That kind of acceptance is foreign to me. It has helped teach me what love can look like.

Brent, thank you for supporting this dream of mine, always, without any pushback. And thank you for giving me the greatest gift of my life—our daughter. To my baby girl, thank you for showing me the purest love I've ever known and for pushing me to be a better human. Before I met you, my greatest goal was to publish this book. Now it is to show you a kinder, more loving world than the one I grew up in. You are my everything.

And finally, to everyone who buys my book with your hard-earned money and then spends your precious time reading it, thank *you*. This right here—you holding my book in your hands—is an impossible dream come true. Thank you for helping me realize that dream.

NOTES

AUTHOR'S NOTE

1. U.S. Department of Defense Casualty Status, www.defense.gov/casualty.pdf.

2. Stop Solider Suicide, page 1, stopsoldiersuicide.org/vet-stats.

3. National Institute on Drug Abuse, Substance Use and Military Life DrugFacts, page 3, nida.nih.gov/publications/drugfacts/substance-use-military-life.

4. Meryl Kornfield, Kyle Rempfer, and Steven Rich, *The Washington Post*, Fentanyl Has Taken a Record Toll on the Army. Families Demand Answers, page 4, www.washingtonpost.com/national-security/2023/06/12/fentanyl-overdoses-military-fort-bragg.

5. Monica Diaz, VA News, Veteran Homelessness Increased by 7.4% in 2023, https://news.va.gov/126913/veteran-homelessness-increased-by-7-4-in-2023/.

6. Ugur Orak, PhD, Counsel on Criminal Justice, From Service to Sentencing: Unraveling Risk Factors for Criminal Justice Involvement Among U.S. Veterans, counciloncj.org/from-service -to-sentencing-unraveling-risk-factors-for-criminal-justice -involvement-among-u-s-veterans/.

7. Jennifer Bronson, PhD; E. Ann Carson, PhD; and Margaret Noonan, BJS Statisticians; Marcus Berzofsky, DrPH, RTI International, U.S. Department of Justice, Office of Justice Programs, Bureau of Justice Statistics, Veterans in Prison and Jail, 2011–12, page 1, bjs.ojp.gov/content/pub/pdf/vpj1112.pdf.

8. US Department of Veterans Affairs, PTSD: National Center for PTSD, How Common Is PTSD in Veterans?, www.ptsd.va.gov/ understand/common/common_veterans.asp.

9. US Government Accountability Office, Domestic Abuse: Actions Needed to Enhance DOD's Prevention, Response, and Oversight, www.gao.gov/assets/gao-21-289.pdf.

ABOUT THE AUTHOR

KARIE FUGETT holds a BA from the University of South Alabama and an MFA in creative nonfiction from Oregon State University. *Alive Day* is her first book.

TikTok: @KarieFugett
X: @KarieWrites
Instagram: @KarieWrites
Threads: @KarieWrites
Substack: kariefugett.substack.com

ABOUT THE TYPE

This book was set in Caslon, a typeface first designed in 1722 by William Caslon (1692–1766). Its widespread use by most English printers in the early eighteenth century soon supplanted the Dutch typefaces that had formerly prevailed. The roman is considered a "workhorse" typeface due to its pleasant, open appearance, while the italic is exceedingly decorative.